The Regulated Businessman

14-120-278

The Regulated

Businessman

**BUSINESS AND GOVERNMENT:
READINGS FROM *FORTUNE***

Edited by JOHN A. LARSON
Northwestern University

*HD 3611
F65*

HOLT, RINEHART AND WINSTON, INC.

New York • Chicago • San Francisco
Toronto • London

32/2.30973
F//79r

Preface

BUSINESSMEN today have a vital interest in what government actions are, why they are taken, and how they will affect business. The long era in which the business of America was business, and in which the ideology of the country was essentially shaped and advanced by business interests, died about the time that *Fortune* came into being. Since neither nostalgic recollection nor calls for a return to the past will bring back that day, it is necessary for today's businessman or student to understand what *is* happening, whether it is pleasant or not. Unfortunately, as government has expanded, and as the maze of agencies and departments has grown, the average businessman who is concerned every day with his company's operations has felt quite remote from Washington, his state capitol, and his city hall. He may rely on experts in his corporation or at his trade association, but always with the disquieting feeling that he cannot understand what is going on or what "those fellows" want (as a *Fortune* editorial in February 1963 put it).

This volume of readings stresses business enterprises and their relations with governmental bodies. Though individuals are always important both in business and in government, the problems examined tend to center on the confrontation of corporate power with governmental power. *Fortune's* excellent corporation stories are used throughout this book to raise questions about governmental behavior and to illustrate concrete business actions and responses. Government is studied in several ways. National, state, and local governmental bodies all affect business, but most stress is on the national government. The Executive Branch plays an important role, but the courts and legal system provide the mechanism by which regulation takes place.

Throughout its history *Fortune* has kept a careful eye on the continuing relationship of business and government. This book uses the words of *Fortune* to clarify some of the complexities and obscurities of that relationship. Because *Fortune's* clear editorial point of view has been preserved in the readings, it is possible to see how the magazine looks at government and public problems, and better understand the conclusions and recommendations offered. However, in spite of the strong statement of *Fortune's* own position, it is still the task of the reader to formulate his own judgments.

A volume of readings about business and government may go quickly out-of-date, because much in the field of American government turns on the strong personalities of changing leaders. *Fortune* has always sought timeliness for its readers, and the magazine is likely to offer an illuminating article very soon after a major governmental change affecting business. Subsequent articles may update or replace the original information and predictions as further events transpire. Though articles used in this book generally have a minimum amount of information likely to be quickly outdated, it is impossible not to take into account major figures in the current administration in Washington. Some outdated or irrelevant material has been eliminated from the articles by the editor, and specific dates inserted to replace such phrases as "this year."

This book is intended for the general reader who wishes to obtain a coherent picture of business-government relations, and for the student who wishes to supplement his textbooks. It is most clearly designed for courses which deal with business and government, but it may be utilized in courses that stress broad understanding of the economy and government rather than the business view of such things. Some sections may also be helpful in more specialized courses on the social control of industry, the legal environment of business, marketing, and business policy. As new courses develop that combine aspects of business-government relations with the study of business responsibilities, this book can be used for offerings in business and society, or business and its environment.

Each section of the book is introduced and organized in a way to make easily available a good grasp of its subject. The five sections are intended as a logical development of some matters of importance covered in a whole term of business and government courses. The order in which they are taken up does not coincide with typical textbooks, however. While most of the book deals with the national government, the first section covers economic goals and policies commonly discussed at the end of text-

books. Two sections on national business regulation are followed
by one on the impact of defense activities on business, and another on state and local governments. Stress throughout is on
government efforts to define or identify corporate power and then
contain it. Hence the emphasis is on government as regulator,
no matter how important other governmental roles are.

The subjects excluded in any brief collection of readings on a
topic as sizable as business and government are many. There is
much more to the role of government as defender than is included
here, yet other aspects of strategy and the international aspects
of government and business are properly the subject of another
book of readings. Another volume of this series, *The Responsible
Businessman,* includes a section on business political action as
well as a discussion of businessmen as responsible citizens, and
none of these materials is repeated here. Only a few of the many
forms of government regulation and promotion are covered in
this volume; some of the obvious omissions include developments
in agriculture, transportation, and labor relations. Nevertheless,
by focusing on business as a system of power and on government as a competing power center, it is possible to give the
reader an indication of the importance of this field.

This volume of readings stresses the confrontation of and continuing relationship between business (both firms and men) and
government (agencies and men). It is concerned with the exercise of power and with efforts to regulate or control this power
through the public institutions of American society. It is addressed to the reader as an individual who will find for himself
a place in this system and stand for matters of importance to
himself and his fellow men. By further reading in *Fortune* and
elsewhere, and by the accumulation of experience, the individual
should find himself more ready to act well when business and
government come together.

JOHN A. LARSON

Evanston, Illinois
December 1965

Contents

The Regulated Businessman

part 1

NATIONAL GOVERNMENT AND NATIONAL ECONOMY

BUSINESS IS regulated or controlled, at least in part, by the impersonal workings of the free market economy. However, any American businessman can tell a listener much about the added burdens of regulations and restrictions that he experiences in dealings with governmental bodies. The most important of these bodies is the powerful national government (or central government or federal government). While its emphasis is on regulation of business, it may also protect, promote, or defend business. Nevertheless, the prevailing attitude of businessmen toward the government is likely to be a feeling of limitation.

The national government, which comes close to managing the whole economy, is in many ways personified by the President. Businessmen often engage in appraisals of and predictions about the performance of the President, who, as manager of prosperity, deals with macroeconomics, fiscal and monetary policy, and the long-run national economic growth and stability. "The Economy Under New Management" looks at President Lyndon B. Johnson after a year in office, and at a new era of economic policy and a new kind of business-oriented manager in Washington. In the present era of good feeling, business is increasingly consulted for advice and consent, even though there is a sizable commitment to calculated and continuous growth with an unprecedented degree of federal management of the economy. In spite of risks, such an atmosphere may offer a new kind of business freedom.

1

Much of the national government's action in guiding the economy toward its goals is seen in fiscal policy. The most daring fiscal action of the past thirty years was the 1964 tax cut. "The Next Turn in Taxes" assesses both the impact of that action and prospects for future tax reductions and reforms. For the most part, liberals look at the overall effect of the general level of reductions, while conservatives examine the impact of specific rate reductions on incentives. Since spending is holding relatively steady, there is a tendency toward the creation of a national government surplus. Debate now centers on the size of the budget and on ways to stimulate the economy by reducing taxes.

A recent national government foray into regulation or control centered on the guideposts or guidelines on prices and wages announced by the Council of Economic Advisers in January 1962, which were the subject of controversy in the temporary steel price rise of April 1962. The general problem arises from the responsibility of a corporate manager to exercise his best judgment of market factors to further his company, even if he makes a price decision with which the President of the United States disagrees. Debate on the guideposts continues, and the impact of steel price changes on inflation is still in dispute.

The expectations of major businessmen toward the Johnson administration center much less on such specifics as tax cuts and price guideposts than on intangibles. Business' terms for preserving this era of good feeling are amazingly lenient, boiling down to a hope for continuity. What business really seems to need most is a better way of communicating with Washington. If the regulated businessman truly accepts a larger role for government as manager of the economy, he will wish to assert himself positively to make his voice heard in the right offices in Washington.

The Economy Under New Management* —

LOUIS BANKS

During the 1965 hearings of the Joint Economic Committee of Congress, Wisconsin's Senator William Proxmire seemed to play a lonely role. Proxmire, a pleasant, balding Yale man ('38), a Democrat of liberal leanings who modestly confines his official biography in the *Congressional Directory* to a single sentence, obviously had taken pains to do his homework. As one after another of the economic great minds of Washington came to testify on the plans and portents, he frowned as he tried to see through the clouds of theory, somewhat deferentially asked the common-sense questions without making long speeches on his own economic prejudices (save for a pardonable concern for the dairy industry back home). And when the week of hearings was over—when the Secretary of the Treasury, the Chairman of the Federal Reserve, the Council of Economic Advisers, the Budget Director, and the assorted advisers and their advisers had filled the record, when all the statistics had been split and neatly stacked like cordwood and all the congressional axes ground— Proxmire alone seemed to stand in wonderment at what he had seen and heard. "As the old carnival barker would say, 'Brother, you ain't seen nothing yet,'" he wrote in an addendum to the Joint Committee majority report. "Hold on to your hats, folks. You're about to be taken for the ride of your lives!"

Proxmire's sense of astonishment was appropriate: nudged along by the 1964 tax cut, certainly the most daring government fiscal experiment in thirty years, the economy had rolled to a gross national product of $623 billion without a breather in four years. And the Council of Economic Advisers, proclaiming "a new era for economic policy is at hand," promised to see it through to $660 billion (give or take $5 billion) by the end of 1965—adding assertively that "no law of nature compels a free market economy to suffer from recessions or periodic inflations." But the skepticism

---

*May 1965

in Proxmire's outcry made him about as popular among Democrats as Li'l Abner's friend Lonesome Polecat. For the Administration *is* confident that it can give the American people the ride
of their lives in an economic sense—and a great many people,
including many members of the business community and not a
few Republicans, are already aboard and rather liking the
experience. Backed by a sizable consensus, the U.S. seems
thoroughly committed to an economy of calculated and continuous growth, to the conception that the federal government is
responsible not just for reducing unemployment but for avoiding
recessions—and doing it all without significant inflation. The
overpowering promise is that by using both the carrot and the
stick the government can help produce an abundance of jobs,
goods, and services almost beyond man's imagination.

Less well understood is the fact that with this commitment
to growth comes, almost by definition, a commitment to a degree
of federal management of the economy unprecedented in peacetime. "Our tools of economic policy are much better tools than
existed a generation ago," wrote the President in his message
to Congress transmitting the 1965 economic report. The principal
tools themselves are old—i.e., expansive monetary policies and a
budget philosophy unashamed of deficits—but in the warm
afterglow of the tax cut the President and his advisers are confident of their ability to use them with new finesse and in untried
combinations. What was put on the statute books as a promise
and a goal in the Employment Act of 1946 has suddenly blos-
somed into the proportions of a dogma. Continued growth has
become the economic equivalent of victory in wartime. Accordingly, other considerations slide down the scale of values and the
justification of government action in new fields slides up. In the
face of a balance-of-payments deficit, for example, the Administration has been loath to apply orthodox monetary discipline lest
it mar prosperity at home. Instead, it has championed for the
short range a system of compulsory and voluntary restrictions on
the movement of capital, and has vowed for the long range to
amend the international monetary system.

The President is clearly the man in charge of it all and, in this
case particularly, consensus is the word for Lyndon. For while
government is moving into an active role in the nation's economic
affairs, it is moving with the advice and consent of business.

Literally hundreds of corporate executives are on the President's famous telephone list, and find their counsel sought and considered on high economic matters; scores have ready access to the White House to argue their cases on matters of policy that might affect them. With a nice disregard of all the old ideological battle lines, Johnson has preached and practiced the gospel that the U.S. rides on its economy, and the economy rides on the state of American business. Even bureaucratic sneering at business has been subdued; all over town the speech writers declaim fervently and almost gratefully on the creative power of the American business system.

Government, in its operations, has come as well to redefine more and more of its functions in a way that business understands. "True economy," Kermit Gordon, the Budget Director, testified recently, "is the most efficient allocation of resources," and he pledged his $98-billion budget to advance that end. Though such entrenched semi-socialist projects as TVA and REA continue to thrive, the new governmental managers have been happy to pass along to industry the major new areas of development, notably commercial satellite communication and atomic power. On business' side some redefining has been going on too. The rising generation of chief executive officers have come to realize their dependence on government in their international operations, and if they have any complaint it is simply that government should be better managed. On the home front, whole industries, such as space, defense, systems planning, ocean mining, etc., look to government as their legitimate parent. "Planning" is not the horrible word it once was; most major corporations have their own long-range plans, and only wish government would help them by planning its own affairs better. "What is at stake in our economic decisions today," President Kennedy said in his Yale speech in 1962, "is not some grand warfare of rival ideologies . . . but the practical management of a modern economy." And it is a fascination with the idea of management on a universe-sized scale that may have something to do with winning the support of the nation's new corporate executives.

In boardrooms Johnson is discussed not as a blankety-blank Democrat but as a Man Who Gets Things Done. He is building a management team—a team of "doer-thinkers" with which business can readily identify itself. A man who apparently wants to dominate his personal staff, he has nevertheless chosen for his principal Cabinet and sub-Cabinet officers the type who make strong and independent-minded divisional managers. His great respect for Secretary of Defense Robert McNamara, the strongest of the Kennedy holdovers, is one indication of this. His nomination of John T. Connor, the fifty-year-old president of Merck, as Secretary of Commerce adds a combatively independent "voice of management" to government councils. Thomas Mann, fifty-two, the recently appointed Under Secretary of State for Economic Affairs, has won the complete respect of such international businessmen as David Rockefeller and J. Peter Grace for his intelligent and realistic handling of the Alliance for Progress as Assistant Secretary of Inter-American Affairs. (The regard for Mann, incidentally, contrasts with the widely held belief in the business and financial world that the State Department's general approach to world economic affairs is sadly inadequate.) The President's selection of Frederick L. Deming, fifty-two, Des Moines-born president of the Minneapolis Federal Reserve Bank, as Under Secretary of the Treasury for Monetary Affairs, sits well with the cautious Federal Reserve System and with bankers around the country who like him for his breezy, approachable middle-western style. And it is likely that no Johnsonian appointment has more long-term significance in terms of the growth economy than that of Henry Hamill Fowler, fifty-six, as Secretary of the Treasury.

Fowler is a Washington corporation lawyer, a veteran of appointive government service, and was for three years Under Secretary of the Treasury and second-in-command to Douglas Dillon. In what the academic economists (but not Fowler) like to call "the Keynesian Revolution" in Washington, Fowler personifies the forces of moderation. He is a "businessman's Keynesian," accepting as necessary and desirable the need for government to stimulate the economy toward the full employment of all its resources, but holding with a ferocious tenacity to the faith that growth will be successful only as it removes the burdens from business and allows the private sector to fill an ever larger role in shaping the nation's, and the world's, economic development.

The merging of private and public talent at the operating level has been accompanied by a synthesis of sorts in economic thought; the academic Keynesian economists are now not too far away from corporate economists and their bosses. Business, heavy in cash flow and richer in net profits because of the tax cut and various investment incentives, is not averse to fiscal and monetary experimentation—as long as it works. There is considerable agreement on the desirability of such additional stimulants as cuts in excise taxes and another cut in taxes across the board, if necessary to maintain demand. Balanced budgets get a certain amount of lip service, but are low on most lists of priorities. Bankers are getting a little nervous about credit, and some advocate higher interest rates, but practically no one wants a credit squeeze that would make the economy breathe hard. One result of the synthesis is that some corporate executives are talking of "business unleashed" and working overtime on big new expansion plans. In a recent issue the careful First National City Bank Letter reported "a marked evolution [in Washington] toward a more pronounced pro-business attitude, combined with an increasing stress on free enterprise and market competition in the allocation of resources." As Arthur Okun, thirty-six, a five-month member of the Council of Economic Advisers, says with a wry smile: "Prosperity is popular."

AN IDEA BY THE EARS

The new era of good feeling is Johnson's doing, beyond question. Yet it was John Kennedy who opened the White House gates to the Keynesians and made the new economics the official faith.[1] No papal emissaries worked any harder on the conversion of Constantine to Christianity than did the Keynesians on Kennedy. A campaign task force under Paul Samuelson of MIT educated him to the evils of lagging growth and gave him the

---

[1] The term "Keynesian," as used journalistically and by journalistic-minded economists, is a kind of catchall designation for those who think of the economy in the aggregate, and hold that government must act, through easy credit and deficit financing, to stimulate the economy to a level that will provide full employment. Lord Keynes might be astonished at some of the particulars of the doctrine promulgated in his name.

base for his "get America moving again" issue. But in office Kennedy at first backslid into an old-fashioned respect for the balanced budget, and promised one in his opening messages. From across West Executive Avenue to the White House thereupon came Walter Heller, the council chairman, to engage Kennedy's fine intellectual curiosity with discussions of Keynesian theory and the virtues of deficits. From across East Executive Avenue came Secretary Dillon, no Keynesian by training, but an increasingly enthusiastic advocate of the argument that a cut in taxes would remove a burden from business and actually increase tax revenue. The Treasury's figures and prestige carried the day. By early 1963, Kennedy was confidently lecturing the nation of the need for a tax cut on top of a deficit as a prerequisite to growth and the best route to a balanced budget.

Lyndon Johnson has none of Kennedy's fascination with economic theory, which takes a lot of the fun out of things for the various presidential economic advisers. "Kennedy was like a man with an ulcer who wants to see the x-rays," says one of them. "Johnson takes your word for it and says, 'Let's get on with the cure.'" The word "elemental" turns up frequently in any erudite discussion of Johnsonian economics. "He has certain elemental ideas about the importance of prosperity and interest rates," says one adviser. "His habits of thinking are quite elemental," says another, "but his understanding of *how* people think is deep." Still another, who finds himself frequently in the loyal opposition, says: "All the time I'm trying to explain my point I can tell he is not listening to my argument but is looking at my hair and ears, wondering, 'Is this guy worth supporting, or should I go along with that other fellow who was in here just ahead of him?'" A friend who has known Johnson longest explains: "He thinks in terms of what is readily understandable to him. He doesn't respond to complex things put together by geniuses."

Put another way, most of this means that Johnson uses his staff advisers as a source of packaged ideas and relies on his own political instincts for decisions. In economics his political instincts, endowed with southwestern Populism, run strongly toward easy money and ever expanding credit. He goes along with the argument that a stiff rise in interest rates could halt the expansion, and likes to call himself a "bigger-pie man" in pushing growth. Yet he certainly is not beyond the reach of disciplinary realities: when Britain raised its bank rate to 7 percent in the fall of 1964 he reluctantly yielded to the Federal Reserve and the Treasury and accepted the half percent rise in the Fed's discount rate—not, of course, without admonishing the banks to keep their prime rates steady. In typical Johnson style, he was on the telephone a couple of weeks later to Congressman Wright Patman of Texas, chairman of the House Banking and Currency Committee, telling him: "Now you take it easy on those bankers. They're cooperating with me just fine." Johnson is coming to have increasing respect for William McChesney Martin, the durable Chairman of the Federal Reserve Board, and while Martin is a long way from being on the "team" (and probably wouldn't think it proper to be anyway), his opinions get a hearing. It is the stressing of the practical—and even the political—over the theoretical and academic that make Lyndon Johnson far more successful than Kennedy in bringing business into the new economics.

TRIAL BALLOONS IN A STORM

In putting the new team together, Johnson's greatest problem was the Treasury. To knowledgeable business, the Treasury has always been the most important department in the federal government. "The Secretary of the Treasury," in the words of Robert Roosa, now a Brown Brothers, Harriman partner and for four years Dillon's distinguished Under Secretary for Monetary Affairs, "is the financial and economic conscience of the government. From D-day minus one he has to be the least popular among the Cabinet officers. He has to be the force for prudence and discipline. The integrity of government and its performance rest upon a sense that the Treasury provides an orderly approach to the whole range of national economic life." Douglas Dillon, without being "the least popular," came to fulfill this description remarkably well. He rebuilt the Treasury into a strong, going organization and won the confidence not only of the bankers but of such diverse elements of economic Washington as the "easy money" congressional committees and the Federal Reserve. Who could replace him? Who could at once have the confidence of the President (Roosa lists that as the No. 1 prerequisite), represent the new economics, and be acceptable to Congress and the business community? . . .

Moving swiftly, in the mysterious manner that he finds so delicious, Johnson tried a number of candidates on bankers, congressional leaders, and Dillon, unobtrusively including in the list the name of his old friend Joe Fowler. . . . Johnson called Fowler out of a bank board of directors' meeting in Alexandria and asked him to come to the oval office secretly through the southwest White House gate. As soon as Fowler was ushered in, the President enveloped him in ardent, patriotic Johnsonian persuasion and squeezed out an acceptance. He got informal ratification from his friends in the Senate by telephone, and a couple of hours later summoned the White House press corps to nominate "one of the ablest and most dedicated men I know." Secretary Dillon, attending an American Bankers Association meeting at Princeton, got the news an hour later.

COMBINING JEFFERSON AND HAMILTON

Fowler is a man of medium height, with a full head of smoothly combed white hair contrasting with his high coloring. At ease he radiates a vestryman's conservatism (Christ Church, Alexandria) with his unruffled manner and his Virginia courtesy, an impression underscored by his dark striped suits with vests and his white tab-collar shirts. When provoked he can, on occasion, glow in memorable anger, his blue eyes snapping through heavy, dark-rimmed glasses and his pointed opinions propelled (providing no ladies are within a half mile) by profanity. In describing his beliefs, he acknowledges a "strong attachment to the old Jeffersonian tradition," and with it a "long-standing admiration" for that strongly nationalist first Treasury Secretary, Alexander Hamilton. If this sounds baffling to scholars, Fowler's political and professional life gives it a certain meaning in contemporary terms.

Born in Roanoke, the son of a locomotive engineer, he worked his way through high school and Roanoke College, went on to Yale Law School to get not only a bachelor of laws but a doctorate of jurisprudence ('33), and served on the editorial board of the *Law Journal.* He hit Washington in the early New Deal, put in a year's apprenticeship with the blue-ribbon law firm of Covington, Burling & Rublee, and then plunged into government as junior counsel for the Tennessee Valley Authority. Thereafter, he was in and out of a half-dozen government bureaus and regulatory agencies before he established his own firm (now Fowler, Leva, Hawes & Symington) in 1946. So far as his economic background is concerned, he was an assistant general counsel of the War Production Board and served with the U.S. Mission for Economic Affairs in London during World War II, later joining the Foreign Economic Administration. (In later years he served on Paul Samuelson's Kennedy task force, on the CED Commission on Money and Credit, and chaired a presidential task force studying ways to bring private investment into play to help solve the drain on dollars.) He made some important personal and professional friendships in the corporate and banking world when he ran the National Production Authority and the Office of Defense Mobilization for Truman toward the end of the Korean war. When the Republicans came to town under Eisenhower, a number of Fowler's dollar-a-year "employees" offered him promising corporate jobs, but he preferred to stick with law, where, he says, "if you have five good clients you can afford to lose at least one, and keep your independence."

Fowler has always managed to keep a bristling independence in his politics as well. He is, of course, a birthright Democrat, but in Harry Byrd's Virginia he has consistently supported the national ticket, sometimes to the displeasure of the Byrd forces. The story of Fowler at bay in the 1956 Virginia state convention is legend. One by one all the delegations withdrew their endorsement of Adlai Stevenson, leaving only the delegation from Alexandria, tucked away in the balcony. When the Alexandrians stuck by Stevenson, a chant of "Yankee go home" rose in the convention hall. The chant came to an abrupt end when Joe Fowler leaned over the balcony and roared: "You go to hell!" Yet Fowler has managed to keep Byrd's respect and to avoid acquiring the label of a New Dealer or a Fair Dealer or a New Frontiersman. In the 1964 election he worked with Jack Connor, now the Secretary of Commerce, Sidney Weinberg, and John Loeb in organizing the influential National Independent Committee for Johnson and Humphrey, and, though he is too discreet ever to admit it, he probably finds the Johnson Administration more to his taste than any of its predecessors.

"COME WITH ME TO MACEDONIA"

As Under Secretary of the Treasury, Fowler left a firm mark on domestic economic policy. Once Kennedy was sold on the need for a tax cut, the next question was what kind of tax package could be sold to Congress and the people. Walter Heller, like most academic Keynesians of the day, wanted both a tax cut and stepped-up government spending. He was most concerned with getting a quick stimulus into the economy (which he envisioned as being close to recession) and totally unworried about doubling the size of the deficit. For a time he had Kennedy almost persuaded. But Dillon and Fowler stressed the long-range reform aspects of a tax cut that would ease the progressive load on taxpayers and corporations and argued that an emphasis on big deficits, unaccompanied by efforts to hold down increases in government expenditures, was poor strategy both at home and abroad. Dillon, Fowler, and Chairman Martin of the Federal Reserve ultimately led Kennedy away from the Heller position. But Heller countered by leaking stories about Treasury "conservatism," which got the tax bill in more trouble. Congress balked, and business was apprehensive.

With the bill completely bogged down, Kennedy, in late 1962, recruited Fowler to go out and get the business community over what one Kennedy economist calls "its guilt feeling about deficits." Fowler did far more than that. In touring the country, speaking to any business group that would listen, he evolved a Fowlerian corollary to academic doctrine, in effect reshaping Keynesianism to fit the U.S. business system as he understood it. Its principal tenets were these:

1. A tax cut on top of a deficit is not a good thing in itself, but because oppressive rates of taxation have stifled business expansion, it is necessary.

2. An essential objective of government policy is to make it profitable for business to increase its investment in modern plant and equipment.

3. Unemployment cannot be attacked effectively through indiscriminate stimulation of the economy; but once business can see the prospect of profit through lower taxes it will be incited to a broad expansion of facilities. This, in turn, will result in a lower level of unemployment.

4. As the economy expands and revenues increase, government spending must be held in check so that the U.S. can look forward to a balanced budget in the not too distant future.

5. Relying primarily on government spending for growth means expanding forever governmental influence on the allocation of labor and capital.

6. An efficient, modernized private sector, producing near capacity, keeps the U.S. competitive in world markets, provides a trade surplus for the balance of payments, and ultimately provides a better living standard for all the trading world.

During the time that he was trying to fight the tax bill through Congress, and was being hectored by Heller, Fowler sometimes directed the attention of visitors to a quotation from Livy on a plaque on his desk. The quotation is an excerpt from a speech by Lucius Aemilius Paulus, a Roman consul bound for his command in the Macedonian war: "If anyone thinks himself qualified to give advice respecting the war which I am to conduct, which may prove advantageous to the public, let him not refuse his assistance to the State, but let him come with me to Macedonia. . . . But if he thinks this is too much trouble and prefers the repose of a city life to the trials of war, let him not on land assume the office of a pilot."

Fowler won his Macedonian battle resoundingly. Within months there were 3,000 top executives enrolled in the Business Committee for Tax Reduction. ("He wiped off eight years of Eisenhower lectures in six months," says an admiring Administration economist.) Then with President Johnson's powerful help the Treasury's tax-cut bill (with a Heller-backed provision that withholding taxes be cut in one sweep in March 1964) got through Congress. For his part Johnson turned off the lights in the White House to show that he was serious about the low level of government spending.

THE ELUSIVE BALANCE

As it looks to the future, the Johnson team finds itself something of a prisoner of its own success in keeping the boom going. Chairman Gardner Ackley and his fellow Economic Councilmen can rightly pay tribute to the "remarkable balance" in the private sector that provided much of the "durability" of the expansion. But in the final analysis the balance was the result of private decision, the chemistry of which is pretty elusive. The tax cut has moved into history as the principal agent of today's prosperity—"a watershed in economic policy," Ackley calls it. And yet, as the Republican minority on the Joint Economic Committee pointed out, had Walter Heller's original tax cut been passed in the way and at the time he wanted it, the inflationary pressures might well have blown the economy through the roof. Moreover, the stimulus of the tax cut helped balance the depressive effects of the cuts in defense spending in fiscal 1964, which were not expected when the tax-cut bill was drawn.

But this series of lucky coincidences raises the question, as both Proxmire and the Republican minority raise it, of whether a tax cut can be counted on to work the same way another time. Other delicate questions abound. Assuming that a tax cut will work the same way again, how much new stimulus do we need to offset some of the depressing factors already in view? One such depressant is the impending mop-up of some $5 billion in purchasing power involved in the new social-security payroll-tax increases that take effect on January 1, 1966. The Administration is talking vaguely of doing spadework with the tax-writing House Ways and Means Committee (after the excise-tax cuts are out of the way) so that a clean "quickie" cut in income-tax rates could be put through Congress early, if needed. Over the longer range a plan is being revived that would feed some of the rising federal revenues to the states for public-service projects. And the Great Society is already laying the groundwork for public-works programs that, in the President's words, "are capable of quick acceleration" should private demand falter. But the variables are many and the timing is trickier than the nation has been led to believe.

One question that is still wide open is how far stimulation can be pressed in reducing unemployment without creating bottlenecks (i.e., incipient inflation). The Administration's announced goal-by-stimulus is 4 percent, and in April 1965, the Labor Department reported the rate down to 4.7 percent, the lowest since 1957. But was this a solid decline? So liberal has credit been, observed Bill Martin in February 1965, that the banks "have people out trying hard to place loans. This is speculative credit. If you get people in jobs that are really not going to last very long, you haven't done much for them. You've got to get them in something a little better than just jobs created by aggregate demand."

AN ATTACK AT THE ROOTS

At no point has allegiance to growth brought more agonized thinking than in the attempt to deal with the continuing deficit in the U.S. balance of payments. Before growth became an imperative, such an outflow of gold and dollars, whatever the cause, would probably have been dealt with by monetary methods, which would have had the effect of slowing domestic expansion. But Washington today finds even a whiff of deflation intolerable; higher interest rates, in Secretary Dillon's words, "would surely move us toward domestic recession." In the presidential campaign of 1964, Lyndon Johnson proudly took credit for controlling the "time bomb" of foreign dollar holdings without resorting to "damaging controls and restrictions that would have curbed economic freedom." Three months later, as things got steadily worse, the President put into operation his stringent program of controls, some voluntary and some compulsory, over capital movements.

The Treasury's position, as Fowler took over, was that: (1) voluntary controls are working now and might in fact bring a temporary surplus by the third quarter; (2) European nations are as responsible as the U.S. for the drain on American short-term funds because they are relying too heavily on monetary policy—i.e., high interest rates—rather than fiscal to cope with their own difficulties; (3) in any case, with controls on American capital outflow and the trimming of U.S. corporate spending abroad, there will be less inflationary pressure on the European countries, and their rates may case, thus easing as well the American problem.

Fowler, in his first speech as Secretary, seemed to go out of his way to say that the "voluntary program cannot and should not be looked upon as a permanent solution." The U.S. can still help itself by becoming "more competitive in world markets" and by "encouraging capital flows into the U.S." But beyond that, he said, "we cannot escape the complex and difficult task—a task that must be shared by our European friends—of attacking at its roots the basic source of the disequilibrium in world capital markets."

The "complex and difficult task" may well absorb the energies not only of Joe Fowler but of a number of his successors at the Treasury as well. One large part of the task is to revise the international monetary system to protect the dollar from the built-in hazards of being the world's principal reserve currency. In its preliminary studies the Treasury leans toward a plan to create some sort of international payment unit set up under the International Monetary Fund, but under present policy the U.S. will make no move until it gets out from under the gun of its payments deficit. Getting major powers to agree to an international unit that is beyond the reach of their sovereignty will take some doing.

But there is a growing belief that no international monetary system can, by itself, rectify the imbalance among modern industrial nations if they are all pursuing growth at different rates or in different phases. It was to this that Fowler alluded in his speech, and it was on this note that Dillon bowed out of office in a major pronouncement at Princeton in March 1965. "None of us likes controls," Dillon said, ". . . but if we are to dispense with them the nations of the free world, working together, simply must develop better means for influencing capital flows within a basic framework of free markets and national objectives—and without placing intolerable burdens either upon monetary policy or upon the resources of the international monetary system." So the Treasury is seeking a way to keep national fiscal policies as well as monetary policies in balance. The commitment to growth has widespread repercussions.

WHO CAN BEAT THE SYSTEM?

Like all unexplored territory, the new economics offers some perilous risks along with the great promises. At least, "risks" in the terms that the American economic and political system has come to define them. In politics the control of the economic tools and the sanction of growth-above-all give the party in power a tremendous advantage. Samuel Lubell, the political analyst, commented just after the 1964 presidential election: "For the first time in modern American history this nation faces a really serious threat of one-party dominance on the national level." Studies of voting in key counties had persuaded him that Johnson's 1964 victory should be read, primarily, as a plebiscite on the going economic system and fears that Barry Goldwater might change it. "For better or for worse," said Lubell, "we are married to the System—call it what you will, a managed or a mismanaged economy, semi-socialism or the Great Society. If it collapses it will take the Democratic party with it. But Goldwater's rout showed that the System *itself* will not be voted out." The proper role for an opposition party, he suggests, is to make clear what's going on and to advocate effective alternatives.

With "full employment" the central objective, politicians can afford less and less tolerance for anything that interferes with the smooth progression of the economy. Thus such disruptions as major strikes probably will come to be judged not as labor vs. management conflicts but as serious hazards to the whole economic structure. Eisenhower is already being blamed by economists for laying the groundwork for the 1960 recession by "letting the 1959 steel strike go on so long." Pressures will increase to keep wage and price rises, in the aggregate, within the CEA guidelines—i.e., within the productivity gains of the economy as a whole. Even such an economic moderate as Bob Roosa observes matter-of-factly that "national policies for incomes, as well as for interest rates and credit availabilities, seem to be, or be becoming, a normal part of the responsibilities which all governments now acknowledge in varying degrees for promoting growth, avoiding instability, and achieving external balance."

Risks of another magnitude could show themselves if today's "moderate" policies fail to keep the growth rate up to the trend line. Seymour E. Harris, an influential Keynesian who served as chairman of a Treasury advisory committee under Dillon, is willing to accept, if necessary to hold down unemployment, such drastic alternatives as more "teeth in the guidelines," a 2 percent annual inflation rate, an end to the Federal Reserve's independent management of monetary policy, stiff controls on foreign transactions, and, if need be, devaluation of the dollar. Chances are good that under the present management of the economy, moderation would triumph over such academic extremism, but under pressure of rising unemployment a struggle would be almost certain.

A HEALTHY DISCIPLINE

Yet not all the logic implicit in the growth argument is quite so hair raising. To begin with, growth itself, far from constricting business, has produced more capital for innovation, enterprise, modernization, risk taking, etc., hence in a very basic sense has expanded business "freedom." Second, under the rules that the Johnsonian economists have set for themselves, a growth economy demands the highest possible level of national economic efficiency, or the most efficient allocation of resources; the less efficiency the less increase in productivity to share. The market economy is recognized as the best allocator of resources. Under this discipline, government cannot long delay taking a new look at the far-ranging wasteful program of quotas and subsidies.

In this spirit, Kermit Gordon has championed a revision of the woefully inefficient federal regulation of transportation, and has spoken out publicly for changes in the farm price-support program (but in an election year was called off by fearful farm-belt Democrats). Joe Fowler, speaking in his capacity of private citizen and corporation lawyer, pointed out to the Business Council in October 1964 the inefficiencies of the current administration of antitrust laws. "Our concern," he said, "should be with establishing, in a manner consistent with our competitive enterprise system, a climate of opportunity for growth and attainment of size, as a means of greater productivity, better distribution of goods and income, and the greater well-being and strength of the country for its tasks at home and abroad."

It has never been easy to describe the American economy and probably never will be, because it doesn't stand still long enough. Theorists of one persuasion or another have always been laying claim to its achievement. But through some special chemistry of its own—of its people, its heritage, its geography—it has taken the best of the theories and avoided the worst, and gone on its merry productive way to challenge another generation of theorists all over again. Today the powerful economic doctrine of growth has settled in as if to stay, and intelligent and capable men are searching for the best in it. Yet once again perhaps the important point is that they recognize the power and strength of the American economy as the beginning of progress.

The Next Turn in Taxes*

EDMUND K. FALTERMAYER

. . . The whole problem of tax reduction and revision is obviously being dealt with in a more hopeful atmosphere. For years most economic discussion has centered not on tax reduction but on government spending. Now a new national consensus is emerging in which it is recognized that revision of taxes is one of the government's most potent devices for maintaining a healthy, growing economy.

The consensus found expression in the Revenue Act of 1964, when Congress took the unprecedented step of revising corporate and personal income taxes downward over a two-year period in the face of a large budget deficit. This revision did two things. First it cut the Treasury's "tax take" from the private sector by nearly $13 billion a year, thus releasing the over-all fiscal brake on the economy. Equally important, it strengthened incentives by lowering the corporate profits tax four points and by flattening the steep progression in upper-bracket individual tax rates; the top

*December 1964

personal rate was cut from 91 percent to 70. Economists differ as to which aspect of the 1964 law is of greater importance for the future, but most agree that the experiment worked. Says Arthur F. Burns, president of the National Bureau of Economic Research, "Both positions were right the way the 1964 tax bill came out. Both can claim victory."

While further cuts in personal and corporate taxes may have to wait until 1966 or 1967, the prospect of frequent tax revision has been brightened considerably by some recent trends in the administrative federal budget. Thanks in large part to the economies exercised by Secretary of Defense Robert S. McNamara, federal spending has declined somewhat for the first time since President Kennedy took office in 1961. While outlays are almost certain to rise again, they may increase at a slower rate than in the past. Meanwhile the federal tax system, which is still basically an engine for wartime financing even after the 1964 law, may grind out $5 billion to $6 billion of additional revenue each year, or more than is likely to be spent. While there is a deficit right now, to be sure, this new *tendency* toward surplus gives promise of a whole series of possible tax reductions. According to current thinking, these need not be delayed each time until the budget is in the black because in most circumstances—except inflation—it will be desirable to release the money to the private sector as quickly as possible. Tax policy is particularly important these days—so runs the new argument—because the U.S. balance-of-payments deficit limits the use of monetary policy to stimulate the economy. A full-throttle "easy money" policy at the Federal Reserve Board would cause more U.S. capital to seek higher interest rates abroad, and renew the gold drain.

So big has been the impact of this kind of thinking that in the last election both candidates came out for more tax cuts. While Senator Goldwater denounced the 1964 tax bill as "politically motivated" as to size and timing, he proposed during the campaign not only further revision of the tax structure but a reduction in the government's tax take by 5 percent annually during the next five years. President Johnson was more circumspect, promising the reduction of excises in 1965 and further "carefully timed" tax cuts later on. "In the future," he said, "we will not permit federal revenues to become a drag on the economy." With both major political leaders talking this way, the layman might almost assume that all that remains to be done is to draw up a master tax plan and then let Congress go home. Except for differences in timing, it would seem, there is nothing more to argue about.

HOW MUCH REFORM?

Actually, there will be plenty to argue about. A broad bipartisan consensus on the possibility and desirability of further tax reduction is a long way from agreement on specific proposals. Moreover, there is no guarantee that the money for tax cuts will actually turn up. The economy, after all, might not grow fast enough to generate the additional revenues. And the Democratic Administration, with its strong new mandate from the electorate, might abandon its recent frugality. If the money does appear— and chances are pretty good that it will—there is the important question of how much should be used for tax cuts. Should some of it, for example, be applied to reducing the $312-billion national debt or, as some have recently proposed, turned over to the hard-pressed state governments? Should taxes be cut during a recession in order to stimulate a business upturn, even when the budget is running a heavy deficit? Given the complexity of the legislative process, will Congress act speedily on future tax cuts or drag its feet? Will a series of tax reductions weaken the tax system's much-praised effectiveness as a "built-in stabilizer" of the economy? Finally, how much tax reform will be coupled with future tax reduction?

The last question is particularly important, because reform efforts can be both bad and good. An effort at reform can delay tax reduction; this is one of the reasons why the 1964 Revenue Act took thirteen months to get through Congress. But rate changes designed to strengthen incentives, to many economists, are more important than reducing the government's tax take, and they stand a far better chance of passage if they are proposed in connection with a general tax reduction for everybody. Similarly, the best time to close so-called tax loopholes—which divert a good deal of human and corporate effort into tax-avoidance gimmicks—is during a general reduction that softens the impact on those who will no longer be able to use them.

Many of the unsettled issues in federal tax policy have a nonpartisan character. But on two key questions some rather deeply rooted differences of viewpoint are certain to intrude. One question concerns the form that future tax reduction will take—i.e., the *way* in which it will be tailored to stimulate the economy. The other is the perennial debate over the size of the federal budget. How much Washington spends, after all, will have a rather direct bearing on how much of that potential $5-billion to $6-billion-a-year melon of additional revenues will be available for tax cuts, and how often. Continuing differences of opinion are strikingly apparent in the contrasting views of the impact of the February 1964 tax law, and what it means for future fiscal policy.

MACRO VS. MICRO

It is highly important to understand these differing viewpoints because they will affect the shape of the tax legislation to come. One major split is between those who tend to emphasize the so-called *macro*economic effects of general tax reduction on the economy, and those who stress the *micro*economic effects of specific *rate* changes on incentives. Both "macros" and "micros" turn up almost anywhere in the political spectrum, and the distinction cuts across conventional group labels. But in general the macro approach is taken by liberals and the micro approach is taken by conservatives.

The liberals see the over-all reduction in governmental takeout from the economy as the prime reason why the gross national product will rise by about $38 billion during 1964—about $10 billion to $15 billion more than would have otherwise been the case, they say—to about $623 billion. Walter Heller, outgoing chairman of the President's Council of Economic Advisers, says the tax reduction probably enabled the U.S. to "skip a recession" that many considered long overdue.

Government economists buttress the liberal argument with some figures. Pre-tax personal income, at an annual rate, increased $13 billion during the first half of 1964 over the fourth quarter of 1963, one points out. Normally, this would have caused an increase of about $10 billion in personal consumption. Instead, consumption rose $15 billion. Conclusion: the extra $5 billion must have been the result of the tax cut. The stimulus of the personal income-tax cut continued into the third quarter. By then, consumers, who at first spent only half the extra money and saved the rest, were spending most of it.[1]

Conservatives do not necessarily disagree with this line of reasoning. Indeed, some of them fear that the tax cut may have been too much of a good thing all at once; that it may have enabled the U.S. to skip a recession in 1964 but it increased the danger of one in 1965. Whatever their misgivings, though, most conservatives believe the stimulus came primarily from the incentive effects of the 1964 Revenue Act. The gentler slope of progression that the new law provides at the upper end of the personal-income-tax schedule, they say, is the most important change of all. For this is far more than a tax reduction to those affected; it is a major rate reform that will stimulate individual effort and permit more saving in the high-income brackets from which so much of the country's investment capital comes. Meanwhile, these economists say, the reduction of the corporate profits tax from 52 to 48 percent, coming on the heels of the 7 percent investment credit voted by Congress in 1962 and the speedup in depreciation allowed by the Treasury that same year, has helped push plant and equipment spending to record levels.

These new incentives—or, more correctly, the reduction of previous disincentives—provide considerable lift. George Terborgh, of the Machinery and Allied Products Institute, has calculated that the corporate tax changes of the last three years have increased the rate of return on a typical piece of new equipment by 35 to 45 percent. Individuals, too, are enjoying the effects. Previously, the Internal Revenue Service took 50 percent

---

[1] Most of the economic stimulus to date has come from the $9.2-billion personal-income-tax cut provided by the recent law. In theory, this is spread over two years, with two-thirds of the reduction in 1964 and the rest in 1965. But because the personal withholding schedules were reduced to the 1965 rate in one stroke, at President Johnson's request, the individual tax reduction, for all practical purposes, has already taken place. Corporations, on the other hand, will not get any additional cash for several years because their $2.4-billion reduction in taxes was coupled with a speedup in payment procedures. Because the economy has grown, the over-all size of the tax cut has grown, too, from $11.5 billion a year, when it was first proposed in 1963, to nearly $13 billion in 1964 and, according to Secretary of the Treasury Douglas Dillon, $14 billion in 1965.

of a $1,000-a-year pay increase awarded to an ambitious bachelor earning $17,600 entirely from wages. Beginning in 1965, his salary can climb to $23,600 before Uncle Sam gets half of his raises. The lowering of upper-bracket rates has already caused some corporations to reappraise their stock-option plans, which may no longer offer any particular advantage over straight salary increases. Just as important as the specific tax changes of 1962 and 1964, the conservatives say, is the dramatic change they have brought in the U.S. business climate. For they symbolize an abandonment, first by Kennedy, and then by Johnson, of the "soak-the-rich" and anti-business philosophies that had lingered on in muted form from New Deal days.

Obviously, there is considerable overlap between the liberal and conservative viewpoints. What matters for the future is the difference in emphasis, for each camp will press for its own kind of tax cut. The fact that there was no head-on clash of viewpoints in the formulation of the 1964 tax law proves little, for this was a massive tax reduction—the first in a decade—big enough to give something to both camps. But if taxes are cut more often in the future, as most economists believe they should be, the bag of goodies will be small each time. Liberal politicians may want to concentrate most of the benefits in the lower-income brackets, so they will be big enough to be noticed, while conservatives will want to keep chipping away at corporate taxes and at the top personal-tax rates.

"KEYNESIAN" OR CONSERVATIVE?

Another important split, also essentially along liberal-conservative lines, is certain to influence future tax legislation. This is the ancient debate on the size of the federal budget. The debate is far from dead; this is clear from the contrasting liberal and conservative notions of the fiscal doctrine embedded in the 1964 Revenue Act. Both camps see the law as a "breakthrough" and a victory for their side. The liberals have hailed it as the first "Keynesian" tax cut—i.e., the first one legislated during a time of deficit for the express purpose of stimulating the economy. The conservatives, on the other hand, see it as a turning of the tide against ever higher federal spending. Because of the tax cut's disciplinary effect on spending, conservatives say, the federal budget will now begin to decline as a percentage of GNP, or at least level off.

On balance, though, the conservatives came out ahead. What speeded the lagging tax-reduction bill through Congress, after all, was President Johnson's January 1964 budget message, which called for the first reduction in federal spending in five years. It symbolized a retreat by the liberals from the doctrine of federal pump priming. In the early months of his Administration, President Kennedy had tried to "get the country moving again" by spending more money, but Congress had refused to appropriate all of the funds he sought. Only then did the emphasis shift from spend more to tax less. Tax-cut money, many liberals are now saying, finds its way into the economy more quickly, in the form of refrigerator or car sales, than money appropriated for new post offices. "There is nothing sacred, or even desirable, about the expenditure route," says Budget Director Kermit Gordon.

The liberal "breakthrough," while of lesser magnitude than the conservative one, was in selling a sophisticated new rationale for cutting taxes when the budget is in deficit. Without this rationale, the conservatives might not have agreed to reduce taxes as quickly as they did, despite their instinctive yearning to do so. The prospect during Congress' final deliberations on the tax bill was for a whopping $10-billion deficit in fiscal 1964 if taxes were cut (the final figure was $8.3 billion). It went against the conservative grain to give a surplus away, in the form of a tax cut, before it arrived.

Liberal arguments eased many conservatives' misgivings. What mattered, the liberals said, was not the actual deficit but the fact that if the economy were operating at its full potential and federal spending remained the same, the tax system would produce a surplus. Yet it was precisely the federal tax structure, with its progressive individual rates and heavy over-all "tax take," that was stunting economic growth and, in effect, preventing the surplus from ever appearing. With the tax brake released, economic growth would accelerate and produce enough new revenue to offset much of the tax cut. Walter Heller, in pressing the argument, saw a justification for immediate tax reduction in the so-called "full-employment surplus," i.e., the surplus that would exist if the U.S. economy were operating at its theoretical "full employment" level. While the "full employment" concept is frowned upon by many conservatives, the notion of a latent tendency to surplus persuaded many of them that tax reduction offered the only hope of ever getting the budget in the black. Thus an essentially conservative tax bill was expedited by some liberal, "Keynesian" thinking.

This could represent a dangerous precedent, to be sure. For it is likely that from now on the mere prospect of a surplus, say, twelve or eighteen months hence, will be considered sufficient justification for reducing taxes at once, particularly if the economy is operating substantially below its potential. Those who wish to delay tax reduction will be answered with the "full-employment surplus" doctrine and similar arguments. If this becomes the general pattern—i.e., if surpluses are repeatedly postponed through tax reduction—the national debt will continue to rise, though perhaps at a slower rate than in recent years. The obvious exception would be during a period of severe inflation, when even liberals would favor a budget surplus, combined with debt reduction, as a means of damping down an overheated economy.

While the 1964 law marks a major narrowing of liberal and conservative differences, the two camps will continue to disagree on the over-all level of federal expenditures. Liberals, for all their new-found appreciation of the private sector, will still look favorably on proposals for stepped-up federal spending for mass transit, urban renewal, and the poverty war; many conservatives will go right on opposing them. The precise outcome of this dialogue, which will determine the amount available for tax reduction, is impossible to forecast. But assuming that a middle course is followed, it is possible to look down the road and see what form a pattern of future tax cuts might take.

THOSE REVENUES KEEP RISING

When Washington officials speculate on tax reduction they look primarily at the expenditure curve in the federal administrative budget. This is smaller than the comprehensive "national income accounts" budget—which includes such items as Social Security and the federal highway trust fund—but it also contains all the activities that lend themselves to economizing—i.e., defense, foreign aid, farm price supports, and the rest. The other variable is the state of the economy, for this will determine how much additional tax revenue comes in each year. This is impossible to foretell, of course. But if GNP were to grow by 5 percent annually, in current prices, for the next several years —not on overly optimistic assumption, in view of the recent performance—revenues would rise about $5 billion to $6 billion a year.

Though it may sound incredible, almost nobody in Washington can figure out ways to spend all that extra money. Expenditures on defense, space, and interest on the public debt account, which absorb about $70 billion of the current $97.2-billion budget, are all tending to level off or grow more slowly than in the past. It is extremely unlikely that the $27-billion civilian portion could absorb the bulk of the revenue increases, even with a stepped-up anti-poverty war. A reasonable guess, therefore, is that total expenditures will rise only $2.5 billion to $3 billion a year. This, in turn, would leave room for tax cuts averaging $2 billion to $3.5 billion annually.

The bulk of this money would, indeed, probably go for tax cuts, rather than for some other alternatives. If recent history proves anything, there will be little sentiment for applying the money to the national debt, except during a period of strong inflation. There will also be little sentiment for finding new ways to spend the money. Many Washington politicians believe that, with state and local budgets growing faster than GNP, the federal budget must grow more slowly. Otherwise the total tax burden on the economy, which rose from 23 percent of GNP in 1948 to 29 percent in 1963, will become still heavier. There is more support for a third alternative—giving some of the money to the states in the form of a "fiscal dividend," with no strings attached. Curiously enough, this is favored by both Walter Heller and Barry Goldwater. But it also raises a host of thorny problems. Should the money be apportioned to states on the basis of area, population, per capita income, or what? President Johnson, who supports the idea in principle, has authorized a study of possible methods for channeling a portion of federal revenues back to the states. But even if he recommends a plan and Congress approves it, the scheme would probably be only a partial substitute for tax reduction.

Assuming, though, that most of the extra money would go for tax reduction, there remains the all-important question of timing. The federal administrative budget might reach a surplus late in fiscal 1967—i.e., between January and June of that year. But a tax cut might be desirable before then, many economists argue. This is because the national income accounts budget, reflecting a rise in social-security taxes scheduled for January 1, 1966, may come into balance a year sooner. Meanwhile, the stimulus of the 1964 tax cut will have played out by mid-1965, just when some economists see a possible business downturn. According to this reasoning, a $2-billion to $3-billion excise-tax cut would appear not only possible but desirable. If this is done, the earliest date at which personal and corporate taxes could be reduced would be 1967. If the proposed tax reduction included a lot of reform, Congress would have to start working on a bill as early as 1966. The cut might run as high as $5 billion, with another one of similar dimensions possible in 1969 and perhaps every two years after that.

At least two things could upset this admittedly tentative schedule. One would be a new rise in defense spending. A stepped-up U.S. military involvement in South Vietnam, for example, could push defense costs up, and so could the development by the Soviet Union of an effective defense against ballistic missiles. In the latter case, this country might have to spend $20 billion or more for an anti-missile system of its own. The other upsetting factor would be a recession, for this would slow the projected increase in revenues, but strengthen the argument for stimulating the economy somehow.

SUPPORT FOR "QUICKIE" TAX CUTS

This latter possibility raises one of the most serious questions about future tax policy. Most of the discussion preceding the 1964 law focused on tax reduction for promoting long-term economic growth—i.e., for preventing recessions from occurring in the first place. But what if a recession does come, as it inevitably must? Should taxes be cut anyway to counter the recession, even though the tax-cut "ammunition" may already have been expended and the budget is in substantial deficit? Congress has never cut taxes in the midst of a recession, and many believe that doing so is not only fiscally irresponsible but likely to boomerang because of its effect on public confidence. Arthur Burns and some other economists urged a tax cut during the 1957–58 recession, but the Eisenhower Administration shied away from it, partly because Congress had voted a massive step-up in anti-recession spending. The prospective deficit seemed so large—it hit a postwar high of $12.4 billion in fiscal 1959—that a tax cut seemed out of the question. President Kennedy briefly considered a "quickie" tax cut in 1962 to ward off what then appeared to be an oncoming recession, but the idea got a cool reception from Wilbur Mills, chairman of the House Ways and Means Committee, where tax bills must originate, and was dropped.

Nevertheless, the idea of an anti-recession tax cut is very much alive. One reason, Administration officials say, is that Congress is unlikely to go overboard on spending in a future recession because of the disappointing results of past pump priming. Therefore, the deficit might not be so large as it was during the 1958 recession. And Congress might be more receptive to a quick tax cut if it were temporary in nature—if it were made clear that taxes would revert to their previous rates after, say, nine months. One of Mr. Mills's objections to the quickie tax cut proposed in 1962 was that it would have been a permanent one, and the reform-minded committee chairman would have none of a permanent tax reduction that did not also include some improvements in the tax system. The biggest imponderable, of course, is whether a temporary tax cut would move the U.S. out of a recession even if Congress passed it. The prevailing view in the Johnson Administration is that it would, if it were properly formulated and quickly acted upon by Congress.

To lay the groundwork for such action the Treasury is considering some sort of "sense of Congress" legislation that would spell out in advance the form a quick and temporary anti-recession tax cut would take. There is far less agreement on this kind of action, however, than on the general proposition that taxes should go down over the years, in good times as well as bad. Goldwater's five-year tax-reduction plan, while criticized as unduly rigid, is not so far from the mainstream as it might appear. The main idea, Goldwater advisers said during the recent campaign, would be to get Congress committed to a series of tax cuts. If fiscal conditions changed, the reductions could always be postponed by new legislation. Arthur Burns, who is impressed by the fact that Japan has been cutting taxes annually since 1950, thinks Congress should reduce taxes every year. He has doubts, however, about Goldwater's 5 percent, which he considers too high, and he also questions the desirability of a "mechanical" five-year timetable. President Johnson has been cool to a long-range program of tax reduction, partly because it would give less latitude for increases in federal spending if these should later prove desirable.

WORRIES ABOUT THE AUTOMATIC STABILIZER

Frequent tax reduction, some observers fear, would reduce the tax system's potency, as a "built-in" stabilizer of the economy. Because corporate profits fluctuate sharply and because of the progression in individual tax rates, federal revenues fall when business levels off or turns down, and rise more rapidly than the GNP during an upswing. Constant whittling away at federal taxes might lessen this effect, some argue. First, over-all tax revenues would decline as a percentage of GNP, giving the tax system less anti-cyclical leverage. And second, a lowering of corporate rates and a flattening of the slope of progression in the middle and upper brackets of the personal-income tax—an almost inevitable result of a series of tax cuts—would further dampen the stabilizing effect.

Actually, this effect is less than some enthusiasts of the "built-in stabilizer" believe. In fiscal 1958, during the deepest postwar recession, revenues for the administrative budget fell only $2 billion, or 3 percent—not enough, in the opinion of many economists, to provide effective anti-cyclical uplift. Whatever its effect, automatic stabilization will continue to be an important feature of the tax system. Even if the federal budget shrinks in relation to GNP, it will still be quite substantial. Corporate tax revenues would fluctuate even if the corporate tax rate fell to, say, 35 percent, because the profits on which they are based would continue to be volatile. A lowering of top individual tax rates would have little effect on the built-in stabilizer, because these rates produce only a negligible percentage of the total revenue. Indeed, if all upper bracket tax rates were reduced to 50 percent—i.e., if the progression curve were absolutely flat above $22,000 of taxable income for single persons and $44,000 for married couples—the Treasury would lose only $250 million to $300 million a year. Much of the built-in stabilization would continue to take place where it does at present—at the relatively flat, lower end of the scale, where exemptions and standard deductions produce considerable progression.[2]

THE SIMPLIFIED INCOME TAX

Tax reform is almost bound to intrude into most future legislation, other than "quickie" tax cuts. Wilbur Mills is only one of many people who believe it should, even if it delays the release of the fiscal brake on the economy, because the best time to rejigger the system is in connection with tax reduction. Tax reform, of course, means different things to different people. To many conservatives, as already noted, the most important kind of reform is the flattening of the gradient of progression in the personal-income tax and reduction of the corporate tax. To them reduction of the top individual rate to 70 percent—the lowest it has been since 1936—is an enormous advance. Many believe that this should be carried further, with the top rate reduced eventually to 50 percent.

But tax reform also means simplification of the tax laws, the elimination of special hardships and price-distorting effects, and the ending of such special privileges as the oil-depletion allowance. From the standpoint of structural reform, says Professor Richard A. Musgrave of Princeton University, the recent law was "pretty miserable." When the tax bill was originally proposed by President Kennedy in January 1963, it included some $3.3 billion

---

[2] A married couple with two children, for example, using the new "minimum" standard deduction of $600 and taking its four $600 exemptions, will pay no taxes whatever in 1965 on its first $3,000 of income. For such a family an increase of only 25 percent in total income, from $4,000 to $5,000 a year, will mean a *doubling* of the portion on which it pays taxes, and these will shoot up by 107 percent from $140 to $290. Short-term fluctuations in income are common in the $4,000 to $6,000 bracket, since this includes the bulk of hourly paid workers who work overtime during a boom but may be temporarily laid off during a recession.

of such reforms, i.e., non-rate changes, designed to offset the expected loss in revenue. The biggest single item, the plan to limit individuals' itemized deductions to those exceeding 5 percent of adjusted gross income, ran into a storm of opposition. Nevertheless, some structural reformers are encouraged by the fact that the final bill included quite a few non-rate changes. Many people, such as Henry H. Fowler, who as Under Secretary of the Treasury helped push the 1964 law through Congress, consider this a turning of the tide against the opening up of more so-called loopholes. The new law, he said just after its passage, represents a decision "to arrest the gradual erosion of the tax base through special preferences."

The prospect, then, is that the reformers will try to hitch a ride on future tax-cut legislation. Drastic changes are unlikely, however, and they will proceed in piecemeal fashion. The two most exciting current proposals for structural change are intriguing because of the effect they would have on incentives. One is a plan developed by Senator Russell Long of Louisiana, which would offer wealthy individuals a top tax rate of 50 percent if they waive most deductions and provide a larger standard deduction for middle-income taxpayers. The other is a "value-added" tax that would partly replace the corporate profits tax. Of the two, Senator Long's plan is far more likely to be adopted in the near future. The Senate Finance Committee almost approved it as an amendment to the 1964 law, and the Senator has recently brought out a revised version, whose basic principle, at least, appeals to the Treasury. The Senator says he will introduce his bill, which would cost the Treasury $700 million annually, sometime during the next two years.

Few Washington politicians are ready to commit themselves yet to something as novel as a value-added tax on business, though France and the state of Michigan already have one. But support for it, as a substitute for at least part of the corporate income tax, has been growing lately in academic circles. For years, economists have been unable to agree on whether the corporate profits tax is passed along to consumers in the form of higher prices. But the theory that at least part of the burden is shifted to consumers is gaining ground. If this is so, argues Professor Dan Throop Smith of the Harvard Business School, the shifted portion is in effect a "capricious sort of excise tax that increases prices more than a general excise would." To the extent it is not shifted, he says, it "has a discouraging effect on investment," which is also bad. Further, it puts U.S. exporters at a disadvantage because the GATT agreement prohibits rebates to them of income taxes. The value-added tax, which would be levied on a company's total sales minus the cost of purchased materials, has a number of possible advantages, its proponents claim. Unlike the corporate tax, it would be paid by all firms, unprofitable as well as profitable; it would not be a "tax on efficiency." The tax base would be broad, so that 1 percent of value-added tax could replace as much as five points of the corporate income tax. And it could be rebated to exporters under the GATT agreement. . . .

Behind U.S. Steel's Price Blunder* _____

RICHARD AUSTIN SMITH

The afternoon of April 10, 1962 was a tranquil one in New York, mild and sunny, as if the west wind had become charged with the balm of national well-being in its sweep across the land. The specter of a steel strike had been quietly laid to rest in the agreements labor and management had been signing since April 6, and the agreements themselves, providing a package settlement of 10 cents an hour, were among the most moderate in the postwar history of steel. Down on Varick Street the big Miehle multicolor presses of Lind Brothers were happily clattering away on an expression of euphoria, a lead article in the monthly survey of the Morgan Guaranty Trust Co. It began: "To a business community eager for good news, the labor agreement in the steel industry has provided the brightest word of recent weeks. . . . If it proves to set a pattern for other industries, the bargaining outcome could encourage investment spending by easing apprehensions over a further profits squeeze in industry generally and,

_____

*August 1962

over a period of time, could help the competitive position of U.S. goods in world markets."

Certainly nobody other than the handful of men gathered together in a big paneled room at 71 Broadway could have had any idea that the afternoon's tranquillity was about to be shattered by a sudden action on the part of U.S. Steel. The top men at Morgan Guaranty obviously didn't expect it, though bank officers had sat on U.S. Steel's board ever since the corporation had sprung full-blown from the heads of J. P. Morgan and Charlie Schwab, sixty-one years before; they learned the news over the radio that evening, after the monthly survey, embarrassingly, was in the mail. Nor was it expected by those who keep an attentive eye on the doings of the steel industry. Only the day before the *Wall Street Journal* had reported from Pittsburgh that the nation's leading steel producers were saying they didn't expect any significant improvement in business before autumn and as a result "many of them have about given up any hope of generally boosting prices this year." Nevertheless, that was what happened; U.S. Steel's executive committee voted an across-the-board price increase in the big paneled room that April afternoon. And at 5:45 P.M. Chairman Roger M. Blough handed the President of the U.S. a press release to put him on notice of what they had done.

So began the most mystifying episode American business has witnessed in many a year. Roger Blough has been castigated for "stupidity" and President Kennedy's angry reaction has been termed "arrogance." But these judgments divert attention from important lessons of the April crisis. Why did U.S. Steel make just the wrong decisions at just the wrong time? The answer lies partly in the character of the corporation, partly in the changed economic environment. But the place to begin the quest for an explanation of the mystery is with the top men of U.S. Steel as they appeared at the denouement of the drama, on Friday, April 13.

A DAY AT THE CARLYLE

That morning found U.S. Steel's finance-committee chairman, Robert C. Tyson, its president, Leslie B. Worthington, and Chairman Blough closeted with Labor Secretary Goldberg and Clark

Clifford in Goldberg's suite at New York's Hotel Carlyle. Clifford, once special counsel to President Truman and a lawyer of broad corporate experience, had been brought in by Kennedy late on Thursday, April 12. Of the three U.S. Steel men present for the conference, Worthington was described by one of the conferees as silent ("he didn't say a word all day long"), Tyson as "terribly worried," and Blough as "amiable and tenacious" in his "exceedingly unimpressive" arguments rationalizing the general price increase. Those arguments, together with Goldberg's ripostes, took up most of the morning. "Did we help you to get a more favorable settlement?" the Labor Secretary asked at one point, and received an assent from Blough. "Then what do you think we were in there for? Roger, there were eight to ten times during this period when all you had to say was: 'Understand we are taking part in the negotiations, but understand that no one is going to interfere with our right to raise the price of steel.' Did you ever say that?" Blough replied no, because he felt it was implicit that steel had the right to raise prices anytime it chose.

But around midday there was a change in U.S. Steel's tone of voice. Blough had admitted at his press conference the day before that the corporation might have to rescind its price increase if certain competitors didn't go along with it. Now at 12:00 New York time Inland Steel had announced it would not raise its prices and Kaiser had followed suit, as Blough no doubt learned during his frequent telephone calls from an adjoining room at the hotel.

After Inland's announcement, the men in the suite at the Carlyle turned from accusations and rationalizations about the past, and focused their discussion on recision of the price increase. When offers to help him "save face" were reiterated in this context, Blough finally asked "What excuse have we got?" Three face-saving ideas were promptly suggested: (1) U.S. Steel could announce that careful study had indicated the price boost was not in the public interest, consequently it was being rescinded; (2) U.S. Steel could say there had been a "misunderstanding" with the Administration and since the Administration felt so strongly that steel should *not* have raised prices, it was appropriate to remove the source of the controversy and rescind; (3) U.S. Steel could explain that some companies had not gone along with the increase, and since it was not in the best interest of the corporation to engage in this kind of intra-industry contest, it was rescinding. The last suggestion seemed to gain merit as Blough & Co. pondered, especially toward midafternoon. It was then, at 3:25 P.M. to be precise, that the announcement came of Bethlehem's recision. But though it became a little clearer as time went by that U.S. Steel was ready to throw in the sponge, when Blough & Co. left the Carlyle suite at 5:10 P.M. Goldberg and Clifford were still in the dark about just how U.S. Steel would explain its capitulation. They learned a half hour later when a phone call notified them the corporation was rescinding on the ground that other companies had not gone along.

"WE HAD A FUNDAMENTAL PROBLEM"

Three months later many businessmen were still wondering why U.S. Steel had not foreseen both the government's reaction and the purely commercial difficulty of raising prices in a weak steel market. Quotes from three of U.S. Steel's top people offer clues to this part of the mystery. "We looked at the costs of the fourth quarter of 1961 and the first quarter of 1962," said President Worthington, "and we looked ahead to the prospects down the line. We have to invest $400 million in physical properties every year just to stay even. Adding it all up, it was certainly high time we got going. The thing was debated and it was our conclusion that we should announce a general price increase." Added Executive Vice President Richard F. Sentner: "We had a fundamental problem. The company was not making a sufficient margin to do what we needed to do commercially. In the Commercial Department, we wanted new strip mills and we were told, sure, we could have them if the company had the money. It was not anything that happened all at once. It was an accumulation of things dating from 1958 onward." Summed up Chairman Blough: "When would there have been a better time to test the market? In our judgment the cost and commercial factors all warranted it; and, from the competitive angle in a highly competitive industry, one of the best possible times we could elect to increase prices would be one not expected by the rest of the industry."

Certainly if the strategy behind Big Steel's timing was to catch the industry unawares, it succeeded. All the companies *Fortune* has talked to expressed astonishment over the timing, however much each of them considered that it *needed* a price increase. Bethlehem, U.S. Steel's major rival, had previously examined the market and decided against initiating any general boost for reasons that were obvious throughout the industry. Demand for the metal was still soft, as it had been for the past several years; orders were sufficient only to justify industry-wide operation at an estimated 60 percent of capacity, and that was expected to drop to the lower 50's before customers worked off the inventories they had accumulated as a hedge against a strike. Foreign competition was on the rise, nourished by highly efficient new mills and important increases in capacity. Indeed the period would have seemed more appropriate for a major producer to be adjusting itself to the disciplines of international competition. In 1955 the U.S. had exported 4,061,000 net tons of steel products, imported only 973,000. In 1961 exports, down to 1,989,000 tons, were passed by imports, which rose to 3,164,000. By the spring of 1962, foreign nails and staples had grabbed off 47 percent of the U.S. market, drawn wire 9 percent, wire rods 27 percent; reinforcing bars—in which competition is so intense there is no quoted price—25 percent; pipe and tubing 7 to 8 percent, shapes and piling the same proportion. As for materials in competition with steel—aluminum, plastics, concrete—the price increase could be expected only to accelerate their threatening displacement of steel in building construction, containers, automobiles, etc.

THE DECISIVE ROLE OF INLAND

A compelling factor in Bethlehem's earlier decision not to initiate a general price increase was one that U.S. Steel might also have foreseen; Bethlehem had calculated that Inland Steel probably would not go along with an across-the-board boost. U.S. Steel's strategy was based in part on the premise that other companies would follow its lead because they were all in a comparable situation in so far as costs were concerned. But Inland had been able to absorb the greater part of the wage increases of the previous contract (1960–62); indeed its first-quarter net earnings in 1962 were only 6.8 percent below those of the comparable quarter of 1959. Per ton margins of Inland

had dropped only $1.65 below 1959's first quarter (U.S. Steel's
were down $7.90). As late as November 1961, Inland's Chairman
Joseph L. Block had publicly stated his belief that under prevailing conditions an improvement in profits could best be obtained
by cutting costs rather than trying to raise prices. Said he to the
Controllers Institute of America: "Profits can be improved either
by raising prices or by lowering costs. Of these alternatives I
would much prefer the latter. Price levels which would further
weaken the American steel industry's competitive position in
relation to foreign producers would not be in the interest of the
United States or of the employees, customers, and stockholders
of the steel industry." In addition, Inland had a wary eye on the
plant Bethlehem was planning to build nearby, which would
considerably enhance Bethlehem's competitive position in Inland's prime market, Chicago. The company considered maintenance of customer loyalty of vital importance.

Now the character of the steel business is such that if a major
producer in a major market, like Inland in Chicago, does not go
along with somebody else's price increase, it is just a matter of
time before that somebody has to beat a retreat. Indeed this
fundamental truth was succinctly stated in 1957 by none other
than Roger Blough himself: "There isn't certainly any steel company in the first ten or in the first twenty that couldn't require
us to change our prices overnight simply by taking action which
is different than the action that we take." As Joe Block analyzed
the situation that arose in mid-April: "Once Inland announced
it would stay out, Bethlehem rescinded their price increase because they immediately recognized what would happen to them
in the national market if they didn't. In the Chicago area Inland
would be running at full capacity, the rest of the industry at
about 50 percent. To be sure, Chicago is only a part of the national market for steel, but the impact of such action is national,
and with the industry only running at 60 percent nobody could
afford to lose any tonnage anywhere." There was something else.
The customers that Inland, U.S. Steel, and others supply in Chicago also have operations in localities beyond the Chicago marketing area. These companies would bring heavy pressure to
force prices in their areas back to the level Inland maintained in
Chicago. As Block put it: "You can have a lot of different prices,
say for automobiles, because styles are different. But if you are

making steel for fenders for General Motors or whomever, you have to meet the specifications of the automobile company. You either have to supply to these specifications at the lowest competitive price, or you don't get the order. Steel for a particular purpose is standardized and competition forces prices of such steel to be the same at a given time throughout the industry." Logan T. Johnston, president of Armco Steel, next to Inland the steel industry's most profitable producer (1961), echoed Block: "If *we* had raised our prices and Inland's stayed put, Inland would have moved so deep into our territory we'd have to put a moat around our plant in Middletown [Ohio] to keep them out."

SIZE, TRADITION, AND DICHOTOMY

Why, then, did U.S. Steel disregard general and specific factors militating against an across-the-board price increase in the steel industry? There are at least two possible explanations, one an economic reason, the other founded in Big Steel's corporate psychology. The company's outlook on the world has been profoundly influenced by the fact that back in the Twenties it was adjudged a "good trust." This judgment, handed down by the Supreme Court in a four-to-three decision, permitted Big Steel to escape dismemberment at the hands of the Justice Department, but at the price of the aggressiveness that produced big, strong companies out of split-up empires like Standard Oil. U.S. Steel was left intact, but it was inhibited from trying to obtain a larger share of the total market for steel. This somewhat dulled the corporation's competitive instincts. In the 1930's Chairman Myron Taylor complained he was hard pressed "to find men who will leave private business [*sic*] and devote themselves to the corporation." In 1958 a Brookings study found U.S. Steel's pricing policy "colored by a concept of the corporation as the industry leader vested with the responsibilities and subject to the inhibitions of a public utility."[1]

In certain respects, U.S. Steel's "inhibitions" do it credit and help account for the company's survival in the face of anxieties about its vast size and power. There have been a number of

---

[1] *Pricing in Big Business* by A. D. H. Kaplan, Joel B. Dirlam, and Robert F. Lanzillotti; the Brookings Institution.

occasions in the past when U.S. Steel could have raised its prices but refrained from doing so because of its special "inhibitions"; looking inward, it told itself it didn't need the money. But the other side of this "public utility" psychology has been a certain insensitivity to the market pressures that more directly affect the behavior of other companies. In the new situation this habit of thinking again led U.S. Steel to look inward and to justify a price increase on the ground that now it *did* need the money. U.S. Steel's corporate behavior pattern, in short, is partly like that of a public utility (without a regulatory body) and partly like that of a competitive enterprise. Such dichotomy was in the background of the April blunder. President Worthington's public statement defending the price increase was wholly based on U.S. Steel's "need" for more profits, and when a public utility can make a case for *needing* a price increase, one is usually forthcoming. But, to repeat, though U.S. Steel may sometimes think and act like a public utility, its price increases are not granted by some regulatory body; they must always stand the tests of the marketplace.

LEADING FROM WEAKNESS

This other side of the corporation's position—its involvement in a competitive market—merits closer examination, for U.S. Steel did not give it adequate consideration in the price boost of this April. Steel prices are typified by their stability—they are set at levels designed to equate supply and demand over periods of months, even years, rather than fluctuating with short-term changes—and they are customarily set by the industry's price leader. That price leader, though its leadership has always been subject to challenge, has almost always been U.S. Steel. However, in 1958, the year of the last price increase, U.S. Steel made some moves that stand in significant contrast to what it did this April.

In 1958 the corporation's president, in an unprecedented statement, announced U.S. Steel would not increase prices July 1 but would wait and see what might happen. Declared President Hood: "Any adjustment of sales prices can only be made in the light of all known commercial and economic factors, including competitive conditions in the steel industry, competition with other materials, underlying customer product demand, and economic climate and outlook, together with other factors. United States Steel is continuing its study of all of these factors. The only point we have reached to date is not to attempt to change our prices until the situation clarifies itself." This was interpreted in the trade press as a plea for someone else to take the pricing leadership—and Armco eventually did. It increased prices, not across the board but selectively, in a cautious probing of the market. Armco's move was followed in short order by Republic, Jones & Laughlin, then U.S. Steel. Thus on this occasion Big Steel no doubt recognized the heavy pressures price leadership would be under (the market was soft and a congressional investigation of steel prices in the offing) and adopted a new tactic: it would follow suitable selective price increases by others, though its own pattern had been to put up prices across the board at a level of its own choosing. What had made the increases of Armco *et al.* acceptable to the corporation in July of 1958, however, was their being at levels that suited U.S. Steel's needs. But in April of 1962 the situation was quite different. By then U.S. Steel could ill afford to hang back, since it would likely have had to wait for some time before other producers boosted prices. Moreover, when such increases did come they would likely have been selective, rather than across the board, and set at levels that suited the needs of those who announced them, not U.S. Steel. As such they would touch only a part of the corporation's broad product range and provide it only partial relief at that, for U.S. Steel was in worse straits than many of its competitors. The important fact was that in 1958 the corporation was strong enough to do a little experimenting in price leadership; in 1962 it was not. By then it was leading the industry not from strength but from weakness, and that weakness had been on the increase for the past several years.

TRENDING INTO TROUBLE

From 1958 through 1961, the corporation's tonnage of steel shipped had fallen substantially below the level of 1950. Nor had it been able to maintain its percentage of the market—shipments dropped from 30.1 percent of the industry total in 1955 to 25.4 percent in 1961. (A drop of 1 percent in shipments in a 66-million-ton market like 1961's represented roughly a $130-million loss of sales.) Ever since Ben Fairless' testimony before a congressional committee in 1950, U.S. Steel had been on record as intending to "keep in step with the growth of our country"— i.e., finally abandon Judge Gary's old policy of letting its share of the market decline. Now Blough explains that U.S. Steel could not preserve its share of the market and at the same time have a profitable operation. But, in fact, the corporation's profits have declined along with its share of the market. In 1957 it was earning 9.5 percent net on every dollar of sales, the highest since the war; by 1961 this had dropped to 5.8 percent. On profits as a percent of net worth, the drop was from the handsome 14 percent of 1957 to a troubling 5.8 percent in 1961. On sales last year Big Steel earned no more than the average of the seven next-largest steel companies while the steady downward trend of its earnings on net worth had dropped it well below the seven's average in 1961 (5.8 percent vs. 7.1 percent). Inland alone netted $55 million in 1961 on sales of $725 million, while U.S. Steel earned only $190 million on $3.3 billion; as for the seven as a group, their profits were 1.5 times those of the corporation in the first quarter of 1959; by the first quarter of this year they were 2.2 times U.S. Steel's.

The reasons behind this progressive deterioration are difficult to determine with precision, especially since U.S. Steel is an admixture of steelmaking facilities, ore and coal enterprises, railroads, ships, a cement company, and reticence. The best explanation is that during the Fifties the company calculated the future market for steel would be sufficiently big to justify the heavy capital expenditures, principally for raw-material plant, that it had in mind. (Such capital expenditures reached a peak of $469 million in 1952, another peak of $515 million in 1957, still another of $492 million in 1960, and in the long run may pay off.) But market volume proved to be a disappointment: steel shipments never regained their postwar high of 85 million tons (1955), fell off to 60 million tons in the recession year of 1958, stood at 66 million by the end of 1961. The year 1957 marked the end of the sellers' market in steel and the advantage has remained with the buyer ever since. Next the wage-price escalator ended in 1958 (the year of the last price increase) and with it the easy-come easy-go method of raising earnings by boosting prices above whatever level seemed necessary to meet the wage increases. And finally the character of the market changed with a shift from low-profit heavy products (in which U.S. Steel's capacity was concentrated) to high-profit light ones. Inland, among others, drastically revamped its product mix to take full advantage of the increased demand for the lighter steels, U.S. Steel did not; thus today only about 20 percent of U.S. Steel's capacity is devoted to light, flat-rolled steels while Inland has committed 60 percent of its capacity to them.

The cumulative impact of all these developments on the U.S. Steel of 1962 was formidable to say the least. With its competitive edge already dulled by a decade of inflation, it was now confronted by intensified competition both at home and abroad. It had seldom considered the small order worth its while; now it was having to scratch for them in a buyers' market where many buyers were still resentful at being fobbed off by Big Steel in the past. It had obviously miscalculated the product mix of the future, continuing to bank on the heavy steels for the capital-goods industries while the competition put its emphasis on light, flat-rolled steels (for the burgeoning market in containers, appliances, and automobiles); thus this year, when light, flat-rolled products are expected to account for over half of all steel shipments, up from 40 percent in 1951, Big Steel's share is estimated to have dropped to 20 percent (from 25 percent eight years ago).

Financially, the results have been only too visible. With its cash flow (retained earnings plus depreciation) sliding from $509 million in 1957 to half that figure in 1959 and on down to $213 million by the end of last year, U.S. Steel was pinched for funds. Income available for reinvestment in the business (after payment of dividends) plummeted from $117 million in 1960 to $2,700,000 in 1961.

No doubt the corporation had counted on relief during the first quarter of 1962 when it had been generally assumed that U.S. Steel's share of the market would rise as demand for steel recovered from the recession period of 1960–61. But the outlook, as the first-quarter figures came in, was if anything more dismal than before. The corporation's market percentage continued its decline, at 24.9 was the second-lowest share for any quarter in U.S. Steel's history. Profit margins were equally disappointing.

They failed to rise despite the 85-million-ton annual shipment rate the industry was running at in the first quarter; earnings were only half what they had been on the same volume in prior quarters.

NEED IS REASON ENOUGH

Thus on April 10 many factors came together to convince U.S. Steel that an across-the-board price increase was timely. Indeed, Roger Blough has maintained to this day that nothing was wrong with the timing, that there's never a *good* time to raise prices. Considering this in the context of April 10 one can only conclude he was insensitive to the tremendous difference between facing the "normal" resistance to a price boost—the public never takes kindly to one under the best of circumstances —and choosing the *worst* possible time to raise prices. To him and a majority of Big Steel's executive committee, the corporation's need for more profits—a need that was real enough— constituted by itself a sufficient reason for the price increase. And once the increase was decided upon, there was no paving of the way, no preparatory measures to soften the shock. Indeed, Big Steel's public-relations department had only an hour to prepare the release.

BACK TO "THE GOOD OLD DAYS"

What the timing of the price increase has to say about U.S. Steel, however, goes beyond any entries on a profit-and-loss statement. The prices it advanced on April 10 were a failure to read the clock correctly: the corporation thought it was back in "the good old days" of a sellers' market, wage-price escalation, and across-the-board increases. The April 10 increase was an anachronistic reversion to the across-the-board pricing policy the corporation had itself found unsuitable even in 1958. Very likely, economic circumstances would have forced its rapid recision, as increasing discounts and U.S. Steel's own price *cuts* in June suggest; as a matter of fact, if the corporation can take any comfort from the government's antitrust harassment and Internal Revenue pressures, it is that these abuses of federal power have drawn attention away from the basic unsoundness of U.S. Steel's commercial judgment. "Throwing a lot of prices up against the wall to see which ones will stick," as one of the company's executives reportedly explained the rationale of its across-the-board increases, could only further unsettle an already discount-ridden market; "U.S. Steel's increase," recently declared a Wall Street analyst of thirty years' specialization in the industry, "was an open invitation to other producers to start discounting the new mill-based prices. Everyone in the industry had been reconciled to living with the existing price structure, then suddenly they were handed a $6-a-ton increase to fiddle with. An unrealistic price produces all sorts of discounts and once posted prices start being discounted you probably wind up worse than when you started."

A CALL FOR COST LEADERSHIP

Looking back over the whole unfortunate episode, even with the short perspective of four months, one cannot but feel that it provides a valuable insight into a new order of things. For basic industry, the surest road to better profits now obviously lies in cutting costs rather than raising prices. Big Steel itself will have to become more of a *cost* leader—if the corporation is to improve its profitability and remove industry's growing doubts about the validity of its price leadership. Any company following a price leader whose costs are no longer low enough to permit it to meet its competitors in a given market is hardly maximizing its opportunities.

In the present noninflationary economy, across-the-board price increases in a basic industry are unlikely for a long time to come —and for the same reasons (foreign competition, a soft market, and national economic policy) that resulted in recision in the spring; selective price increases, however, are still feasible and may even materialize. Prices of certain items (e.g., galvanized and cold-rolled sheet steel) might be raised if steel demand picks up, as expected, in the second half. Even so, some experts believe steel is in for a new kind of market. Steel prices are going to be more and more responsive to the marketplace: discounting will be more prevalent or the posted mill prices set will endure for shorter periods than has been the custom.

In such circumstances, common sense imposes on the government an obligation to make up in other ways for the price increases it opposes. Worthington's proposition that U.S. steel needs more money to modernize falls apart only when he ties it to a general price increase. The difference between what the industry needs and what it can't get in the way of price increases should be made up by more favorable depreciation provisions and some tax relief.

At the same time one of the most significant lessons of the April crisis concerns this very word "need." It is simply that whenever a great company gets away from market factors and starts talking about its *need,* such talk constitutes an open invitation to government to start applying the fair-return concepts by which public utilities are regulated. How much Washington considered it an invitation is indicated by the emergency measures the President was ready to push on April 13. They would have made Big Steel a quasi-public utility—i.e., forced to announce price rises in advance and justify them in public hearings. Of course, the steel industry is not a public utility in the sense of a legal monopoly. It is—as the upshot of the April crisis demonstrated—regulated by a competitive market. That kind of "regulation" makes government price interventions unnecessary and disruptive; certainly, price decisions should be free from government harassments under the pretext of antitrust and tax investigations. But market "regulation" also requires of the price leader keener insight, better public relations, and sounder commercial judgment than U.S. Steel displayed to the nation in April 1962.

Steel: The Ides of April* _____

EDITORIAL

In April 1962, along came an episode that will reverberate for years to come through the political and economic life of the U.S. The unexpected announcement of a general steel price increase and the subsequent rescinding of it were explosions

---

* *May 1962*

ripping through the bland surface of prosperity and disclosing elements of confusion and weakness—as well as some elements of strength—in the political economy of the U.S. A lot of damage was done, but it may be worth the cost if some of the right lessons are extracted from what happened during the Ides of April, 1962.

Among the points to be noted:

1. The fury of President Kennedy's reaction points up the danger of deep government involvement in labor negotiations.

2. U.S. Steel's action paid inadequate attention to present market conditions.

3. When certain companies, refusing to go along with the price increase, forced U.S. Steel and others to rescind, their action indicated that the framework of business decision had changed greatly—and for the better—since the inflationary years when nobody could go far wrong by taking the lead in increasing prices.

The deepest lesson of the episode is that in our "mixed economy" there is much confusion about who is responsible for what.

GARRISON STATE RHETORIC

In contrast to President Kennedy's be-kind-to-business mood, the depth and anger of his reaction were most significant. The President's language was immoderate and its content reverted to the worst aspects of the Kennedy campaign of 1960. After reciting the foreign perils faced by the U.S. in Berlin and Southeast Asia, he said he found it "hard to accept a situation in which a tiny handful of steel executives whose pursuit of private power and profit exceeds their sense of public responsibility can show such utter contempt for the interests of 185 million Americans." This is the rhetoric of the Garrison State, not the discourse of the Free Society. In U.S. theory, a corporate manager is not acting in "irresponsible defiance" because he makes a price decision with which the President of the United States disagrees; the manager's responsibility is to exercise, within the law, his best judgment of market factors to the furtherance of the short-range and long-range position of his company. The President moved all too easily toward the assumption that the responsibilities of his own office, which are huge on any reading, can be expanded to include the final judgment of such a matter as the price of steel.

Senator Hubert Humphrey adopted this view when he called the steel price increase "an affront to the President." A given price increase may be an affront to economics or to business sense; but how does it get to be an affront to the President of the United States? The President and Secretary of Labor Goldberg properly exerted themselves during the steel negotiations to prevent a strike and to restrain union demands within the limits of the national average productivity increase. Some intervention of this sort is desirable, but it should be held within strict limits. The danger is now made painfully clear. After the Administration received major credit for the settlement of the steel negotiations, it became almost inevitable that a general steel price increase would be regarded as an "affront."

DO MARKETS MATTER?

But if the price increase was not an "affront" and not an "irresponsible defiance," neither was it necessarily a piece of good sense.

U.S. Steel's statement explaining the increase started by recalling that the company's prices had not risen for four years, although production costs had risen. The statement gave only one reason why prices had not increased: the market—"competitive pressures from domestic producers and from imports of foreign-made steel as well as from other materials which are used as a substitute for steel." The statement did not go on to say that the market situation had improved; instead, it explained that "the severity of these competitive pressures has not diminished."

Then the statement swung abruptly into a discussion of why higher profits are desirable. The case for much better profit margins than U.S. Steel has recently enjoyed is an intrinsically good case. U.S. Steel's president, Leslie B. Worthington, among others, has recently argued that the growth of American industry has been hampered by low profit margins. In U.S. Steel's price-increase announcement the case for better profits was well presented, but the statement as a whole had a most unfortunate defect: it gave the impression that the soft market referred to at the beginning did not really matter, that all U.S. Steel had to do to increase its profits was to increase its prices. The impression plays directly into the hands of Senators Kefauver and Gore and of many others who believe that we have moved from a market economy to one of administered prices. The next step in the Kefauver line of reasoning, naturally, is to demand that the government take a larger hand in the "administration" (i.e., fixing) of prices. The weird oversimplification of U.S. Steel's statement suggests (1) that cost is the *only* important factor in determining price and (2) that price and wages are the *only* really important factors in determining profit. If both these propositions were true, then the market would be a myth and we might as well have government wage-cost-profit control.

The facts are different. Competition among American steel companies has been intense. Competition with foreign producers in some important product lines is real. Competition between steel and other products (e.g., aluminum and concrete) is serious. Steel's long-range ability to make more money depends as much on the volume of its sales as on the level of its prices. This truism was glossed over in U.S. Steel's price-increase discussion—though it was an important factor in restraining union demands.

The probabilities are that even without an increase U.S. Steel's profits will rise sharply in 1962. The very low operating rate of 1961 produced a profit of only $3.05 a share; but financial analysts, assuming no general price increase, had expected 1962 profits of $5 to $5.50 a share for U.S. Steel. If the price increase had stayed in effect, the competitive disadvantage to the industry might not have been felt until subsequent years.

It might not have been felt at all. Labor costs of foreign steel producers are rising. U.S. Steel's Roger Blough said he thought the economy was improving. He may have expected rising demand to put an upward pressure on the prices of products competing with steel. In such circumstances, steel-industry profits could have increased markedly. But what "such circumstances" added up to was another round of inflation.

Last September [1961], in his exchange of letters with President Kennedy, Blough had argued eloquently against the notion that steel was a "bellwether" of the great inflationary movement. Once an inflation gets rolling, who can say which segment of the economy leads it? What part of a moving wheel is pulling the rest?

But the situation in the Ides of April, 1962, was different. The general price level had been almost stable for four years. U.S. Steel, after the first major labor contract without a general wage increase in more than a decade, increased prices across the board in the most dramatic manner possible. Let us suppose that rising demand in other industries had indeed led to rising prices. Let us suppose—and surely this is a probability—that the Steelworkers and other unions had taken the steel price increase as a signal to press for further wage increases. Who would have got the blame—whether or not it deserved it? Who but steel?

TO BREAK "JAWBONE CONTROL"?

If this was the prospect, how can the way U.S. Steel handled its announcement be explained? Why was the decision cast in the only possible manner that would draw four-column headlines in the New York *Times* and provoke the President of the U.S. into a vitriolic and demagogic assault?

There is a theory—unsupported by any direct evidence—that Blough was acting as a "business statesman" rather than as a businessman judging his market. According to this theory, Kennedy's letter of last September 6 poised over the industry a threat of "jawbone control" of prices. For the sake of his company, the industry, and the nation, Blough sought a way to break through the bland "harmony" that has recently prevailed between government and business.

This theory could account for the otherwise inexplicable timing and manner of U.S. Steel's announcement. If Blough wanted to create the greatest possible uproar and provoke maximum presidential reaction, his procedure was beautifully calculated.

That the threat of "jawbone control" was no mere bugaboo was borne out by the tone of President Kennedy's reaction and the threats of general business harassment by government that followed the "affront."

THERE WAS A BETTER WAY

Whether his motive was strictly business or partly "statesmanship," there was a better way to do it. Why did U.S. Steel decide to make its price increase on an across-the-board basis? In the past, such increases have been justified by the inflation then rolling. A given company's prices, it was said in those days, were merely being adjusted to the moving dollar. But in the stable price conditions of 1962 this justification for an across-the-board increase did not hold water.

Steel is many markets. Today some are soft and some are firm. Some face outside competition and some don't. Why didn't U.S. Steel wait a couple of months—then market conditions might have clearly justified increases in certain product lines. Such an action would have been a far better answer to "jawbone control." It would have emphasized the fact—and it is a fact—that a company's profits depend upon a market it cannot control, and not merely upon the company's decision to set its prices. A product-by-product price rise would not have exposed the industry to the "administered price" charges of Kefauver & Co. It would not have invited upon the industry's head blame for reviving the threat of inflation.

WHO'S IN CHARGE OF WHAT?

When Inland and Armco refused to go along with U.S. Steel's increase (and Bethlehem rescinded its increase) it became apparent that Blough had miscalculated market factors as well as public-relations factors. Ten years ago, five years ago, the industry would have followed the leader on the theory that even if an increase was premature, inflation would soon catch up with it. Today, with unused capacity not only in steel but many other lines, and with four years of relative price stability in the background, price-rise decisions that were formerly automatic become much more difficult to make on strictly business grounds.

When the increase was rescinded under competitive pressure from the other companies, credit went to Kennedy. This may give rise to the mistaken notion that the President's job is to fight inflation by denouncing price increases. In fact, his responsibility for maintaining a stable price level belongs in an entirely different area.

Inflation cannot happen by cost push alone. The decisive factor is the government's own monetary and fiscal policy. Unless Kennedy stops pressing the federal budget toward more and more unnecessary nondefense expenditures he will create a situation where direct price controls and resumed inflation may be the only alternatives.

The explosions of the Ides of April go all the way back to the decades of undue government support of unions, coupled with inflationary policies in the government's own house. Blough's effort to escape the squeeze was natural, but its main result was to give President Kennedy an opportunity to avoid the politically difficult decisions of sound fiscal policy while denouncing business for price increases. It is to be hoped that the President in the months ahead will have the courage to resist this temptation.

The trouble with the "mixed economy" favored by some of the President's associates is that everybody's responsibility gets mixed with everybody else's. U.S. Steel is telling us what's best for "the strength and security of the nation" and the President is telling us what's the right price for a ton of steel. Now that the excitement is over, this would be a good time for President Kennedy and the leaders of U.S. business to take a hard look at the need to unscramble the irrationally mixed economy.

Do Rising Steel Prices Cause General Inflation? It's Debatable* _____

"As goes steel so goes inflation" has become an article of faith in popular economic thought. Steel's wage and price policies have been widely blamed for leading the economy into a round of "cost-push" inflation during the 1950's, and this history is much on people's minds as the new round of steel wage negotiations gets under way. But is the cause-and-effect conclusion about the experience of the Fifties entirely valid? The learned economists are far from agreed, and in the debates in their journals have been building up a sizable body of new argument. It resolves itself into three basic positions, best illustrated by three important studies.

_____

* *January 1965*

The most specific of these, by Otto Eckstein (now a member of President Johnson's Council of Economic Advisers) and Gary Fromm, gives support to the New Frontier tendency to blame the steel industry for putting inflationary pressures on the economy through rising prices and wages in the 1950's, and so appears to validate government intervention. These two economists made a complex input-output analysis which showed that steel prices accounted for half the rise in the wholesale price index between 1953 and 1958, from which they drew the seemingly obvious conclusion that steel prices pulled the price level of the whole economy upward.

Economist M. A. Adelman of MIT accepted the Eckstein-Fromm method and data but on further analysis came to the opposite conclusion. In the *Quarterly Journal of Economics* (February 1961) he argued that if steel prices are subtracted from the price index the remaining rise in prices is a number so small as not to differ significantly from zero (some random variables are always at work and many products being priced have been upgraded in quality, so that their real higher value has not been reflected in the index). In other words, Adelman says the steel industry is not to blame for inflation; indeed, he reaches the startling conclusion that outside of steel's private cost-push there has been no real inflationary pressure in the economy as a whole since Korea. The rise in steel prices, he holds, is an isolated "sectoral" phenomenon in which labor and industry for their mutual shared benefit pushed steel prices up to a "monopoly" level. But they had to stop in 1959 when steel prices were so high that steel was threatened in the market by substitute products and imports. Because management sensed the ceiling had been reached, the industry took the 116-day strike rather than submit to further large wage demands; after that the unions knew that they could push no further and accepted a modest settlement which has held. Such is Adelman's view.

The third view, expressed by the economist E. Robert Livernash of Harvard in a study for the U.S. Department of Labor, rejects the Eckstein-Fromm estimate of the effect of steel prices as exaggerated and finds both labor and management innocent. The postwar increase in steel prices, Livernash writes, "in large measure reflect increases in employment, material, and capital costs, and have been largely unavoidable. Regardless of the reasons for price increases, however, even large price increases in steel . . . have only small effects upon the general price level in the economy. Within a range of realistic discretion open to the parties in collective bargaining, and to the companies in the determination of prices, their decisions have hardly had a measurable effect upon the general price level."

In sum, Eckstein-Fromm say steel pricing stimulated inflation. Adelman says it did not; there was no general inflation. Livernash, close to Adelman on this but from different data and analyses, says the impact of steel pricing was not so great as usually thought. Livernash sees the rising wage level contributing to price increases like any other rising cost, whereas in Adelman's view some considerable part of the steel wage increase was directly tied to the union's anticipation of higher receipts from higher prices.

These challenges to today's conventional wisdom about steel prices are important. For quite apart from whether the market today will support a higher wage-price level in steel, the new economic debate has reopened the question of whether such a rise would be generally inflationary.

What Business Wants from Lyndon Johnson*

EDMUND K. FALTERMAYER

Washington's ear is cocked toward the business community as it has not been in decades. President Johnson has called for a business-government "partnership" and has actively sought the friendship and advice of the nation's corporate chiefs. He also wants desperately to maintain an atmosphere of business confidence. For these reasons, therefore, the hopes and fears of the nation's corporate leaders have taken on new importance. Pieced together,

---

* *February 1965*

they add up to the business leadership's economic policy for the next four years—or, put more bluntly, its terms for getting along with the President.

In one broad sense, business' terms are remarkably lenient. The basic hopes of U.S. corporate executives can be summed up in one word: continuity. "Business leaders consider the greatest gift to be the status quo," says the head of a large management-consulting firm. They like the policies the President pursued during his first year in office and want more of the same—frugal budgets, a good climate for business expansion, more tax reduction if it does not mean chronic deficits, and relatively easy money. They are willing to go along with the welfare state and the Great Society to some degree. They are not necessarily opposed to wage and price guidelines, so long as they stay just that. In short, they will take a good bit from Lyndon Johnson so long as they feel that he is playing the game right down the middle.

But there are a number of things Johnson could do to violate business' terms. Any hint of a double standard in the application of the guidelines—e.g., a downhold on prices but a wink at excessive wage increases—would revive business fears. So would the appointment of government officials dedicated to tightening up the already painful and maddening restraints in such areas as antitrust and the regulatory agencies. So would an obvious disintegration of the Great Society program into an excuse for lavish spending. To some corporate leaders, the President strayed close to the danger zone by supporting repeal of the "right-to-work" section of the Taft-Hartley law in his 1965 State of the Union Message.

To learn in detail about big business' hopes and fears, *Fortune* interviewed more than thirty chairmen and presidents of nationally known enterprises. Most of these men spoke on a not-for-attribution basis, and the sources of many of the statements in this article must remain anonymous. Men of predominantly middle-of-the-road views were selected—though some of these voted for Goldwater—since they represent the pivotal group to whom Johnson will try to pitch his economic policies. Nearly half of them are on the prestigious Business Council, which meets quarterly to discuss federal policies, and many of them know Johnson personally—a fact driven home by photographs in their offices showing them shaking hands with the President. Many of the more articulate ones have served in important federal posts, or are active in the Committee for Economic Development, a private organization financed by business. Supplementing the interviews are the written suggestions of an additional seventy-two chairmen and presidents, who were asked for their ideas as part of a *Fortune* election survey.

Considerable care must be exercised in separating what businessmen *say* they want from what they really want, and in determining what they want *most*. Corporate leaders are not too articulate on the broader aspects of public policy, and many of their "recommendations" are philosophical generalities that may be at variance with their real desires. One well-traveled executive describes the problem of finding out what businessmen are really for and against. "When I'm in New York," he says, "I ride into the city on the club car from Greenwich. There are about 300 businessmen who ride in these cars from time to time, and the opinions they express aren't worth a damn. If you talk about government 'management' of the economy, for example, they say it should not be managed. But if you get specific and talk about their industry, then they say government should do this and that —embargo Japanese goods, grant depletion allowances, give tariff protection or whatever."

It is true that the most frequently mentioned subjects in the world of business conversation are in the "against sin" category, while some of the most genuine and intense desires rarely get a public airing. On the strength of *Fortune's* interviewing, however, it is possible with fair accuracy to categorize business' "do's" and "don't's" according to increasing degrees of urgency. In the low-pressure area of the "do" sector are the philosophical, often wistful, recommendations that top executives are really not too excited about, but that frequently are the subject of ringing resolutions at various national conventions. Next comes a second category of proposals—concrete ones that corporate leaders will try to promote in Washington, many of them designed to help a particular branch of industry. Most important of all is the third category: the policies the business community will virtually insist upon as its minimum price for getting along with President Johnson. In the same fashion the list of "don't's" should be broken down: first, the things businessmen oppose on philosophical grounds but will tolerate; second, some widely discussed proposals that would displease but not quite alienate them; and, finally, policies that, if pressed, would turn them against the new Administration.

CONCERNED BUT NOT COMMITTED

Among the lowest-pressure "do's" are the familiar executive demands for a halt in the trend toward centralized government, for balancing the budget, and for getting the government out of activities that compete with business. Like many other thoughtful citizens, business leaders are genuinely concerned about the growing number of activities directed from Washington. "The federal government has now come to the point where it frequently interferes with social betterment instead of leaving it to local governments and states," worries a California corporation head. But few executives see much chance of halting or reversing this increasing interference in social affairs. "No doubt Mr. Johnson will take us further down the road to central government," sighs the chairman of a large eastern manufacturing corporation. But, he adds, this trend is not all bad. "There are some problems the federal government must take on." Similarly, businessmen see little hope of getting the federal budget regularly, or even frequently, balanced. Most executives say this should be done before taxes are cut again, but few seem alarmed by deficits as such. They also see little hope of getting the federal government out of such activities as the rural-electrification cooperatives and those TVA steam plants Senator Goldwater wanted to sell—a proposal that won widespread sympathy in the nation's executive suites, but little else.

Surprisingly few top executives appear to be losing sleep over the U.S. balance-of-payments deficit, other than bankers and heads of companies that do a large volume of international trade. In interviews only a handful of executives mentioned trade liberalization, or displayed much interest in the "Kennedy round" negotiations now going on in Geneva. A majority of corporate leaders favor freer trade, of course, but in industries that have been hit by low-cost import competition they want some protection, too. Robert T. Stevens, president of J. P. Stevens & Co., hopes President Johnson will renew the "long-term arrangement" that has held cotton imports to about 7 percent of the domestic market. He would also like a similar arrangement for woolen and worsted fabrics and apparel. Most bankers and financiers have publicly criticized the interest-equalization tax passed by Congress in 1964, which imposes a levy up to 15 percent on U.S. portfolio investment abroad. But if private conversations are any guide, the majority of business leaders would be disappointed, but not infuriated, if the President asked Congress to extend the tax beyond its expiration date in December 1965.

Almost to a man, corporate executives believe unions have too much power, particularly in their ability to shut down an entire multiplant corporation or a whole industry. "How this country ever got into the pattern of national bargaining I'll never know," frets a Philadelphia manufacturer. But few believe very much can be done about it, and a midwestern executive speaks only for a minority when he declares flatly that "unions shouldn't be exempted from the antitrust laws—no other class of citizen is!" By pushing for such legislation, most executives fear, they would reap a whirlwind. "If there's one thing that would unify the labor movement," one says darkly, "it would be a strong drive by management to bring unions under the antitrust laws."

DISTURBED AND DETERMINED

When it comes to the second category—proposals with some chance of success—the list, predictably, includes a host of items designed to benefit particular industries. Henry Ford II says he "especially" wants to see the 10 percent manufacturers' excise tax on new automobiles eliminated. Stuart T. Saunders, chairman of the Pennsylvania Railroad, hopes the President will push a bill, bogged down in the last Congress, that would give the railroads greater flexibility in rate making. He also hopes for a sympathetic attitude toward railroad mergers, including the proposed merger of the Pennsy and the New York Central. Other proposals abound. The chairman of a milling company wants the government to encourage the sale of wheat and flour to Russia and China to work off the farm surplus and help the balance of payments, an oilman wants tighter curbs on crude-petroleum imports, and so on.

But the most frequently recurring recommendations in the

medium-pressure group of "do's" boil down to just two subjects—cutting taxes and reducing "bureaucratic" government interference with business. Whatever their original misgivings about cutting taxes when the budget is in substantial peacetime deficit, business leaders now overwhelmingly believe the 1964 tax cut removed a drag on economic growth. Aware that federal revenues may increase faster than expenditures in the years ahead, thus bringing the budget into surplus, they look forward to further tax reduction. Almost uniformly, they *say* they would like to see a surplus before taxes are pared again. But, the tenor of their remarks indicates, they would not oppose another tax cut in time of deficit provided the gap was small and the economy appeared to need another shot in the arm.

More interesting is the *form* they would like future tax reduction to take. While opposed to selective excise taxes that discriminate against individual products such as autos and fur coats, they believe the U.S., like continental Europe, should rely more on indirect taxes. Therefore they view the present excise taxes, which Congress is certain to cut this year, as a ready-made opportunity for tax reform. Instead of merely eliminating many of these taxes, several business leaders say, Congress should substitute a uniform national sales tax on all commodities or a "value-added" tax on business—an idea supported by the U.S. Chamber of Commerce, among others. Since this is not considered politically feasible as yet, most businessmen would like to see future tax reduction concentrated in personal income taxes, in order to stimulate individual initiative. Strangely, only one executive specifically and emphatically calls for a further cut in the corporate-profits tax, reduced from 52 to 48 percent by the 1964 tax law. Does this mean that big business, after complaining for years about having half its profits taxed away, has grown comfortable on its bed of nails?

Apparently it does. Many big businessmen have become convinced, as have a growing number of economists, that the corporate tax is a cost they can largely pass along to purchasers of their products. If it were removed completely, some of them say, net profits would be about the same as now because of the pressure of competition on prices. "It may sound heretical," says an eastern banker who is not so heretical as he thinks, "but I think the corporate tax is a convenient way for the government to collect revenues, and that it is passed on to consumers." The tax has some genuine virtues, other executives add, because it helps companies in bad years and makes possible such incentive gimmicks as the 7 percent tax credit on business investment in new equipment, passed in 1962.

Some executives would like to see still more incentives. H. G. Bixby, president of Detroit's Ex-Cell-O Corp., a maker of machine tools, would like the Treasury to liberalize further its treatment of depreciation. Despite the 1962 revision of the Treasury's depreciation guidelines, he says, U.S. manufacturers are still treated less liberally than their European counterparts. "It should be a management decision how fast to depreciate," he says, and the government should limit itself to making sure a capital item is not written off more than once. Others, such as Chairman Charles B. ("Tex") Thornton of Litton Industries, Inc., would grant tax concessions to spur research and development by private industry, thus helping to redress the present federal preponderance in this area. "There is a whole new set of needs and demands that private industry should be confronting," he says. "Why not a special tax advantage for those companies creative enough to break ground in new areas? We have too many do-nothing companies that are content to market the results of government research." Another West Coast executive backs a proposal by the National Association of Manufacturers designed to eliminate the "double taxation" of corporate dividends. He would allow a company's dividend payments to be deducted, like an expense item, from its taxable profits. The effect, he says, "would be to put more money into normal investment channels instead of providing an inducement to companies to hold on to their profits and diversify into fields of which they know nothing."

A CRY FOR GOOD APPOINTMENTS

Corporate leaders would also like some relief from the vexations of government regulation. The chief desire of top executives, in the words of a prominent retailer, is "essentially to be left alone." Nobody questions the need for the various regulatory agencies, but many executives complain of "harassment" by mediocre officials. "Some of these agencies," the retailing executive says, "are manned by people whom I would describe generally as leftish idealists. They won't say so in so many words, but these people tend to think there is something wrong with our economic system." In the fall of 1964, he notes, the President told the heads of various agencies, in the presence of a group of visiting executives, that he wanted them to deal fairly with business. "That was during the election campaign," he says. "It remains to be seen whether the President will carry out this philosophy."

One improvement devoutly wished is more consistent rulings by regulatory agencies. The National Labor Relations Board, in the words of one executive, reverses itself with "diabolical delight," and another man believes some of the Federal Trade Commission's investigations have been tantamount to "witch hunts." On the latter point, one critic believes the President should "move to take away some of the prohibitive atmosphere and the feeling that we have to consult with a lawyer before we can do anything." Many of these defects, businessmen say, can be remedied if the President will make good appointments to federal agencies. Utilities men, in particular, will be closely watching President Johnson's appointments to the Federal Power Commission.

ON ANTITRUST: "REWRITE THE LAW!"

On no aspect of "interference" are corporate leaders more outspoken than on the government's current attitude toward mergers. So many executives are demanding a clarification of federal antitrust policy that this must be placed in the third and most urgent category of big business' wants. The mood on merger policy, in the wake of recent Supreme Court decisions and Justice Department proceedings, ranges from bewilderment to anger. "It is now virtually impossible," says one corporation head, for a large corporation to expand by merger without risking litigation. The chief criticism is directed not at the courts, which have gone beyond the Justice Department's recommendations in many proceedings, but against the department for instituting them in the first place. "The Department of Justice has been overzealous," this executive says, with heat. "They're overplaying their hand." Even President Donald C. Cook of American Electric Power Co., a lifelong Democrat and close friend of President Johnson's, asserts that the department has instituted cases for the purpose of "extending the law" beyond the intent of Congress, and that "they are stretching further than they should."

While there is no agreement on what the President should do to reassure big business on antitrust, there is almost universal agreement that he should do something. "If it is a question of the courts stretching the law," says one manufacturer, "then rewrite the law!" This corporate chieftain emphasizes that he would not make present laws less restrictive on mergers; he would simply codify them "in such a way that businessmen know what they can and can't do." If this proves politically impossible, he says, the Attorney General could improve the situation a good deal by clarifying the department's position and administering the present law in less "punitive" fashion. "The President could establish guidelines" on what sorts of mergers are permitted, says another industrialist, and he should also order a "housecleaning" of the Justice Department's staff. Business leaders have been waiting tensely for the President's final choice for Attorney General in his new term. The post is considered so important that one corporation was recently advised by its Washington attorney to delay all merger deals until the decision had been made.

The other items on business' "must" list require little explanation. Fiscal frugality is unquestionably one of the policies that have won many business leaders over to LBJ. While they may no longer insist on a balanced budget every year, they are paying close attention to the over-all size of the federal budget. Currently, leading industrialists regard $100 billion as the proper ceiling. At the same time they are for a continuation of easy-money policies. The *Fortune* survey shows easy-money advocates outnumbering those who want tighter money by seventeen to twelve. In interviews, the critics of the policy of "reasonable ease" that the Federal Reserve Board has pursued in 1964 lack genuine fervor, while those who oppose any tightening speak with real emotion.

Naturally, business leaders want the President to hold inflation down to the slow pace of recent years and, above all, to keep the U.S. out of a recession. They have remarkably few suggestions on how he should avoid a business dip, or get the country out of one, perhaps because of their great confidence in his ability to handle such a situation. "The government's anti-recession tool kit has been pretty well perfected by now," says one executive. Clearly, one of the surest ways for the President to lose his newfound friends in industry would be to fail to use the tool kit properly, or in time.

WHAT THEY DON'T WANT

Some of the business community's "don't's" are merely the reverse of the preceding "do's." In this guise they furnish important additional insights into current thinking. Again, the list must be graded by emotional intensity. The lowest-pressure "don't's" include further expansion of "socialistic" or "welfare-state" programs in general, medicare in particular, and continued subsidies for agriculture. Few executives believe the growth of the welfare state can really be halted, and though nearly all say they are against medicare, few seem to be viscerally disturbed about it. "I don't think business is really concerned with this issue inasmuch as it doesn't directly affect the vital concerns of business," says a California executive. And a southern insurance-company head speaks for an important minority when he says: "When it comes to aged people who can't care for themselves because they haven't earned enough, we can't leave them to die without medical attention. It is not actuarially or economically feasible for the insurance companies to provide medical care plans for those over sixty-five. I would damn sure prefer it if the industry could, but we can't. I recognize that this is letting the nose of the camel under the tent, and that the bureaucrats always try to move further, but I do and will oppose that bitterly." Significantly, none of the executives who oppose medicare volunteer any alternative proposals. Not a single businessman contacted liked the idea of farm subsidies, but, equally important, no one pounded the table about the need to end them.

In the intermediate emotional range, the "don't's" include two important labor items. Big business does not want the minimum wage raised further, though it probably would not be unduly upset by such action. It would also like the federal government to keep out of the collective-bargaining process, except in essential industries such as railroads and shipping. Top executives say they highly disapproved of former Secretary of Labor Arthur Goldberg's penchant for settling strikes in such nonessential enterprises as New York's Metropolitan Opera. They rejoice that his successor, W. Willard Wirtz, has kept out of most disputes and hope that he will continue to do so. The principal reason is summed up by one manufacturer: "When the government comes in, you usually get a shot of inflation." Outside the labor front, many corporate leaders oppose further government interference in the form of "truth in lending" and "truth in packaging" legislation. Each industry, of course, has its own pet "don't's"—e.g., electric-utility men oppose any further "favoritism" toward public power.

As to what business leaders think President Johnson must avoid at all costs, first is any action that would rock the boat of the U.S. economy; second, as is already abundantly clear, rapidly rising budgets. The third item is the one he may have the most difficulty in avoiding: any obvious favoritism to labor, either in legislation or in wage matters. On the legislative side, the President has already incurred some businessmen's displeasure by supporting a bill that would require double-time pay for overtime work in certain industries. But he has opposed another spread-the-work measure more repugnant to industry: a shorter work week. Obviously, if he changed his stand on this one he would lose a lot of business friends in a hurry. Equally infuriating to many corporate leaders would be repeal of Section 14-B of the Taft-Hartley Act, under which twenty states have passed "right-to-work" laws banning the union shop. Many of them concede that repeal would do little to strengthen organized labor, since unions have campaigned successfully against "right-to-work" laws in the northern states where most of their membership is concentrated. But business believes the laws are still weighted in favor of the unions, and that further concessions must be resisted. By coming out for "change" of Section 14-B in his State of the Union Message, therefore, the President has run the grave risk of appearing "pro-labor" in the eyes of many businessmen.

Corporate leaders will be watching especially closely for any signs of pro-union bias in the President's pursuit of wage-price stability. His reputation for impartiality in this area was enhanced by his mediation of the railroad work-rules dispute but subsequently tarnished a bit, in the eyes of business leaders, by his seeming acquiescence in the generous wage increases won by the United Auto Workers. The UAW contract with the automobile companies will boost labor costs nearly 5 percent annually over the next three years—far more than the White House's 3.2 percent "guideline" figure for wage increases. The President kept out of the auto negotiations, so far as the public knows, perhaps because the automobile industry traditionally has opposed federal intervention. But corporate leaders, almost to a man, believe that, without directly involving the government in the bargaining, Johnson could have put pressure on UAW President Walter Reuther to moderate his demands. "A few well-chosen words might have helped," says a prominent Boston businessman.

HOW TO "DISILLUSION" CORPORATE FRIENDS

For most top executives the steel industry, which faces hefty union demands in its upcoming wage negotiations, will provide the crucial testing ground for the President's impartiality. Essentially, corporate leaders say, Johnson's conduct in steel will show whether or not he wants to maintain price stability at the expense of industry's profit margins. The President is already on record against a general rise in steel prices, which, he declared in the summer of 1964, "would strongly conflict with our national interest in price stability." But, warns a corporate admirer of the President, "He could alienate business if he sat quietly by and did nothing about a big steel wage package and then hit the steel companies on the head when they tried to equate the cost in their prices." Such evidence of a "double standard," adds a Republican who joined the businessmen's National Independent Committee for Johnson and Humphrey, "would be disillusioning." Restraining either side will not be easy, even for a Lyndon Johnson, most corporate leaders admit. "This will be another test of his suaveness and his ability," says a leading Chicago executive.

The situation in steel raises a larger question that is causing considerable soul-searching in executive suites these days: To what extent should the federal government try to influence wages and prices through "moral suasion"? Most corporate leaders consider steel a special case, but what about the rest of the economy? Top executive thinking on this fuzzy matter is strongly divided, and neither the interviews nor the questionnaires yield a clear-cut set of "do's" and "don't's."

Most top executives now accept the idea that Washington should influence the economy in a general way through monetary and fiscal policy. But to many, the use of moral suasion to influence such matters as wages and prices amounts to what one Detroit businessman bluntly labels "polite controls." To a Chicago manufacturer who is anything but conservative, the notion of wage-price guidelines smacks of the old National Recovery Act and European cartels, and is therefore repellent. "This economy is complex and business is complex," he argues. "If government starts messing with it, it's going to be like pushing in a finger here and having something pop out somewhere else. No government can manage a complex economy."

The widespread distrust of the general notion of government meddling in wages and prices is documented by one of the questions in the *Fortune* political survey. Executives were asked which of two alternative courses they would prefer—"a relatively free-market economy with its possibility of a cyclical slowdown in business activity" or "stronger government influence over wages and prices in an effort to maintain steady noninflationary economic growth." Of the seventy-four corporate leaders who answered this question, all but eight chose the first alternative.

Along with the widespread "ideological" opposition, there are great doubts that Washington's "jawbone" tactics have much effect, or that Johnson really intends them to. "You can see by the auto settlement that the guidelines mean nothing," snorts a midwestern manufacturer. A Philadelphia executive believes the wage guidelines are self-defeating because "they become a floor under union demands." Ultimately, many corporate leaders say, market forces settle things anyway. "The marketplace is going to take care of inflation," says a Chicago businessman.

GUIDELINES FOR THE GUIDELINES

That might seem to settle the matter, with management as strongly against guidelines as is organized labor. But when the discussion gets away from broad, abstract principles and focuses on specific proposals, it develops that a good many business leaders rather like the idea of White House guideposts. They would agree with Walter H. Wheeler Jr., chairman of Pitney-Bowes Corp., who says: "It would be wonderful if we could make the guidelines work. I don't think we should stop trying, because moral suasion is better than direct government control."

Many of the supporters, however, seem to favor something of

a double standard on the thorny question of how specific the President's moral remonstrations should be. As some of the preceding remarks show, business leaders see nothing wrong with White House pressure on specific unions such as the Auto Workers or the Steelworkers in connection with some very specific wage negotiations. But most of them resent it when the President singles out a particular branch of industry on prices. Johnson's remarks on steel prices, says a Republican executive who otherwise strongly praises the President, were "uncalled for." Similarly, business in general was unhappy when Johnson told the banks, in his speech to the December 1964 meeting of the Business Council, that the recent increase in the Federal Reserve's rediscount rate did not justify "any general increase in the rates which banks charge their customers." On that one, says an eastern businessman, "the President went a little far."

While there is no corporate consensus on the guidelines, the various statements add up to a tentative set of ground rules that big business would accept. First, the guidelines should be promoted delicately and sparingly, lest they lead to the formal controls, which corporate leaders universally oppose. Only a very few executives think the President could push the guidelines harder without crossing the threshold of direct controls. Second, the President must maintain an image of absolute impartiality between labor and management. "If the government is going to get in, it will have to get in on both sides," says a banker. Third, it is all right for the White House occasionally to single out individual industries on pricing, but the industry should be put under no pressure, other than moral, to go along. Otherwise, there may be a repetition of the 1962 confrontation between President Kennedy and the steel industry on prices—a clash that, in the words of President Joseph S. Wright of Zenith Radio Corp., "scared the business community out of its pants." Says one executive: "It is all right for the president to say what the price should be, but not necessarily for industry to listen."

THE GREAT SOCIETY, STRIPPED VERSION

Despite their desire for lean federal budgets and their dislike of the "welfare state," many business leaders are lending cautious support to the antipoverty program, which the President hopes to double in size, and to his larger dream of a Great Society. "I hope he will tackle the Great Society," says Robert Semple, president of Wyandotte Chemicals Corp., "but I hope he will do it recognizing that there is just so much we can afford." As leading citizens in their own communities and as employers, top executives can speak with authority on some of the national problems Johnson seeks to eradicate, such as urban decay, the Negro's economic lag, and unemployment. Many of them see nothing wrong with federal leadership in these areas, provided Washington's role is a minimal one. "A lot of urban renewal is happening naturally," says a San Francisco executive, but he adds that "some government encouragement will be helpful if it is not used as a boondoggle thing." Most top executives, many of them heads of companies participating in the President's Committee on Equal Employment Opportunity, are convinced the Negro problem can be solved only by better education, particularly in the earliest years. But many of them doubt that a new federal program to expand pre-school education in needy areas, which President Johnson has proposed, is necessary. Local funds, they say, are sufficient to do the job.

Most corporate leaders, while conceding that unemployment is too high, believe the problem is far less serious than the current 5 percent jobless rate would indicate. "Those statistics are treacherous things," says a utilities executive who believes they should be revised. The main objection is that they are based on a definition of the "labor force" that includes teenagers who have nobody to support and married women who work only sporadically. Howard C. Petersen, president of Fidelity-Philadelphia Trust Co., notes that the jobless rate among male heads of households was only 2.7 percent in December 1964. "Hell, that's full employment for that group," he says, adding that in many skilled trades jobs are going unfilled.

Another criticism is that welfare and unemployment-compensation programs have become liberalized to the point where many of the so-called "unemployed" are people who would rather stay home than take menial or domestic jobs. As a partial solution, says Chairman Thomas B. McCabe of Scott Paper Co., "a concerted effort should be made to improve the image of domestic employment." Beyond that, he says, President Johnson has a big enough election mandate to undertake a broad-gauge study of the causes of unemployment. Given their view of the problem, most executives are against any artificial stimulation of the economy to bring down the unemployment rate. They also take a dim view of pressures on business to hire more of the so-called "unemployables." "They want us to hire 2,000 dropouts and have them pillage the warehouse!" scoffs a Chicago business-man.

THE CLOUD CALLED HUMPHREY

In the last analysis, many top executives are less concerned about what the federal government does than how it does it and who's in charge. One well-known executive, who heard anti-poverty chief Sargent Shriver address the recent Business Council meeting, came away declaring: "My God, he's an impressive man! No doubt he will support some programs that are poorly conceived, but he's conservative in his approach and has his head screwed on tight." To a large extent, business will back these programs—or refrain from actively opposing them—if it continues to have confidence in the man in the White House.

Some corporate leaders doubt that the confidence can survive the test of time. Sooner or later, one executive says, Johnson will have to face up to some hard problems whose solutions are bound to offend somebody, particularly if the current prosperity wanes. Otherwise, he warns, there will be a danger of "expediency, ac-commodation, and drift." But a majority of top executives, who repeatedly praise Johnson as an "astute politician," believe his efforts to please everybody and be President "of all the people" are the mark of a great chief executive. Moreover, they say, Johnson will try to maintain his new rapport with corporate leaders because he considers it essential to business confidence—confidence without which the economy will not grow rapidly enough to generate the tax revenues needed for the Great Society program. "He said he would seek the advice and counsel of busi-ness and I believe he means it," says David Kennedy, chairman of Chicago's Continental Illinois National Bank & Trust Co.

The opposite extreme—an openly anti-business posture at the White House—is rated extremely unlikely, no matter how rough the going gets. "Nobody that's President of this country can take an anti-business position," says President William B. Murphy of the Campbell Soup Co., who was recently elected chairman of the Business Council. "Being anti-business is like being anti-people."

If businessmen are reasonably sure about Johnson, they are far less so about his Vice President, whom they regard as a potential successor. "Hubert Humphrey would be a disaster as President," says a West Coast businessman, "and I'm afraid there's a damn good chance we'll get him." Few business leaders are quite so outspokenly anti-Humphrey, but many are disturbed because they are not sure just how close to the middle of the road the Vice President has moved in recent years. Some have already discarded their fears about Humphrey. "He has a balanced view," says a midwestern banker. "He's smart as a whip, and I'd rather have him ten to one over most of the other ones they were talking about." Nevertheless, the widespread doubts suggests that one of the principal items on Johnson's agenda will be to increase further the contacts between Humphrey and corporate leaders.

NEEDED: A BIGGER VOICE

Meanwhile, the nation's business leadership has an important item on its own agenda: to communicate more effectively with Washington. "All sorts of things should be done" to improve the business-government dialogue, says Thomas McCabe of Scott Paper. "Business leaders have been derelict in not making their views known," echoes the Pennsy's Stuart Saunders. The Business Committee for Tax Reduction, of which he and Henry Ford II were co-chairmen, is an excellent example of how corporate leaders can mobilize support for important measures, he says.

The problem is partly psychological, leading executives say. Business leaders are still too negative in their thinking about Washington. "It might be well for businessmen," President Lynn A. Townsend of Chrysler Corp. recently told the NAM, "to talk just a little less about the evils of government and a little more about the many ways in which government can help business do its work more effectively."

But the problem is also organizational. There are too few effective channels for bringing top-executive thinking to bear on vital national problems, economic or otherwise. The U.S. Chamber of Commerce and the NAM perform a vital function in guarding business' interests across the whole spectrum of proposed legislation. But they speak for many other elements of business besides the chief executives of the country's giant corporations. Many of these corporate leaders are in the Business Council, before which President Johnson has made several appearances. But this body is essentially a two-way, informal channel through which the government solicits top businessmen's views of the state of the economy and gets their reaction to proposed policies.

What is needed, beyond mere reaction, is policy-making initiative. Perhaps the most effective mechanism for this, in its limited way, has been the Committee for Economic Development, composed entirely of top executives of corporations plus a few college presidents. In the last few years the CED's broad-gauge studies have strongly influenced government policy in such areas as tariff policy and tax reduction. Some consider the CED's relative smallness a virtue; if it were any bigger its proposals might become so watered down by compromise as to be useless. But this also means that, at any given time, the organization is addressing itself to only two or three major problems.

The solution, some business leaders think, is to have several organizations, some permanent and some purely of an ad hoc character, some national in their representation and some regional. The important thing is to articulate the views of the men who head giant corporations—men whose unique combination of inventiveness and practicality, shaped by the highly competitive world in which they live, would provide an important counterweight to the more high-flown visions of college professors, politicians, and labor leaders. The cost of inarticulateness is high. "Too often," says *Enterprise*, a magazine published by Scott Paper Co., "there is strong public support for a course of action detrimental to the cause of free enterprise in general or to a particular industry only because there are no alternatives offered."

part 2

CORPORATE POWER AND ANTITRUST ACTION

ONE WAY by which the national government manages or regulates the economy is by setting rules, and some of the most conspicuous and most debatable of these are the antitrust laws. Today businessmen feel great uncertainty about these laws, and are urgently requesting revisions that would take into account both merger policy and corporate pricing actions as quite legitimate means to enhance market power and improve profits. While the laws may be interpreted either as a charter of freedom or as an instrument of economic planning, "Antitrust: The Sacred Cow Needs a Vet" suggests that today the planners have the upper hand. A committee of the National Association of Business Economists responded favorably to this editorial, but asked for stress in any debate on economic realities and not legal concepts, and on the affirmative promotion of forms of competition rather than negative anti-bigness ideas.

Yale Professors Bork and Bowman find much to criticize in recent court interpretations of the antitrust laws, enough so that they call the situation one of crisis. They see the problem as arising from a fundamental misconception of the nature and virtues of the competitive process. They applaud the great early accomplishment of flat prohibitions against cartels and price-fixing, while calling harmful laws on mergers that purport to block actions that might injure competitors. They find three fallacious doctrines in recent cases, and conclude that suits to block conglomerate mergers have reached their logical conclusion in attacks on efficiency. Columbia Professors Blake and Jones offer a direct answer, stressing the multiple objectives of the laws. They recognize that reliance on self-interest may lead to actions that will harm efficiency, but that efficiency may be less important than self-policing. They believe the case for economies arising from mergers is tenuous, and that the present approach of antitrust policy is a compromise. Their conclusion is that there is no crisis, but only a long struggle to shape meaningful antitrust doctrines in the face of uncertainties and hostility.

Since even critics of the antitrust laws generally applaud prosecutions of cartels and price-fixing arrangements, it is not surprising that many serious questions about corporate power and corporate ethics were raised after sentences were handed down for "The Incredible Electrical Conspiracy." This conspiracy was clearly illegal, even though the heavy electrical equipment producers were faced with pressures from chronic overcapacity and difficulties in profit planning. The article stresses management failures, yet it is unresolved how persons in an industry with similar structures and practices can be expected to avoid running afoul of the laws.

One agency concerned with antitrust enforcement is the Federal Trade Commission, which has other functions besides its responsibilities concerning mergers and price fixing. "The Root of FTC's Confusion" illustrates the wide range of powers of the Commission, and the problems arising from confusing and ambiguous laws. As an important independent regulatory agency, particularly in the field of corporate power, it is watched with care by businessmen because it possesses so much discretionary authority. *Fortune* has called for repeal of the Robinson-Patman Act, perhaps the most ambiguous and troublesome of the laws the FTC enforces. This law is an important factor in the problem of determining a pricing policy in a price war, discussed in "The Strange Case of Sun Oil." The case provides only one example of the contradictions with which all businessmen with responsibility for pricing must live, in a world of active federal regulators.

Antitrust:
*The Sacred Cow Needs a Vet** _____

EDITORIAL

The U.S. owes so much to the Sherman Act that we tend to accept as right everything that is done in the name of this statute and the laws that purport to supplement it. But antitrust, like other good things, can be dangerous. Nowadays, scarcely a week passes without a front-page notice that antitrust is being used by government in some way that would have been considered startling a decade or more ago. Uncertainty about how the laws will be interpreted hangs over almost every major piece of business planning. . . .

For every case that reaches the front pages there are a dozen in which the Justice Department or some other federal agency quietly nudges a business into a decision that businessmen would not make on the basis of their own judgment. And for every case where the government acts quietly there are a thousand instances where business lawyers advise their clients to avoid steps that some agency or court, someday, might declare in violation of antitrust.

Recent interpretation has moved so fast (and has involved so many contradictory principles) that lawyers simply cannot say with reasonable certainty what antitrust law is in a host of practical situations that arise in business. Being lawyers, they work on the principle "when in doubt, don't." If clients insist, lawyers may find ways to mask actions that should be done openly and forthrightly. More often, clients take the counsel of caution and the result is probably a decrease in the competitive, innovating, expansionist spirit of U.S. business. In commerce, no less than in the ring, "he who doesn't fight to win, fights to get hurt."

_____

* *November 1962*

TIME FOR A DEBATE

One of the unwholesome characteristics of the recent trend in antitrust enforcement and interpretation has been an almost total absence of any fundamental public debate. Of course, anybody will yell when *his* ox is gored, but there has not been enough effort to connect the individual cases and add up the score. This may be because business lawyers are so busy with suits and questions arising out of the new uncertainties of antitrust that they don't have time to assist in a vigorous public questioning of recent trends; or some of them may fear that if they do speak out they will invite Justice Department attention to their clients. In any case there is only a kind of sullen, muffled resentment in business circles matched by a kind of sly glee in anti-business circles, so that neither side is stating its case in a way that might clarify the differences. But unless such a debate starts soon, this nation may find that it has quietly drifted into the kind of government direction and consequent economic stagnation antitrust is supposed to avoid. . . . Nearly everybody has fallen into the habit of treating antitrust as a sacred cow. Particular cases can be sharply argued, but on the broad trends in antitrust few are willing to make statements that would stimulate debate. . . .

LET'S NOT FORGET

In the minds of some men in 1890, including the statesman whose name it bears, the Sherman Act was a progressive charter accepting the marketplace as the arbiter of economic activity. Pro-business groups were so sure that the Sherman Act was a charter of market freedom that they became too confident that *their* motives and *their* interpretations would prevail over those who wished to check the development of a business economy. They forgot that the necessarily broad terms of the Sherman Act can be interpreted in two different spirits, as is the case with many another broad legal document.

It is no coincidence that the U.S., which until recently had the only antitrust laws in the world, was the nation that developed business competition to the highest degree. Who can be sure that, if the Sherman Act had never been passed, American business would have escaped the deadening cartels and cozy collusions that characterized much of European business until recently? After World War II, when productivity teams from other countries began to inquire seriously into the secret of American efficiency, they found the answer in the higher degree of U.S. competition. These outsiders saw a connection between the U.S. antitrust laws and the stimulating competition that prevailed in the U.S. Accordingly, a number of industrial nations adopted antitrust laws more or less modeled on those of the U.S. In Europe these efforts are still heavily compromised by medieval resistance to economic change, by notions of "fair trade" and "accepted practice." Nevertheless, the recent progress of the European economy is connected to the liberating influence of antitrust principles. Now that those principles are proving their efficacy in other lands, it would be a pity if Americans abandoned them— either by turning away from antitrust or by allowing it to become a vehicle for government direction of economic life.

TIME TO FIGHT BACK

Antitrust will always be a battleground between those who see it as a charter of free competition and those who wish it used to shape the specifics of economic life in accordance with "public policy," as defined by government. This issue is not disposed of by asserting that antitrust is good for business or bad for business. Antitrust is good or bad according to the spirit in which the laws are written and interpreted.

The record of the last twenty years, at least, indicates that the initiative is in the hands of those who, distrusting the market's capacity to protect the public, would substitute government standards of desirable economic behavior. This monopoly of political initiative ought to be broken. Instead of merely deploring singly each court decision or administrative action, business should seek a public airing of the issues involved. A demand for the repeal of Robinson-Patman would be an easy place to start. The Clayton Act's language has been made the basis for some extraordinary decisions in the field of corporate mergers; amendment might clarify the bounds of what is permitted and what is not. As to the Sherman Act, it has undergone in the last generation "a vivid transformation" by court interpretation. Possibly this transformation could be reversed without changing the statute itself; a public debate might disclose a climate of opinion very different from that in which the courts seem to think they are operating. But if necessary the act itself could be amended to inhibit interpretations that pervert its liberating intent. Unless it is kept under constant review, antitrust can become dangerously anti-business.

The Crisis in Antitrust* _____

ROBERT H. BORK AND WARD S. BOWMAN JR.

Long-standing contradictions at the root of antitrust doctrine have today brought it to a crisis of policy. From its inception with the passage of the Sherman Act in 1890, antitrust has vacillated between the policy of preserving competition and the policy of preserving competitors from their more energetic and efficient rivals. It is the rapid acceleration of the latter "protectionist" trends in antitrust that has brought on the present crisis. Anti-free-market forces now have the upper hand and are steadily broadening and consolidating their victory. The continued acceptance and expansion of their doctrine, which now constitutes antitrust's growing edge, threaten within the foreseeable future to destroy the antitrust laws as guarantors of a competitive economy.

The situation would be sufficiently serious if antitrust were merely a set of economic prescriptions applicable to a sector of the economy, but it is much more than that; it is also an expression of a social philosophy, an educative force, and a political symbol

* December 1963. The authors of this article are both on the faculty of Yale Law School, Ward S. Bowman Jr. as a professor of law and economics, Robert H. Bork as an associate professor of law. Bowman was with the Antitrust Division of the Department of Justice during most of the years from 1938 to 1946. Bork formerly practiced law, primarily in the field of antitrust, with the Chicago firm of Kirkland, Ellis, Hodson, Chaffetz & Masters.

of extraordinary potency. Its capture by the opponents of the free market is thus likely to have effects far beyond the confines of antitrust itself.

The very existence of this crisis—and the basic societal changes it portends—seems unsuspected by most Americans. Even the general business community, which will be most directly affected, though it is conscious of hostility, appears to understand neither the nature nor the immediacy of the threat. To be sure, businessmen and their lawyers may frequently be heard inveighing against some particular action of the courts or of the governmental enforcement agencies. Calls from industry for mutual reasonableness and understanding between government and business are common. But such responses to the situation are dangerously beside the point. The problem is not created by a temporary aberration of the courts or the unreasonableness of a particular set of officials who can be jollied out of it or, if not, who will eventually be replaced with a more reasonable crew. The danger arises from a fundamental and widespread misconception of the nature and virtues of the competitive process. This misconception, coupled occasionally with real hostility toward the free market, exists in varying degrees in the courts, in the governmental enforcement agencies, and in the Congress, with the result that in crucial areas the doctrines of antitrust are performing a 180-degree turn away from competition.

The nature of the present crisis in the law can be demonstrated by comparing the law concerning price fixing and the developing law of mergers. The comparison illustrates the schizophrenia afflicting basic antitrust policy.

The rule that price fixing and similar cartel arrangements are illegal *per se*, that is, incapable of legal justification, must be ranked one of the greatest accomplishments of antitrust. Though its wisdom may seem obvious now, it was not always apparent that this was the correct rule or that the courts would adopt it. The first price-fixing case to reach the Supreme Court (in 1897) was the government's Sherman Act suit against the Trans-Missouri Freight Association, an association of railroads that agreed upon rates to be charged shippers. Both the trial court and the court of appeals agreed that the government's bill should be dismissed because the agreement provided for "reasonable" rates and the new Sherman Act only struck down unreasonable restraints of trade. The Supreme Court, by a five-to-four vote, rejected this view. If one vote had been cast the other way the "reasonableness" of the price agreed upon would have determined legality and the Sherman Act might easily have become not the symbol of the free market but a judicial version of the NRA. To many observers at the time the Supreme Court's Trans-Missouri decision seemed disastrous. Were businessmen to be helpless to defend themselves by reasonable agreement from "ruinous competition"? Would not the small and perhaps less efficient producer be at the mercy of the more efficient? The Supreme Court majority rejected such arguments for judicially supervised cartels. A year later William Howard Taft, then a circuit-court judge, rejected a similiar defense in the Addyston Pipe & Steel case, saying that to adopt such a standard was to "set sail on a sea of doubt" and that courts that had done it had "assumed the power to say . . . how much restraint of competition is in the public interest, and how much is not." Since then, with very few exceptions, the Supreme Court has hewed to the rule of *per se* illegality for cartel agreements.

The reason behind the characterization of this rule as one of the supreme achievements of antitrust goes straight to fundamentals. Why should we want to preserve competition anyway? The answer is simply that it is the chief glory of competition that it gives society the maximum output that can be achieved at any given time with the resources at its command. Under a competitive regime productive resources are combined and separated, shuffled and reshuffled ever anew in the endless search for greater profits through greater efficiency. Each productive resource moves to that employment where the value of its marginal product, and hence the return paid to it, is greatest. Output is seen to be maximized because there is no possible rearrangement of resources that could increase the value to consumers of total output. We want competition, then, because we want our society to be as rich as possible and because we want individual consumers to determine by their actions what goods and services they want most. This preference for material prosperity requires no apology. Aside from its obvious advantages, prosperity is important both in our long-run competition with the Communist world and for humanitarian reasons. There is much justifiable concern about relative poverty in our society and about particular groups that are thought to be disadvantaged in one way or another. It should be obvious that such groups will achieve major gains in prosperity only by sharing in the general increase of wealth. Competition allows us to use our resources most effectively to this end.

Price fixing is antisocial precisely because it lessens the total output of the society. When competitors agree on higher prices and put them into effect, they necessarily restrict output and so reduce total wealth. Some of the resources in the industry are then unused or are forced to migrate to other employment where the value placed on them by consumers is not so high. Over time, of course, such resources will move back into the industry as new firms, attracted by the higher rate of return there, move in. Usually the only way for the cartelists to prevent that is to persuade the government to impose legal barriers on entry into the industry, but that is not always possible. The tendency of competition to erode cartels does not, however, disprove the value of the rule against price fixing. Though its life is limited, the cartel may last long enough to cause a substantial loss in output.

The *per se* rule fashioned by the Supreme Court is thus a model antitrust law. It is at once a clear, workable rule and the expression of sound social policy. In dismal contrast has been the record of the courts in the field of mergers and of practices that are thought to injure competition by injuring competitors. Such practices as exclusive dealing and price discrimination fall within this latter category. It is here that antitrust has gone awry and that the immediate cause of its crisis lies. In order to understand the crisis, it is essential to understand the doctrines that underlie the courts' performance. These consist primarily of the theories of: (1) monopoly-gaining or exclusionary practices; (2) incipiency; and (3) the "social" purposes of the antitrust law. Though they enjoy nearly universal acceptance and provide the impetus and intellectual support for the law's current growth, these doctrines in their present form are demonstrably fallacious in concept and visibly hurtful in application.

Economic theory indicates that present notions of the exclusionary practices are fallacious. This was first perceived by Professor Aaron Director, of the University of Chicago Law School, who noted that practices conventionally labeled "exclusionary"—notably, price discrimination, vertical mergers, exclusive-dealing contracts, and the like—appeared to be either competitive tactics equally available to all firms or means of maximizing the returns from a market position already held. Director's analysis indicates that, absent special factors which have not been shown to exist, so-called exclusionary practices are not means of injuring the competitive process. The example of requirements contracts (i.e., contracts by which a customer agrees to take all his requirements of a product from a particular supplier) can be used to illustrate the point. The theory of exclusionary tactics underlying the law appears to be that firm X, which already has 10 percent of the market, can sign up more than 10 percent of the retailers, perhaps 20 percent, and, by thus "foreclosing" rivals from retail outlets, obtain a larger share of the market. One must then ask why so many retailers are willing to limit themselves to selling X's product. Why do not 90 percent of them turn to X's rival? Because X has greater market acceptance? But then X's share of the market would grow for that reason and the requirements contracts have nothing to do with it. Because X offers them some extra inducement? But that sounds like competition, it is equivalent to a price cut, and surely X's competitors can be relied upon to meet competition.

The theory of exclusionary practices, here exemplified in the use of requirements contracts, seems to require one of two additional assumptions to be made theoretically plausible. One is the assumption that there are practices by which a competitor can impose greater costs upon his rivals than upon himself. That would mean that X could somehow make it more expensive for his rivals to sign retailers to requirements contracts than it is for X to do so. It would be as though X could offer a retailer a $1 price reduction and it would cost any rival $2 to match the offer. It is difficult to imagine that such a mechanism exists in the case of requirements contracts, price cutting, or the usual examples of predatory or exclusionary practices, but it is perhaps conceivable. One possibility, though of limited applicability, would be the case where the only seller of a full line required retailers to deal with him exclusively or not at all. He might be able to get more retailers than his initial market share would seem to command if it would be difficult or impossible for the retailers to assemble a full line from the remaining suppliers.

The other assumption upon which the theory of exclusionary practices might rest is that there are imperfections in or difficulties of access to the capital market that enable X to offer a $1 inducement (it has a bankroll) and prevent its rivals from responding (they have no bankroll and, though the offering of the inducement is a responsible business tactic, for some reason cannot borrow the money). No general case has been made showing that imperfections of this type exist in the capital market.

MYTH AND FACT IN THE STANDARD OIL CASE

Professor Director's reasoning applies to all practices thought to be exclusionary or monopoly gaining. A moment's thought indicates, moreover, that the notion of exclusionary practices is not merely theoretically weak but is, for such a widely accepted idea, remarkably lacking in factual support. Has anybody ever seen a firm gain a monopoly or anything like one through the use of requirements contracts? Or through price discrimination? One may begin to suspect that antitrust is less a science than an elaborate mythology, that it has operated for years on hearsay and legends rather than on reality. The few supposedly verified cases of the successful use of exclusionary tactics to achieve monopoly are primarily in the early history of antitrust. The story of the old Standard Oil trust is probably the classic example. The Supreme Court's 1911 Standard Oil opinion is pivotal not merely because it is thought to have launched the famous "rule of reason," nor because it decreed dissolution which made the oil industry more competitive. Its greatest significance is that it gave weight, substance, and seeming historical veracity to the whole theory of exclusionary and monopoly-gaining techniques. It thus provided much of the impetus for the passage of the Clayton and Federal Trade Commission Acts in 1914. Such intellectual support as can be mustered for the law against price discrimination derives primarily from the lessons supposedly taught by that case.

The factual accuracy of the Standard Oil legend is under attack and is coming to seem as dubious as the theory that it is thought to support. Professor John McGee, an economist now at Duke University, reviewed the entire case record of the Standard Oil litigation and reported that there is not one clear episode of the successful use by Standard Oil of local price cutting or other predatory practices. The other supposed instances of monopolies gained through such tactics deserve similar investigation.

It would be claiming too much to say that there is no merit to the theory of exclusionary practices, but it is fair to say that theory has been seriously challenged at both the theoretical and the empirical levels. Perhaps a sound theoretical base can be constructed. The law could then be directed at those practices that in particular settings may be exclusionary. So far as is known, however, this task has not been undertaken or even recognized by the Antitrust Division, the Federal Trade Commission, or any court.

THE TREES DON'T GROW UP TO THE SKY

The incipiency theory starts from the idea that it is possible to nip restraints of trade and monopolies in the bud before they blossom to Sherman Act proportions. It underlies the Clayton Act, the Robinson-Patman Act, and the Federal Trade Commission Act. Though the idea initially sounds plausible, its consequences have proved calamitous. The courts have used the incipiency notion as a license for almost unlimited extrapolation, reasoning from any trend toward concentration in an industry that there is an incipient lessening of competition. The difficulty with stopping a trend toward a more concentrated condition at a very early stage is that the existence of the trend is prima facie evidence that greater concentration is socially desirable. The trend indicates that there are emerging efficiencies or economies of scale—whether due to engineering and production developments or to new control and management techniques—which make larger size more efficient. This increased efficiency is valuable to the society at large, for it means that fewer of our available resources are being used to accomplish the same amount of production and distribution. By striking at such trends in their very earliest stages the concept of incipiency prevents the realization of those very efficiencies that competition is supposed to encourage. But it is when the incipiency concept works in tandem with the unsophisticated theory of exclusionary practices currently in use that its results are most anticompetitive. Where a court or the Federal Trade Commission lacks the means to distinguish between tactics that impose greater costs on rivals and those that are normal means of competing, what evidence can it look to in its effort to discern an incipient lessening of competition? The obvious resort is to evidence that a competitor has been injured, for it is through the infliction of injury upon competitors that the exclusionary devices are thought ultimately to injure the competitive process itself. There seems no way to tell that a competitor has been "injured," however, except that he has lost business. And this is precisely the meaning that the statutory test of incipient lessening of competition or tendency toward monopoly is coming to have. In case after case the FTC, for example, nails down its finding that competition is injured with the testimony of competitors of the respondent that his activities and aggressiveness may or have cost them sales. The conduct that threatens such "injury" is then prohibited. That this result is itself profoundly anticompetitive seems never to occur to the commission or to most courts.

When the anti-efficiency impact of the law is occasionally perceived, the third theory—the social purpose of the antitrust laws—is called upon to provide a rationalization. Judge Learned Hand's Alcoa opinion contains the most famous exposition of this view. Hand suggested that Congress, in passing the Sherman Act, had not necessarily been actuated by economic motives alone, and continued: "It is possible, because of its indirect social or moral effect, to prefer a system of small producers, each dependent for his success upon his own skill and character, to one in which the great mass of those engaged must accept the direction of a few." He went on to say: "Throughout the history of these statutes it has been constantly assumed that one of their purposes was to perpetuate and preserve, for its own sake and in spite of possible cost, an organization of industry in small units which can effectively compete with each other."

Hand's rhetoric has commended itself to most commentators on the topic, but it seems clear upon reflection that it is a position which is inaccurate as a description of congressional intent, dubious as social policy, and impossible as antitrust doctrine.

It is simply not accurate to say that Congress ever squarely decided to prefer the preservation of small business to the preservation of a free market in which the forces of competition worked themselves out. There was much rhetoric in Congress about the virtues of small business but no clear indication that antitrust should create shelters for the inefficient. In fact, the statutory language of all the major antitrust laws after the Sherman Act explicitly requires the preservation of *competition*. That places an enormous burden of persuasion upon those who purport to find in the legislative history a direction to value small business above competition.

Hand's notion, moreover, is dubious, and indeed radical, social policy. It would be hard to demonstrate that the independent druggist or groceryman is any more solid and virtuous a citizen than the local manager of a chain operation. The notion that such persons are entitled to special consideration has typified some of the ugliest European social movements. It hardly seems suited to the U.S., whose dominant ideal, though doubtless often enough flouted in practice, has been that each business should survive only by serving consumers as they want to be served. If that ideal is to be departed from here, if antitrust is to turn from its role as the maintainer of free markets to become the industrial and commercial equivalent of the farm price-support program, then we are entitled to an unequivocal policy choice by Congress and not to vague philosophizing by judges who lack the qualifications and the mandate to behave as philosopher kings.

It is clear, in addition, that the "social purpose" concept is impossible as antitrust doctrine. It runs into head-on conflict with the *per se* rules against cartel agreements. Those rules leave it entirely to the play of competitive forces to determine which competitors shall grow and which shall shrink and disappear. If the social-policy argument makes sense, then we had better drop the *per se* rule in favor of one permitting the defense that cartels benefit small businessmen. Co-existence of the social-policy argument with the pro-competitive rules would introduce so vague a factor that prediction of the court's behavior would become little more than a guessing game. How could one know in a particular case whether the court would apply a rigorously pro-competitive rule or the social policy of preserving small business units from aggressive behavior? When the person whose conduct is to be judged is in doubt concerning which of two completely contradictory policies will be applied, the system hardly deserves the name of law.

THE CRASH OF MERGER POLICY

The three theories discussed are active in many areas of antitrust, but perhaps they may be best illustrated in the law that is now developing under the antimerger statute, amended Section 7 of the Clayton Act. Their collaboration produced the crash of antitrust merger policy in Chief Justice Warren's opinion for the Supreme Court in Brown Shoe Co. *v.* United States. The Court there held illegal the merger of Brown, primarily a shoe manufacturer, with G. R. Kinney Co., primarily a retailer. Their respective shares of the nation's shoe output were 4 percent and 0.5 percent. Kinney had 1.2 percent of total national retail shoe sales by dollar volume (no figure was given for Brown), and together the companies had 2.3 percent of total retail shoe outlets. With over 800 shoe manufacturers, the industry was as close to pure competition as is possible outside a classroom model. Yet the seven Justices participating in the case managed to see a threat to competition at both the manufacturing and the retailing levels, and they did so by using the three concepts already discussed.

The Court held the merger illegal for both its vertical and its horizontal aspects. The Court generally views vertical integration as a form of exclusionary practice, since it is always possible that the manufacturing level will sell to the retail level of the same firm and thereby "foreclose" a share of the retail market otherwise open to competing manufacturers. In the Brown Shoe case the Court said the share of the market foreclosed was not enough by itself to make the merger illegal but that it became illegal when two other factors were examined: ". . . the trend toward vertical integration in the shoe industry, [and] . . . Brown's avowed policy of forcing its own shoes upon its retail subsidiaries. . . ." It is enlightening to examine the facts upon which that conclusion rests. The "trend toward vertical integration" was seen in the fact that a number of manufacturers had acquired retailing chains. The district court found that the thirteen largest shoe manufacturers, for example, operated 21 percent of the census shoe stores. Accepting that figure for the moment, it is impossible to see any harm to competition. On a straight extrapolation, there would be room for over sixty manufacturers of equal size to integrate to the same extent, and that would result in as pure competition as is conceivable. In fact, since these were the largest shoe manufacturers, there would be room for many more manufacturers. But that is by no means all; the category of census shoe stores includes only those that make at least half their income from selling shoes. It thus leaves out about two-thirds of the outlets that actually sell shoes, including such key ones as department and clothing stores. Even if, as there was no reason to expect, complete vertical integration took place in the industry, there would obviously be room for hundreds of shoe manufacturers, and given the ease of entry into shoe retailing, no basis for imagining that any new manufacturer could not find or create outlets any time he chose. The Court's cited "trend toward vertical integration" was thus impossible to visualize as a threat to competition.

IMAGINARY "FORECLOSURE"

Brown's "avowed policy of forcing its own shoes upon its retail subsidiaries" turns out, upon inspection of the Court's footnotes, to spring from the testimony of its president that Brown's motive in making the deal was to get distribution in a range of prices it was not covering, and also, as Kinney moved into stores in higher income neighborhoods and needed to upgrade and add new lines, ". . . it would give us an opportunity, we hoped, to be able to sell them in that category." The empirical evidence of coercion was no more impressive than this "avowal." At the time of the merger Kinney bought no shoes from Brown, but two years later Brown was supplying 7.9 percent of Kinney's needs. (Brown's sales to its other outlets apparently had risen no higher than 33 percent of requirements, except in one case in which Brown supplied over 50 percent.) The "trend toward vertical integration" and the "avowed policy of forcing its own shoes upon its retail subsidiaries" were thus almost entirely imaginary. But even if they were accepted at face value, it ought to be noted that, since Kinney supplied about 30 percent of its own retail requirements, less than 1 percent of the nation's total retail shoe sales was open to "foreclosure" by Brown through this merger and it had actually "foreclosed" slightly less than one-tenth of 1 percent.

The idea of vertical integration as an exclusionary device had to be coupled with almost unlimited extrapolation in the name of incipiency to reach the incredible result that the Court achieved on the vertical aspect of the case.

"IT IS COMPETITION . . . THE ACT PROTECTS. BUT, . . ."

The horizontal aspect—the putting together of Brown's and Kinney's retail outlets—was held illegal on similar reasoning. The Court found the creation of market shares of as low as 5 percent of shoe retailing in any city illegal, stating: "If a merger achieving 5 percent control were now approved, we might be required to approve future merger efforts by Brown's competitors seeking similar market shares. The oligopoly Congress sought to avoid would then be furthered. . . ." On this reasoning every merger "furthers" oligopoly no matter how small a share of the market is taken over. To imagine that every firm would then merge up to 5 percent is to indulge in sheer conjecture, and in any event the result would be competition. Twenty firms in an industry is far too many to act as oligopolists. Given the ease and rapidity of entry into shoe retailing, the Supreme Court's fear of oligopoly is simply incomprehensible.

Then, apparently without realizing the inconsistency with its earlier prediction that Brown would "force" its shoes upon Kinney, the Court suggested that the merger was also bad because Kinney's new ability to get Brown's shoes more cheaply would give it an advantage over other retailers. "The retail outlets of integrated companies, by eliminating wholesalers and by increasing the volume of purchases from the manufacturing division of the enterprise, can market their own brands at prices below those of competing independent retailers." The merger was therefore bad both because Brown might "force" Kinney and because Kinney wanted to be "forced." This fascinating holding creates an antitrust analogue to the crime of statutory rape.

Apparently concerned that the achievement of efficiency and low prices through merger seemed to be illegal under this formulation, the Court then stated: "Of course, some of the results of large integrated or chain operations are beneficial to consumers. Their expansion is not rendered unlawful by the mere fact that small independent stores may be adversely affected. It is competition, not competitors, which the Act protects. But we cannot fail to recognize Congress' desire to promote competition through the protection of viable, small, locally owned businesses. Congress appreciated that occasional higher costs and prices might result from the maintenance of fragmented industries and markets. It resolved these competing considerations in favor of decentralization." No matter how many times you read it, that passage states: Although mergers are not rendered unlawful by the mere fact that small independent stores may be adversely affected, we must recognize that mergers are unlawful when small independent stores may be adversely affected.

The Brown Shoe case employed the theory of exclusionary practices to outlaw vertical integration that promised lower prices, the theory of incipiency to foresee danger in a presumably desirable trend that was barely started, and the theory of "social purpose" to justify the fact that it prevented the realization of efficiencies by a merger that, realistically viewed, did not even remotely threaten competition.

THE ATTACK ON CONGLOMERATES

The FTC and some of the lower federal courts are now pushing these doctrines to their logical conclusion—an attack on efficiency itself as anticompetitive. This is seen most clearly in the rash of suits challenging conglomerate mergers. A conglomerate merger is one between parties that are neither competitors nor related as supplier and customer, an example being the acquisition by a locomotive manufacturer of an underwear maker. It neither increases any firm's share of a market nor forecloses anybody from a market or source of supply. The government's attack on such mergers, therefore, has had to be on the theory that they create a "competitive advantage" which may enable the new firm to injure rivals. The competitive advantage, upon inspection, turns out to be efficiency. Thus a district court recently entered a preliminary injunction at the government's request restraining Ingersoll-Rand Co. from acquiring three manufacturers of underground coal-mining machinery and equipment. Though the opinion rested in part upon the competing status of the acquired companies, it stressed the conglomerate aspects of the merger.

One of the court's explicit fears was that the merger would create "economies of scale" (efficiencies due to size) which would put other companies at a competitive disadvantage. The court of appeals affirmed, noting as anti-competitive the fact that Ingersoll-Rand would be able "to offer a complete line of equipment to its consumers and to further enhance its position and dominance in the market by extending consumer financing to prospective purchasers through its wholly owned subsidiary finance company." This is a decision that illegality attaches when the merger enables better service to consumers.

On a similar theory the FTC attacked Procter & Gamble's acquisition of the Clorox Chemical Co. The hearing examiner held the acquisition illegal, assigning as major reasons the fact that, by integrating Clorox advertising with its own, P&G had realized substantial savings over what Clorox alone had had to spend, and the supposition that P&G might sell Clorox through its own existing sales force and thus lower the costs of distribution. The examiner thought the creation of such efficiencies anticompetitive because they might hurt the sales of other liquid-bleach manufacturers. Neither the Ingersoll-Rand case nor the Procter & Gamble decision considers that the creation of just such efficiencies is the main benefit competition has to offer society. If it now takes fewer salesmen and distribution personnel to move a product from the factory to the consumer than it used to, that is a net gain to society. We are all richer to that extent. Multiply that by hundreds and thousands of transactions and an enormously important social phenomenon is perceived. Any law that makes the creation of efficiency the touchstone of illegality can only tend to impoverish us as a nation.

PRESERVING THE DODOES

Too few people understand that it is the essential mechanism of competition and its prime virtue that more efficient firms take business away from the less efficient. Some businesses will shrink and some will disappear. Competition is an evolutionary process. Evolution requires the extinction of some species as well as the survival of others. The business equivalents of the dodoes, the dinosaurs, and the great ground sloths are in for a bad time—

and they should be. It is fortunate for all of us that there was no Federal Biological Commission around when the first small furry mammals appeared and began eating dinosaur eggs. The commission would undoubtedly have perceived a "competitive advantage," labeled it an "unfair method of evolution," and stopped the whole process right there.

It is important to try to understand why this anticompetitive strain has developed in antitrust. The institutions primarily responsible are the Supreme Court, the enforcement agencies, and Congress.

It would be difficult to overestimate the role of the Supreme Court. Though not compelled by the wording or the legislative history of the laws, the Court has with increasing frequency taken extreme anticompetitive positions. In many cases the Court has materially changed the law as it had previously been understood. This means that the Court is making major social policy, and the policy it chooses to make today is predominantly anticompetitive. It is naive to imagine that Congress can always correct the Court when it legislates in this fashion. When the Court, consciously or unconsciously, changes the meaning of a statute or the direction of a body of law, it may very well accomplish a change that Congress was politically incapable of making but is equally incapable of reversing. In fact, the prestige of the Court is so high that by taking the lead in formulating new policy it may make further legislative change in the same direction much easier. The propriety of this process and of the Court's rather unrestrained use of its power and influence depends of course upon one's view of the correct roles and relationships of the judiciary and the legislature. It seems at least highly doubtful that it is appropriate for major policy shifts to come through the judicial process when they could not initially have been arrived at by the political process.

The Antitrust Division and the FTC have also played leading parts in pushing the law in the direction it has taken. This is to be expected because of the natural partisan feeling that springs up in any group of men who are always on one side of litigation as well as the fact that such specialized agencies are likely to attract and hold men who take personal satisfaction in prosecuting "business culprits." Then, too, there is the tendency of men to see what they are told is there. If a congressional committee were to suggest to the FTC that vampires were injuring competition, the Government Purchasing Office would shortly be asked to lay in a supply of holly stakes.

When the head of the Antitrust Division or the FTC reports to a congressional committee, protocol requires that he wear a suitable number of bloody scalps of businessmen at his belt. It would be unthinkable, moreover, that he report no need for fresh powers. It is established ritual that there is always grave danger to the American economy, if indeed it is not already too late, and that new restrictions are imperative. If an antitrust chieftain did not bring in the scalps and follow the ritual, his own scalp would shortly be hanging from the committee's lodgepole. Scolding the enforcement agencies, therefore, while it is highly diverting sport at bar-association meetings—a sort of sedentary version of bull-baiting suitable for middle-aged lawyers—is ultimately rather beside the point.

Congress, through legislation and through pressure on the enforcement agencies, is a prime source of the tendencies we are discussing. The men who seek and receive the key posts in congressional committees concerned with antitrust generally display an active dislike of large business units and antipathy toward the free market. The old native Populist strain in American thought, which identifies virtue with the small local businessman and evil with the banks, the railroads, and big corporations, has been strongly represented in recent Congresses by Wright Patman, Hubert Humphrey, the late Senator Kefauver, and many others.

The present trend in Congress is shown by the antitrust bills now pending. They uniformly seek less competition. The so-called quality-stabilization bill, now likely to become law, is nothing more than a federal resale price-fixing law. Its aim is to prevent volume distributors from selling to the public at lower prices than less efficient outlets charge. Senator Humphrey sponsored a bill that would make the vague, little-used prohibitions of Section 3 of the Robinson-Patman Act, now solely a criminal statute, available to private triple-damage litigants and for government civil suits. Humphrey proclaimed as virtues that the bill would outlaw not only "unreasonably low prices," whatever they might be, but would also prevent a seller who offered one customer a lower price than another from defending himself, as he may under present law, on the ground that he did so only to meet the equally low price of a rival seller. The destruction of that defense would mean, of course, that the seller might have to lower all his prices everywhere or let the customer go. If sellers must lower all prices or none, it is an excellent bet that customers in general are going to pay higher prices. If consumers are required to subsidize inefficiency, antitrust is on its way to becoming the businessman's version of the farm price-support program.

INCANTATIONS WON'T HELP

What can be done to arrest and reverse these trends? The basic difficulty is lack of understanding of the competitive process, and this failure exists not merely in the courts, the federal agencies, and the Congress but also in the nation at large. We have inherited a marvelously responsive and intricate mechanism, the free market, which we do not understand or appreciate, and so, like savages left a tractor, we poke and rip at it, hit it with clubs and mutter incantations, all in the vain hope of improving its performance. The courts and the legislature preside like a body of medicine men, giving the tribe a new set of chants and directing that yet another piston rod be ripped out or spark plug smashed in order to make the mysterious mechanism behave. This pattern of behavior will take a long time to correct. An educational process of such magnitude is necessarily slow, particularly when there are strong know-nothing forces in the society who will vehemently oppose and vilify the ideas themselves.

The best short-run hope is the more active and direct participation of the business community in those aspects of congressional activity that bear upon the free market. Efficient businesses will lose most directly by the "protectionist" trend of antitrust, for they will be denied the returns that accrue in a competitive economy to initiative, imagination, and good management. If the business community does not inform itself of what is taking place and take an active, intelligent role in the political arena in support of competition, the antitrust laws are condemned to become parodies of themselves and the most potent political symbol of the free market ever known to our society will be lost to the forces of economic regimentation.

In Defense of Antitrust* _____

HARLAN M. BLAKE AND WILLIAM K. JONES

A new attack on antitrust is being launched. With the strident call of "crisis," Professors Bork and Bowman of the Yale Law School warn that the Sherman and Clayton acts are today being enforced in a way that is "anti-competitive" rather than toward their proper purpose of preserving competition and protecting consumers. The attack is of deep significance. It lends intellectual support to those who periodically seek to persuade Congress to weaken the antitrust laws—laws that provide the chief bulwark against economic and political forces which historically lead first to a monopolized and then to a socialized economy.

Bork and Bowman charge that the antitrust laws are being directed toward a "protectionist . . . policy of preserving competitors from their more energetic and efficient rivals," at the expense of businessmen's freedom to serve both their own and the public's best interests. They level a scathing indictment against the enforcement agencies and the courts for limiting the freedom of business firms to engage in a number of types of rivalrous behavior. They criticize restrictions that have been placed on such "exclusionary" practices as "vertical" mergers, exclusive dealing arrangements, and price discrimination. And they attack the Clayton Act rule that condemns all these practices—and "horizontal" and "conglomerate" mergers as well—even when they constitute merely "incipient" threats to competition.

The pillar of their argument is that antitrust should be enforced solely to promote and preserve free-market processes and thereby assure maximum efficiency in the allocation of economic resources. This is, indeed, a major objective of antitrust and one that we fully support. But antitrust, as an integral part of the eco-

---

* August 1964. This reply is by two members of the faculty of Columbia Law School.

nomic constitution of the U.S., is not limited to the single objective assigned to it by the new critics.

Competitive markets are fundamental to the American system not simply because they encourage economic efficiency and material progress. They also advance several basic political objectives. One of the great virtues of the competitive process is that it largely polices itself, thus making it possible to secure a viable economy *with a minimum of political intervention.* Antitrust operates to forestall concentrations of economic power that, if allowed to develop unhindered, would call for much more direct and intrusive government supervision of the economy. Reliance on competitive markets accommodates our interest in material well-being to our distrust of concentrations of political and economic power in private or governmental hands.

A "CHARTER OF LIBERTY"

Another political objective of antitrust is the enlargement of individual liberty. The freedom of the individual as a consumer is obviously curtailed if his choice is limited to the offerings of a monopolist or of a few sellers acting in concert. And the individual who wants to be an entrepreneur rather than an employee ought not to have his range of opportunities restricted by unnecessary barriers to entry or by trade practices designed specifically to eliminate him from the field. To be sure, it was not the purpose of the antitrust laws to create havens for inefficient small businessmen. But it *was* the purpose of the antitrust laws to expand the range of consumer choice and entrepreneurial opportunity by encouraging the formation of markets of numerous buyers and sellers, assuring ease of entry to such markets, and protecting participants—particularly small businessmen—against exclusionary practices.

Unlike Professors Bork and Bowman, we do not dismiss these aspects of antitrust policy as so much "rhetoric." From the very beginning, antitrust—as a "charter of liberty"—was considered a bulwark against arbitrary action and oppression by the economically powerful, much as our constitutional guarantees and political institutions were designed to guard against abusive actions by the government. Can it be seriously doubted that the primary motivation of Congress in enacting antitrust measures was concern about the wrongful behavior of economic giants, real or imagined, and sympathy for their victims, consumers and businessmen deprived of alternatives and opportunities? Is it even conceivable that a U.S. Congress—particularly one with the level of economic sophistication prevailing in 1890—would pass an emotionally charged measure like the Sherman Act out of an exclusive preoccupation with the idea that prices should always equal marginal costs?

Antitrust focuses on a basic paradox in business motivation. On the one hand, the market economy relies on the self-interest of the businessman, in seeking to maximize profits, as the dynamic force of the system. On the other hand, businessmen may seek to increase profits by methods that do nothing to improve resource utilization or efficiency or to increase consumer satisfactions in relation to the price paid.

The paradox is most obvious in the willingness of competitors to form cartels in order to eliminate competition with one another and to share the increased profits that result from noncompetitive pricing. The means may be agreement as to prices, spheres of operations, production quotas, or assignment of customers.

With a high degree of consistency, the courts have held that the antitrust laws bar all such practices as *per se* offenses—i.e., without regard to surrounding circumstances or possible justifications. Bork and Bowman heartily approve of this blanket condemnation of cartel practices. Indeed, they describe the *per se* rule as a "model antitrust law." But they neglect to discuss the full implications of the rule as it has been judicially interpreted.

The usual defense of cartels is that they improve the efficiency of industry performance. It is argued that they permit a closer adaptation of supply to demand, thereby minimizing expensive errors in investment and production; that they reduce distribution costs by curtailing the need for advertising, salesmen, and cross-hauling; and that they facilitate joint action in such areas as research and product standardization. Cartels not infrequently claim maximum efficiency, minimum prices compatible with costs, and notable records of progressiveness.

In rejecting such claims, the courts have not merely found them to be untrue or incapable of proof; they have found them to be irrelevant. The economic objective of maximum efficiency is subordinated to the political objective of maintaining a self-policing system.

In some cases the defense has contended that the challenged cartel has been unsuccessful in affecting market conditions, or is incapable of doing so because of the presence of still vigorous outside competition. In rejecting this argument, the courts have acted on the supposition that an ineffective cartel would eventually correct its mistakes and expand its efforts to embrace or crush any troublesome outside competition. The prohibition of cartels even when they are ineffective in controlling the market was one of the earliest applications of antitrust to "incipient" threats to competition.

It is interesting to consider the attitudes of the courts when confronted with competitor collaboration that is not of the cartel variety—i.e., that is not necessarily directed at altering the interplay of supply and demand in a competitive market. The courts have been remarkably tolerant about joint statistical services, industry research, and joint advertising and marketing efforts. When there is no direct challenge to the political objective of a self-regulating system, the judiciary shows great willingness to approve arrangements that promote economic efficiency—even though these may restrict in some measure the areas of competition among business rivals.

THE WILL OF CONGRESS

In keeping with this distinction, the courts for a long time have treated mergers differently from cartels. They have been much more tolerant toward the former, although a merger eliminates competition more effectively than any cartel could. Mergers of competitors were so rarely thwarted in the years prior to 1950 that some entire industries were consolidated into a few surviving companies. Industries thus concentrated found that formal cartels were unnecessary for maintaining noncompetitive prices. The steel industry showed the way: all that was needed was a mutual recognition of the common interest in curtailing competition and a willingness to go along with the policies of a price leader. Thus the *per se* rule against cartels was circumvented in many important sectors of the American economy. And once industries became concentrated through mergers, it was exceedingly difficult as a practical matter to undo the damage at a later date.

In 1914, and again in 1950, Congress, through amendments to the antitrust laws, showed its dissatisfaction with the judiciary's approach to mergers by demanding more stringent standards. Is it at all surprising that the courts have at last reacted to congressional directives and have subjected horizontal mergers to closer scrutiny? There is no *per se* rule against such mergers; nor has a large percentage of such transactions been challenged or invalidated. But the courts, prodded by Congress, have become increasingly alert to the possibility that mergers of competitors may destroy competitive markets.

Congressional concern extended not only to the emergence of monopolies, but also to the creation of oligopolies—concentrated markets in which competing firms are so few that by responding to market situations in parallel fashion they may jointly exercise monopoly power. In criticizing recent merger decisions, Professors Bork and Bowman ignore the entire background of the antimerger legislation and the fact that courts are simply responding at long last to the will of Congress.

THE VERTICAL RESTRAINTS

Everyone recognizes that the competitive interplay has to proceed within boundaries fixed by law. We do not allow rivals to compete with one another in seeing which can practice the greatest deceit, or sell the most adulterated or unsafe product, or impose the most unconscionable working conditions upon employees. At issue now is the question of drawing boundaries affecting the practices of which Professors Bork and Bowman are so extremely solicitous: vertical mergers, exclusive dealing and tying arrangements, and price discrimination. They view these as techniques by which more energetic and efficient businessmen seek to outperform their less enterprising rivals; they consider that the application of antitrust in this area simply protects the inefficient.

But the idea of the competitive "game" is not to win at all costs. It is efficiency that is the goal, not economic power. An effort has been made by Congress and the courts, therefore, to isolate and condemn practices which tend to distort the competitive process by giving an undue advantage to the powerful firm over smaller firms that may be more efficient in performance. We will focus on vertical integration, as did Professors Bowman and Bork.

When a long-term contract or vertical merger is used to gain exclusive access to a processor, an outlet, or a source of supply, subsequent business dealings are not based solely on the merits of competing products. Nor does such competition exist when economic power over one product is used to promote sales of more competitive items—through tying arrangements, block booking, and full-line forcing. A market from which rivals are fenced out is not a free market in any meaningful sense of the word.

Vertical arrangements designed to gain exclusive access to an outlet or a source of supply—either by contract or by merger—have been condemned by the Supreme Court primarily in two contexts. First, where the Court concluded that the transaction placed an unduly large share of the market under the control of one or a few firms—a single firm with 40 or 50 percent, or several firms with 60 percent or 75 percent among them. And, second, where the primary motivation for the transaction appeared to be to gain a preempted market of substantial size rather than to achieve any improvement in technical efficiency. When the statements of management, or the nature of the transaction, make it plain that the impetus for the arrangement was a desire to build fences about markets, one cannot blame the courts for being reluctant to listen to glowing accounts of the economies and efficiencies that might also be achieved.

But Professors Bowman and Bork doubt that there is any real possibility of subverting the market process. Vertical arrangements, they say, are open to any competitor to adopt or not as he sees fit. If a vertically integrated concern prevails over one not so integrated, it is simply a sign that vertical integration is more efficient than operation of successive stages as independent enterprises; to upset the arrangement is to stand in the way of progress and to impoverish the nation.

What this position overlooks is the substantial monopoly power now present in the economy as a result of the defective antimerger policies of earlier years, the patent system, vast and sustained advertising outlays, and other factors. Such power may be exploited in a variety of ways. The monopolist might seek to charge a uniformly high price in order to maximize immediate returns. But such a policy would encourage competitors to enter the monopolized market and invite governmental and consumer attention to the power being exercised. And it might not produce the greatest return even in the short run. Another way the monopolist may increase his monopoly "tribute" is to sell to different groups of customers at different prices, or at prices yielding different profit margins—thus taking into account that some customers are willing to pay more than others. This practice may placate the customers who are most likely to call for government action, and it is likely to discourage entry of new firms into those branches of the business that are most vulnerable to competition. Thus, differential pricing may be an effective tool both in exploiting and in perpetuating monopoly power. Vertical integration can play a similar role. It facilitates the separation of customers into distinct groups to which sales at different prices or profit margins may be made. It assists in camouflaging from the public and the government the monopoly profits being earned. And it makes entry into the monopolized market more difficult. This final element creates the greatest problem for antitrust policy.

HOW COMPETITORS ARE DISCOURAGED

Vertical integration in markets that are already less than perfectly competitive tends to perpetuate monopoly profits by creating financial and psychological barriers to the entry of new competitors. In the extreme case of a fully integrated industry— where one or a few manufacturers own the key sources of supply and the existing channels of distribution—it is not feasible for a new firm to come in unless it comes in at all levels. Hence, a firm intending to go into such an industry requires vast amounts of capital—a factor that tends to discourage prospective entrants. It is well recognized that the capital market does not operate like the textbook "model," providing unlimited funds to all comers, strictly in relation to profits and risks. Moreover, even if perfect knowledge and infinite flexibility were present, the greater risks involved in entering an industry at all levels would greatly increase the cost of the capital required. Since the total venture must fail if operation at any stage is unsuccessful, this cost will reflect the cumulative nature of the risks involved, rather than the risk at each separate stage.

Where the industry is less than fully integrated—i.e., where some unintegrated firms remain at some levels—this effect is somewhat less strongly felt but may nonetheless be decisive. In such cases the unintegrated firms may not provide the necessary outlets or sources of supply for the prospective entrant because they are too few in number or poorly situated, or because they are unlikely to pursue business policies that oppose the interests of the vertically integrated company upon which they are dependent. Congressional hearings on problems of distribution recount the fears of the unintegrated distributor who finds himself in competition with the distributor branch of his vertically integrated supplier.

Professors Bork and Bowman do not see these dangers in vertical integration. They rest their case on the assumptions of "static" economic theory—perfect knowledge and perfect mobility in the capital market and among entrepreneurs. The trouble with such an approach is that it has little relation to the dynamics of the business world. It is therefore unhelpful in determining what antitrust enforcement agencies and courts should or should not do in dealing with that world. Indeed, if Bork and Bowman were to follow their assumptions to their logical conclusion, they could hardly approve of the outlawing of cartels, because in their theoretical world cartels and price-fixing arrangements would be promptly frustrated by a flow of new entrepreneurs and capital into the cartelized market, attracted by the abnormally high rates of return, and there would be no need for laws on the subject.

If the courts attach so much importance to the anticompetitive threat posed by vertical arrangements, it is in part because they have been taught to do so by the business community. Perhaps there would be more readiness to listen to the gospel of the new critics of antitrust if management reports and stockholders' letters ceased pointing up the virtues of "securing" outlets and obtaining "assured" sources of supply.

To be sure, vertical transactions can be a means of promoting competition as well as thwarting it. They may reflect genuine efficiencies in rearranged production techniques rather than efforts to obtain or protect market positions. In some cases, vertical integrations may have both favorable and unfavorable aspects in roughly equal proportions. How is one to deal with such ambiguity? This question raises the central issue of antitrust: the extent to which economic efficiencies may have to be sacrificed in order to achieve the political objectives of antitrust.

There is no simple and unqualified relation between antitrust policy and economic efficiency. The problems confronted are too varied; the efficiencies asserted are not all of the same order. However, some general conclusions are possible.

First, we can put to one side the asserted efficiencies of an administratively directed economy. The decision to reject that kind of economy was implicit in the enactment of the antitrust laws and the firmly established *per se* approach to cartels.

Second, efficiencies derived from physical production and distribution techniques are almost never at issue. We can think of no case in which antitrust was invoked to condemn the construction of a plant, store, or transportation facility of any particular size or design. The antitrust policies to which Bowman and Bork object—those restricting mergers and vertical integration—have no significant impact on efficiencies of this kind. If one businessman takes advantage of a more efficient technique, or produces at levels permitting economies of scale, he is free to outstrip his competitors in the marketplace without fear of antitrust conviction. It is possible to found a lawful monopoly on superior efficiency or economies of scale, provided that it has been achieved without merger or vertical arrangements that tend to exclude competitors.

This makes sense in terms of the objectives of antitrust policy. In an industry where, because of technical factors or superior efficiency, only one or a few producers are needed to supply the market, other competitors could be kept afloat only by sustained political intervention—e.g., to fix minimum prices or license areas of operation. In this kind of situation, self-policing by competition is simply not feasible. Since political intervention is unavoidable, the most satisfactory course is to capture the benefits of technology by imposing utility-type controls on the monopolist, as we have done in the case of gas, electric, telephone, and pipeline companies.

A third class of efficiencies—relating to the better utilization of *intangible* resources—presents the most difficulty. It is efficiencies of this kind that the prohibitions of mergers and vertical restraints are said to thwart; all of the examples given by Bowman and Bork fall in this category. What are some of the efficiencies commonly asserted?

• *Increased advertising effectiveness.* But do consumers necessarily gain because a merger facilitates larger and larger expenditures for advertising, or more advertising for less money? In the Procter & Gamble acquisition of Clorox, the FTC found that the merger facilitated greater advertising and promotion of Clorox, already the dominant household bleach, and that this would impede the entry and expansion of competitive products. This "efficiency" stemmed largely from the fact that Clorox's advertising outlay would buy up to 33 percent more coverage if added to P&G's enormous budget, because of lower "quantity discount" rates available from the mass media. (Whether such "quantity discounts"—which seem to place an unhealthy premium on size in industries to which advertising is crucial—are in themselves subject to legal challenge is a question which should be examined.) All household bleaches were chemically identical, and the only effect of previous Clorox advertising had been to gain a large market share at a *higher* price to the consumer. So the FTC concluded that the asserted advantage of cheaper advertising would not redound to the benefit of consumers, and it invalidated the merger as potentially hurtful to competition. While this is an extreme example, it illustrates pointedly the dubious nature of the "efficiencies" of advertising economies.

• *Reduced capital costs.* While large companies can obtain funds in the capital market at less net expense than small companies, the source of the advantage is not always clear. To the extent that the reduced capital costs reflect the reduced risks of monopolized operation, the asserted economy is a product of market control and may be disallowed in accordance with our first principle. To the extent that the lower capital costs relate to lower risks of absolute size or the economies of scale that result from dealing in large amounts, the efficiency is real, but it need not be achieved by a merger that curbs competition. Any form of increase in company size will yield the same economies, as many of our large, diversified corporations have shown.

• *Quantity buying and bypassing intermediaries.* Here genuine economies are possible, but they are difficult to disentangle from (*a*) price concessions attributable to the bargaining power of the buyer rather than to reduced seller costs, and (b) the elimination of brokers and wholesalers coupled with a shift of their risks and functions to some other party in the distribution sequence. The fact that a powerful buyer can demand a lower price, or can insist that the seller eliminate a broker and assume the broker's functions, does not necessarily mean that greater over-all efficiency has been achieved. Savings of this kind produce no real gains for society unless the net costs of the entire distribution sequence are reduced rather than merely reshuffled.

• *More efficient utilization of personnel.* This economy, and the related one of providing better service with the same personnel, may be genuine enough. But it is frequently difficult to determine whether the savings are offset by increased costs of administering and supervising an expanded organization. This judgment cannot be left wholly to business management, since a net loss in efficiency might be outweighed by the gains derived from reduced competition.

Taken as a whole, the case for economies arising from mergers is tenuous. As a result, the approach of antitrust policy is essentially a compromise. If a particular efficiency is so pronounced that firms in a position to employ it gain market control without engaging in mergers or vertical restraints, the result is wholly compatible with the antitrust laws. If, on the other hand, a merger or vertical restraint threatens the efficacy of the market process— as by putting together a concentrated industry structure or erecting barriers to entry—the practice is proscribed despite protestations of increased efficiency. Since the asserted efficiencies have such an ambiguous character, it appears reasonable to give weight to the political objectives of antitrust. Congress was certainly prepared to sacrifice *some* promises of efficiency in order to maintain competitive markets.

The extent of government action against the debatable transactions is quite limited. Exclusive dealing arrangements are not attacked with great frequency. And the vast majority of mergers proceed without hindrance. In the three-year period ending June 30, 1962, some 3,705 mergers were of sufficient significance to come to the attention of the Federal Trade Commission through examination of financial newspapers, trade journals, manuals of investment, and the like. During the same period antitrust enforcement agencies filed fifty-five complaints challenging 182 acquisitions—less than 5 percent of the total of publicly reported mergers. Even allowing for the discouragement of transactions not formally challenged as antitrust violations, it is hard to conceive that this "crash of merger policy," as Bowman and Bork describe it, is going to stultify corporate realignments throughout the length and breadth of the economy.

Indeed, it might be defensible to take a more extreme position against vertical mergers and restraints, condemning them whenever they exclude competitors from any substantial market. This more or less automatic approach has the arguable advantage of preventing prolonged litigation, with endless economic evidence of a questionable nature, and of eliminating the possibility that judges will be overly impressed by business expertise. But we believe that the risks and costs of the present approach are worth bearing. If genuine efficiencies seem likely, and if the market process is not threatened, the transaction should be upheld.

We agree with Bowman and Bork that a competitor who loses business because of relative inefficiency is not entitled to protection; he is not the victim of economic oppression, but of his own inefficient methods. Thus, we heartily concur in their condemnations of resale-price maintenance and of the excessive enforcement of the Robinson-Patman Act. The idea that small business is entitled to protection simply because it *is* small business is a corrosive force that has been a threat to antitrust since its inception.

The concept of "incipiency," and its relation to improvements in efficiency, presents a more difficult problem. First, there is great uncertainty about the exact point at which industry concentration along horizontal lines confers market power, and also the point at which vertical restraints pose significant barriers to entry. Second, the very concept of incipiency implies an acceptance of the virtues of the possible efficiencies involved; otherwise the practice could be proscribed as a *per se* offense in the same manner as price fixing. There is a risk that any merger or vertical restraint might sooner or later lead to an impairment of market processes. If this risk seems slight, however, and the gains in efficiency are great, the risks should be endured and continued surveillance maintained against further steps that might be more threatening. Only when impairment of market processes becomes imminent should possible efficiencies be sacrificed. On the other hand, if the asserted efficiencies are not persuasive, the courts are justified in proscribing even those threats that are far removed. Why run unnecessary risks and incur avoidable burdens of continued surveillance?

Our approach to the problem may be illustrated by two recent cases. In the Philadelphia National Bank case, the Supreme Court held that a merger between competitors was presumptively unlawful if the merging firms accounted for as much as 30 percent of the relevant market—in this case commercial banking in Philadelphia. The threat of price leadership in such a market is so great that arguments relating to efficiency can properly be excluded; and other issues also may be simplified in the interest of conserving judicial energies.

By contrast, the Brown Shoe case, discussed at length by Bowman and Bork, requires closer scrutiny. We would argue that the threat there to the competitive process, though slight, was worth noticing. The merger united the fourth-largest shoe manufacturer with the largest chain of family-style retail shoe stores, came on the heels of a number of similar consolidations and was about the largest single step that could have been taken to make entry into the industry more difficult. It was also a transaction that might have been motivated principally by a desire to fence out competitors, without regard to efficiency. But because of the remoteness of the threat posed, the claims of increased efficiency should have been considered on their merits; if found to be valid and sufficiently substantial, they should have resulted in approval of the transaction. However, it is nonsense to conclude, as Bowman and Bork do, that a trend toward concentration in the industry should argue for rather than against a merger—that such a trend "is prima facie evidence that greater concentration is socially desirable." One could as readily infer that an increase in price-fixing efforts indicates that cartelization is socially desirable.

THE PRINCIPAL ARCHITECTS OF POLICY

Although our analysis of the Brown Shoe case is somewhat different from that of Bowman and Bork, we agree that the Court's opinion is an unfortunate one. The Supreme Court should do better in endeavoring to reconcile the varied objectives of antitrust policy. But we believe that it is quite unfair to characterize the Court's work as a whole as being subversive of sound antitrust policy or as being contrary to a congressional purpose more favorable to competition. If anything, the Court has been unfaithful to congressional intentions only in drawing some of the worst stingers from the anticompetitive federal price-discrimination law and "fair-trade" statutes. Its role has generally been a creative and constructive one within the province delegated to it by statute. The principal architects of sound antitrust policy—particularly the aspects approved by Bowman and Bork—have been on the Supreme Court and not in the Congress.

We close by concluding that there is no crisis in antitrust—only a long, continuing struggle to shape meaningful doctrines in the face of great uncertainties and in the presence of hostile elements of considerable proportions. These include, to be sure, the inefficient firms that seek to use antitrust as a protective barrier against competition. But real competition is hardly welcomed by the powerful firms in concentrated industries and other monopolistic elements in our economy. In fighting off one enemy of antitrust, it is not necessary to lay open a clear road for the other.

*The Incredible Electrical Conspiracy** ——

RICHARD AUSTIN SMITH

As befitted the biggest criminal case in the history of the Sherman Act, most of the forty-five defendants arrived early, knocking the snow of Philadelphia's Chestnut Street from their shoes before taking the elevator to federal courtroom No. 3. Some seemed to find it as chill inside as out, for they kept their coats on and shifted from one foot to another in the corridor, waiting silently for the big mahogany doors to open. On the other side of those doors was something none of them relished: judgment for having conspired to fix prices, rig bids, and divide markets on electrical equipment valued at $1,750,000,000 annually. The twenty indict-

* *April and May 1961*

ments, under which they were now to be sentenced, charged they had conspired on everything from tiny $2 insulators to multi-million-dollar turbine generators and had persisted in the conspiracies for as long as eight years. . . .

Shortly after ten o'clock, Judge J. Cullen Ganey, chief judge of the U.S. District Court, entered the courtroom. He had earned a reputation in his twenty years on the bench for tolerance and moderation. But it was clear almost immediately that he took a stern view of this conspiracy: "This is a shocking indictment of a vast section of our economy, for what is really at stake here is the survival of the kind of economy under which this country has grown great, the free-enterprise system." The first targets of his censure were the twenty-nine corporations and their top management. He acknowledged that the Justice Department did not have enough evidence to convict men in the highest echelons of the corporations before the court, but in a broader sense the "real blame" should be laid at their doorstep: "One would be most naive indeed to believe that these violations of the law, so long persisted in, affecting so large a segment of the industry and finally involving so many millions upon millions of dollars, were facts unknown to those responsible for the corporation and its conduct. . . ." Heavy fines, he said, would be imposed on the corporations themselves.

Next he turned a cold blue eye on the forty-five corporation executives who had not escaped the nets of Antitrust. Many of the individual defendants he saw "torn between conscience and an approved corporate policy . . . the company man, the conformist, who goes along with his superiors and finds balm for his conscience in additional comforts and the security of his place in the corporate setup." The judge said that individuals "with ultimate responsibility for corporate conduct, among those indicted," were going to jail. . . .

By lunchtime the second day it was all over. The little game that lawyers from GE and Westinghouse had been playing against each other—predicting sentences and total fines—was ended. GE had "lost," receiving $437,500 in total fines to Westinghouse's $372,500. All told, $1,924,500 worth of fines were levied, seven jail sentences and twenty-four suspended jail sentences handed down. But sentencing, far from closing the case, has raised it to new importance.

THE PROBLEMS OF PREDOMINANCE

No thoughtful person could have left that courtroom untroubled by the problems of corporate power and corporate ethics. We live in a corporate society. Big business determines institutionally our rate of capital formation, technological innovation, and economic growth; it establishes the kind of competition that is typical of our system and sets the moral tone of the market place. The streets of every city in the U.S. are crowded with small businesses that take their cue from great corporations, whether it trickles down from what some executive tells a crop of college graduates about free enterprise or the way he himself chooses to compete. Their lawyers pleaded that the way the electrical-equipment executives did compete was not collusion at its *worst*. To be sure, it was not so vulgar as the strong-arm price fixing of the Gulf Coast shrimpers or the rough stuff employed by a certain Philadelphia linen-supply company. But by flouting the law, the executives of the great companies set an example that was bound to make small companies feel they had similar license, and never mind the kid gloves. As Robert A. Bicks, then head of Antitrust, declared early in the proceedings, "These men and companies have in a true sense mocked the image of that economic system which we profess to the world."

This being so, it is highly important to understand what went wrong with the electrical-equipment industry and with General Electric, the biggest company of them all and the one without which the conspiracies could not have existed.

"SECURITY, COMPLACENCY, MEDIOCRITY"

When Ralph Cordiner took over the presidency of GE from Charles E. Wilson in December of 1950, it was clear from the outset that the corporation was in for some teeth-rattling changes. Cordiner had spent the previous five years working up a reorganization plan that would give GE the new plants, the new additions to capital, and the new management setup he thought essential to its revitalization. Moreover, he had long made plain his distaste for running any big company the way GE had been run by his predecessors, with authority tightly concentrated in the president's office. *De*centralization was a thing with him: he had never forgotten how the "layers of fat" in a centralized GE had slowed his own incessant drive for recognition to a point where he'd once quit to take the presidency of Schick. The simple fact was that intellectually and temperamentally a centralized organization went against his grain, whether it be run with Electric Charlie Wilson's relaxed conviviality or the clockwork autocracy of Gerard ("You have four minutes") Swope.

The corporation at large learned almost immediately what the new boss had in store for it and from Cordiner himself. Within six weeks he rode circuit from New York to Bridgeport, Chicago, Lynn-Boston, Schenectady, spreading the word to some 6,000 GE executives. The gist of his message could be divided into three parts. First, GE was in sorry shape. It was dedicated principally to "security, complacency, and mediocrity." Second, decentralization and rewards based on performance were going to be relied on in the rapid transformation of this "sinecure of mediocrity" into a dynamic corporation. GE would be split into twenty-seven autonomous divisions comprising 110 small companies. The 110 would be run just as if they were individual enterprises, the local boss setting his own budget, even making capital expenditures up to $200,000. But with authority and responsibility would go accountability and measurement, measurement by higher, harder standards. Third, GE's new philosophy of decentralized management specifically prohibited meeting with competitors on prices, bids, or market shares. Charlie Wilson's General Instruction 2.35[1] on compliance with the antitrust laws, first issued in 1946 and re-issued in 1948 and 1950, would remain very much in force.

There was good reason for stressing this last point. Antitrust was then a very sore subject at GE. In the decade just ended (1940–50), the corporation had been involved in thirteen antitrust cases, the offenses ranging from production limitation and patent pooling to price fixing and division of markets. Moreover, GE had long been something of a battleground for two divergent schools of economic thought. One school was straight Adam Smith and dedicated to the classical concept that corporate prog-

---

[1] "It has been and is the policy of this Company to conform strictly to the antitrust laws . . . special care should be taken that any proposed action is in conformity with the law as presently interpreted. If there is any doubt as to the legality of any proposed action . . . the advice of the Law Department must be obtained."

ress, like national progress, was best secured by freedom of private initiative within the bonds of justice. Its advocates believed that nothing was less intelligent than entering into price restrictions with competitors, for this just put GE on a par with companies that had neither its research facilities nor its market power. Ralph Cordiner, the company's most articulate advocate of this viewpoint, prided himself on the fact that it was at his insistence that the three GE employees implicated in illegal price fixing got the sack in 1949; his philosophy, at its most eloquent, was simply: "Every company and every industry—yes, and every country— that is operated on a basis of cartel systems is liquidating its present strength and future opportunities."

The second school of thought held that competition, particularly price competition, was for the birds. Getting together with competitors was looked on as a way of life, a convention, "just as a manager's office always has a desk with a swivel chair." It was considered easier to negotiate market percentages than fight for one's share, less wearing to take turns on rigged bids than play the rugged individualist. Besides, the rationale went, they were all "gentlemen" and no more inclined to gouge the consumer than to crowd a competitor. Admittedly, all of them knew they were breaking the law—Section 1 of the Sherman Act is as explicit as a traffic ordinance. Their justification was on other grounds. "Sure, collusion was illegal," explained an old GE hand, "but it wasn't *unethical*. It wasn't any more unethical than if the companies had a summit conference the way Russia and the West meet. Those competitor meetings were just attended by a group of distressed individuals who wanted to know where they were going."

One important reason for the strength of GE's anti-competition school was a change that occurred in the electrical industry after World War II. Smaller companies were becoming bigger and they were broadening their product lines. Customers had a wider choice of heavy electrical equipment, alike in quality and design. Price, consequently, became the decisive selling point. To turn this situation to their best advantage, buyers adopted a new technique: the competitive bid. When the utilities took it up, it became so prevalent that some manufacturers came to believe certain types of equipment would be treated like commodities with prices expected to fluctuate from day to day. This produced

serious instability in the market and made profit planning difficult. The conspiracies proliferated at GE and elsewhere because
the manufacturers lacked the gumption to shift the buyers' attention from price to higher quality, better service, and improved
design. . . .

A WAY OF LIFE FOR CLARENCE BURKE

One of the more attentive listeners to what the incoming president had to say about antitrust was Clarence Burke, a hard-
driving, tenacious executive in his middle forties (who was to
become the $42,000-a-year general manager of the High Voltage
Switchgear Department and one of fifteen GE executives sentenced in Philadelphia). Burke had come to the heavy-equipment
end of GE in 1926, fresh from the Georgia Institute of Technology (B.S. in electrical engineering), and his entire corporate
life had been spent there. The heavy-equipment division was
more than just the group that accounted for some 25 percent of
GE sales; it was the oldest division, and the foundation upon
which the whole company had been built. Moreover, it was the
stronghold of the collusionists. All of the nineteen indictments to
which GE pleaded either guilty or no contest in Philadelphia
sprang from price fixing, bid rigging, market division in heavy
equipment.

Burke's introduction to the heavy-equipment conspiracies was
easy as falling off a log. It occurred when he reported to Pittsfield, Massachusetts, on June 1, 1945, as sales manager of distribution transformers. A month or so after Burke's arrival, H. L.
"Buster" Brown, sales manager of the whole Transformer Department, called the new man in and told him he'd be expected
to attend a Pittsburgh meeting of the transformer section of the
National Electrical Manufacturers' Association. It was a regularly
scheduled affair, held during OPA days, in what is now the
Penn-Sheraton Hotel, and it was attended by thirty or forty industry people plus the NEMA secretaries from New York. But after
adjournment—when the NEMA secretaries had departed—the
company men reassembled within the hour for a cozier meeting.
The talk this time was about prices, OPA-regulated prices, and
how the industry could best argue Washington into jacking up
the ceilings. Burke didn't consider this illegal, and he took part

in several subsequent monthly meetings before OPA was abolished.

The convenient price klatsches following the regular NEMA meetings continued after OPA's demise. But instead of discussing pricing under government controls, the conspirators turned to fixing prices among themselves. . . . [However,] the post-OPA agreement [did not] seem to some of the participants like Burke to put them any more outside the law than agreements under the OPA. . . . [Said Burke,] "Buster Brown assured us that [the company's antitrust directive] didn't mean the kind of thing we were doing, that Antitrust would have to say we had *gouged* the public to say we were doing anything illegal." . . .

In 1946 [this rationale] was demolished by the company lawyers. Teams of them made the rounds of GE departments, no doubt in response to federal probings that were to result in the successful antitrust prosecutions of GE two years later. The lawyers put everyone in GE on notice that it certainly was illegal to discuss prices with competitors, whether the public was gouged or not. Then the head office followed this up by barring anybody who had anything to do with the pricing from attending NEMA meetings. . . .This situation continued for about nine months, during which everyone received a copy of Electric Charlie's antitrust admonition and during which GE's competitors kept the Pittsfield shut-ins informed by telephone of their own price agreements. Then, abruptly, the iron curtain was raised. . . .

The conspiracy operated, although sporadically, for the next several years of Burke's Pittsfield assignment (he was reassigned February 1, 1950). Every so often, the GE participants would retire behind the iron curtain, until it seemed necessary to bring about some general price increases. Then there would be a resumption of quiet talks with the men from other major manufacturers like Westinghouse. The antitrust-compliance directives they had all initialed? "When anybody raised a question about that, they would be told it doesn't apply now."

By 1951, however, at the time Burke was listening to Ralph Cordiner's antitrust exhortations, the Pittsfield conspiracy had closed down—to make matters simpler if, as everyone correctly suspected, Cordiner was going to clamp down on such cabals. But bigger and better conspiracies were in the offing. In September 1951, not very long after the Cordiner meeting, Clarence Burke walked into a new job at GE—and into membership in probably the oldest conspiracy then extant. The conspiracy was in circuit breakers[2] and it had been operative over the span of a quarter-century. Burke's new job was manager of all switchgear marketing, which included circuit breakers, switchgear, and other items of heavy electrical equipment. . . .

Burke's boss when he first went to switchgear in 1951 was Henry V. Erben, [who] had risen to the No. 3 spot in GE—executive vice president, Apparatus Group. . . . [Burke recalls:] "Erben's theory had been live and let live, contact the competitors. He gave us that theory at every opportunity and we took it down to other levels and had no trouble getting the most innocent persons to go along. Mr. Erben thought it was all right, and if they didn't want to do it, they knew we would replace them. Not replace them for that reason, of course. We would have said the man isn't *broad* enough for this job, he hasn't grown into it yet."

One man, ironically enough, who had not yet "grown" into the job was George Burens, the new boss of the whole switchgear operations. Burens had started out in GE as a laborer; he had the additional disadvantage of being a junior-high-school man in a corporate world full of college men, but during the next thirty years he had steadily risen by sheer competitive spirit. Part of his zest for competition had been acquired in the Lamp Division, where he had spent the bulk of his career. Lamps had long been noted as the most profitable of GE divisions and the most independent, a constant trial to Gerard Swope in the days when he tried to centralize all administrative authority in GE's New York headquarters. But most of Burens' competitive spirit was simply in the nature of the man. "He had grown up hating competitors," was the way a colleague put it. "They were the enemy."

"THIS IS BOB, WHAT IS 7'S BID?"

Burens arrived on the scene in September of 1951 and busied himself solely with the job of splitting switchgear into three independent companies (high, medium, and low voltage), each with

---

[2] Like their household counterparts, circuit breakers are used to interrupt the flow of electricity when it reaches dangerous voltages. The industrial versions are sometimes forty feet long, twenty-six feet high, and weigh eighty-five tons.

a general manager and himself as general manager of the division. Once decentralization was accomplished, he was content for a time to let his new departmental general managers like Clarence Burke run the conspiracy. And some conspiracy it was.

Some $650 million in sales was involved, according to Justice Department estimates, from 1951 through 1958. The annual total amounted to roughly $75 million and was broken down into two categories, sealed bids and open bids. The sealed-bid business (between $15 million and $18 million per year) was done with public agencies, city, state, and federal. The private-sector business was conducted with private utilities and totaled some $55 million to $60 million per annum.

The object of the conspiracy, in so far as the sealed-bid business was concerned, was to rotate that business on a fixed-percentage basis among four participating companies, then the only circuit-breaker manufacturers in the U.S. GE got 45 percent, Westinghouse 35, Allis-Chalmers 10, Federal Pacific 10. Every ten days to two weeks working-level meetings were called in order to decide whose turn was next. Turns were determined by the "ledger list," a table of who had got what in recent weeks, and after that the only thing left to decide was the price that the company picked to "win" would submit as the lowest bid.

Above this working-level group was a second tier of conspirators who dealt generally with the over-all scheme of rigging the sealed bids but whose prime purpose was maintenance of book prices (quoted prices) and market shares in the yearly $55 million to $60 million worth of private-sector business. Once each week, the top executives (general managers and vice-presidents) responsible for carrying out the conspiracy would get the word to each other via intercompany memo. A different executive would have the "duty" over each thirty-day period. That involved initiating the memos, which all dealt with the same subject matter: the jobs coming up that week, the book price each company was setting, comments on the general level of equipment prices.

The conspiracies had their own lingo and their own standard operating procedures. The attendance list was known as the "Christmas-card list," meetings as "choir practices." Companies had code numbers—GE 1, Westinghouse 2, Allis-Chalmers 3, Federal Pacific 7—which were used in conjunction with first names when calling a conspirator at home for price information

("This is Bob, what is 7's bid?"). At the hotel meetings it was
S.O.P. not to list one's employer when registering and not to have
breakfast with fellow conspirators in the dining room. The GE
men observed two additional precautions: never to be the ones
who kept the records and never to tell GE's lawyers anything.

WHERE TO CUT THROATS

But things were not always smooth even inside this well-oiled
machine, for the conspirators actually had no more compunction
at breaking the rules of the conspiracy than at breaching the
Sherman Act. "Everyone accused the others of not living up to
the agreement," Clarence Burke recalled, "and the ones they complained about tried to shift the blame onto someone else." The
most constant source of irritation occurred in the sealed-bid
business, where chiseling was difficult to detect. But breaks in
book price to the utilities in the open-bid business also generated ill will and vituperation. Indeed, one of the many ironies
of the whole affair is that the conspiracy couldn't entirely sup-
press the competitive instinct. Every so often some company
would decide that cutthroat competition outside was preferable
to the throat-cutting that went on in the cartel; they would break
contact and sit out the conspiracy for a couple of years.

What prompted their return? Chronic overcapacity, for one
thing, overcapacity that put a constant pressure on prices. Soon
after he went to Washington as defense mobilization chief in
1950, Electric Charlie Wilson announced that the nation's electric-
power capacity needed to be increased 30 percent over the next
three years. The equipment industry jumped to match that figure,
and added a little more as well. Thus an executive, who ebul-
liently increased capacity one year, a few years later might join
a price conspiracy to escape the consequences of that increase.
"This is a feast or famine business," summed up Clarence Burke.
"At one time everybody was loaded with orders, and ever since
they wanted to stay that way. When utilities decide they need
more generating capacity, they start buying and we have three
years of good business—and then three years of bad. The decision
to build capacity was delegated down to the managers [under
decentralization]."

A more human explanation of why the conspiracy snarled on

for eight years was corporate pressure, the pressure to perform. "All we got from Lexington Avenue," said Burke, "was 'get your percentage of available business up, the General Electric Co. is slipping.' " Cordiner himself has remarked: "I would say the company was more than slightly nervous in 1951–52–53."

Certainly corporate pressure no more exculpates an executive who enters into an illegal conspiracy than the relatively low pay of a bank clerk justifies his dipping into the till. But that is not to say it didn't carry weight with the conspirators from GE. For the company was not only experiencing the increased pressure that goes with new presidents but was adjusting to a whole new organizational setup. Said one observer of the scene, Vice President Harold Smiddy, GE's management expert: "Some thought . . . that he was going too fast. But Cordiner's asset is stretching men. He can push them and he did." Said another observer, GE director Sidney Weinberg: "If you did something wrong, Cordiner would send for you and tell you you were through. That's all there would be to it."

Down the line, where the pressure must have been intense, Clarence Burke had this to say of it as a factor in continuing the conspiracy: "We did feel that this was the only way to reach part of our goals as managers. Each year we had to budget for more profit as a percent of net sales, as well as for a larger percentage of available business. My boss, George Burens, wouldn't approve a budget unless it was a 'reach' budget. We couldn't accomplish a greater percent of net profit to sales without getting together with competitors. Part of the pressure was the will to get ahead and the desire to have the good will of the man above you. He had only to get the approval of the man above *him* to replace you, and if you wouldn't cooperate he could find lots of other faults to use to get you out.". . .

[General Electric's participation in the circuit-breaker cartel continued sporadically. In May 1953, Burke got out, and GE's boycott went on through 1954. That was a bad year for the industry and for GE. When corporate executives sought to prevent underbidding by competition, the celebrated "white sale" of 1954–55 began. In late 1955, the cartel was cranked up again. This worked fairly well until the first part of 1957, when McGregor Smith of Florida Power & Light blew it up. Prices went down even further than during the "white sale."]

CORDINER'S "PIECES OF PAPER"

GE was involved in at least seven other conspiracies during the time the circuit-breaker cartel was inoperative. The one in power transformers (GE Vice President Raymond W. Smith) was going, for GE had yet to develop the "black box" (a design breakthrough using standard components to produce tailor-made transformers), which two years later would enable it to take price leadership away from Westinghouse. The one in turbine generators (GE Vice President William S. Ginn) was functioning too. In the fall of 1957 it was agreed at the Barclay Hotel[3] to give GE "position" in bidding on a 500,000-kilowatt TVA unit.

The question that naturally arises, the cartels being so numerous, is why didn't GE's top management stop them? Cordiner has been criticized within the company, and rightly so, for sitting aloofly in New York and sending out "pieces of paper"—his 20.5 antitrust directive—rather than having 20.5 personally handed to the local staff by the local boss. But there was also a failure in human relations. A warmer man might have been close enough to his people to divine what was going on. According to T. K. Quinn (*I Quit Monster Business*), the GE vice president who had helped him up the ladder, Ralph Cordiner, was "first class in every aspect of management except human relations."

After the conspiracy case broke, the question of top-level complicity came up. GE hired Gerhard Gesell of the Washington law firm of Covington & Burling to come to a conclusion one way or another as to whether Cordiner, Paxton, or any other member of the Executive Office had knowledge of the cartels. No corroborated evidence ever came to light that Cordiner knew of them; quite the opposite. As Clarence Burke put it last month: "Cordiner was sincere but undersold by people beneath him who rescinded his orders." . . .

Judge Ganey, however, expressed a more definite view: "I am not naive enough to believe General Electric didn't know about

---

[3] On February 2, 1960, the hotel jocularly described its *spécialité de maison* in a small New York *Times* ad: "Antitrust-corporation secrets are best discussed in the privacy of an executive suite at the Barclay. It's convenient, attractive, and financially practical."

it and it didn't meet with their hearty approbation." In Ganey's opinion, Directive 20.5 was "observed in its breach rather than in its enforcement." To say the least, there was a serious management failure at GE. . . .

[THE CASE BREAKS OPEN]

In 1958 the circuit breaker-switchgear conspiracy started up again. George Burens struggled with it for the next three months at a round of meetings at the old hotels and some swanky new places. Circuit-breaker prices inched up. Then in January 1959, Burens was promoted out. [His successor was Lewis Burger.] Burger promptly joined the circuit-breaker conspiracy. But the day was not far off, indeed it was only nine months away, when a phone call would set in motion the forces that would shatter the conspiracy and send Burger along with Burens off to prison.

Shortly before ten o'clock on the morning of September 28, 1959, an urgent long-distance call came in to GE's vast Transformer Division at Pittsfield, Massachusetts. It was for Edward L. Dobbins, the divisional lawyer, and the person on the line was another attorney, representing Lapp Insulator Co. He just wanted to say that one of Lapp's officers had been subpoenaed by a Philadelphia grand jury and was going to tell the whole story. "What story?" said Dobbins pleasantly, then listened to an account that sent him, filled with concern, into the office of the divisional vice president, Raymond W. Smith. . . .

The story Dobbins had, which the man from Lapp was about to spill before a Philadelphia grand jury, was that Paul Hartig, one of Ray Smith's departmental general managers, had been conspiring with Lapp Insulator and a half-dozen other manufacturers to fix prices on insulators. Such news was unsettling enough to any boss, but Smith's alarm had its roots in something deeper than the derelictions of a subordinate. He was himself "Mr. Big" of another cartel, one involving $210 million worth of transformers a year, and he didn't need the gift of prescience to sense the danger to his own position. Nevertheless, Smith concluded that he had no choice but to report the trouble to New York. . . .

It was no wonder, then, that Cordiner was upset by what he heard about the insulator department. And this was only the beginning. GE's general counsel, Ray Luebbe, was brought into the case, and within a matter of days Paul Hartig was in Luebbe's New York office implicating Vice President Ray Smith. Smith made a clean breast of things, detailing the operation of the transformer cartel (bids on government contracts were rotated to ensure that GE and Westinghouse each got 30 percent of the business, the remaining 40 being split among four other manufacturers; book prices were agreed upon at meetings held everywhere from Chicago's Drake Hotel to the Homestead at Hot Springs, Virginia; secrecy was safeguarded by channeling all phone calls and mail to the homes, destroying written memoranda upon receipt).

Then Smith implicated a second GE vice president, William S. Ginn. Head of the Turbine Division at forty-one, Ginn was considered a comer in the company. Unfortunately for him, he was just as much of a wheel in conspiracy, an important man in *two* cartels, the one in transformers, which he had passed on to Ray Smith, and the one in turbine generators, which only the year before had aroused the suspicions of TVA by bringing about some very rapid price increases. . . .

BIG FISH IN SMALL COMPANIES

The Justice Department was also looking for answers. It had got started on the case because of TVA's suspicions and because Senator Estes Kefauver had threatened an investigation of the electrical industry, putting the executive branch of government on notice that if it didn't get on with the job, the legislative branch would. Robert A. Bicks, the most vigorous chief of Antitrust since Thurman Arnold, certainly had plenty of will to get on with the job, but the way was clouded. The Antitrust Division had once before—in 1951–52—tried to find a pattern of collusive pricing in the maze of transformer bids, but had wound up with no indictments. Now, as Bicks and William Maher, the head of the division's Philadelphia office, moved into the situation, proof seemed just as elusive as ever.

The tactics of the Antitrust Division were based on using the Philadelphia grand jury to subpoena documents, and then, after study of these, to subpoena individuals—the corporation executives who would logically have been involved if a conspiracy existed. The ultimate objective was to determine whether the biggest electrical manufacturers and their top executives had participated in a cartel, but the approach had to be oblique. As Maher put it: "Even if we had proof of a meeting where Paxton [president of GE] and Cresap [president of Westinghouse] had sat down and agreed to fix prices, we would still have to follow the product lines down through to the illegal acts. You have to invert it, start with what happened at a lower level and build it up step by step. The idea is to go after the biggest fish in the *smallest* companies, then hope to get enough information to land the biggest fish in the biggest companies."

In mid-November a second Philadelphia grand jury was empaneled, and Justice Department attorneys began ringing doorbells across the land. As more of these rang and the trust busters took more testimony (under grand jury subpoena), a sudden shiver of apprehension ran through the industry. The grapevine, probably the most sensitive in American business, began to buzz with talk that the feds were really on to something—moreover, that jail impended for the guilty. Everyone by then was only too well aware than an Ohio judge had just clapped three executives behind bars for ninety days for participating in a hand-tool cartel.

CORDINER'S COMMAND DECISION

Back at GE, meanwhile, Cordiner had issued instructions that all apparatus general managers, including those few who so far had been implicated, were to be interviewed by the company attorneys about participation in cartels. Most of the guilty lied, gambling that the exposures would not go any further than they had. Cordiner, accepting their stories, began to formulate what he thought would be GE's best defense. It would have two principal salients: first, the company itself was not guilty of the conspiracies; what had occurred was without the encouragement or even the knowledge of the chairman, the president, and the Executive Office. GE's corporate position on antitrust compliance was a matter of record, embodied in Directive 20.5, which Cordiner had personally written and promulgated five years before. Furthermore, illegal conduct of any individuals involved was clearly beyond the authority granted to them by the company, and therefore the company, as distinguished from the individuals, should not be held criminally responsible. Second, those employees who had violated Directive 20.5 were in for corporate punishment. "Stale offenses" were not to be counted, but a three-year company "statute of limitations" would govern liability (the federal limitation: five years).

Punishment of necessity had to go hand in hand with a corporate not-guilty stance. If GE's defense was to be that the conspiracies had taken place in contravention of written policy (Directive 20.5), then unpunished offenders would be walking proof to a jury that 20.5 was just a scrap of paper. On the other hand, here was a clear management failure on the part of the Executive Office—a failure to detect over a period of almost a decade the cartels that were an open secret to the rest of the industry. As GE was to learn to its sorrow, lots of people who approved of punishment for the offenders did not think this permitted GE to wash its hands of responsibility. Westinghouse's president, Mark W. Cresap Jr., spoke for many executives both inside the industry and out when he stated his position this January: "Corporate punishment of these people . . . would only be self-serving on my part . . . this is a management failure."

But aside from the moral question, the legal basis of GE's not-guilty stance was shaky to say the least. Its lawyers felt bound to inform the Executive Office: "The trend of the law appears to be that a business corporation will be held criminally liable for the acts of an employee so long as these acts are reasonably related to the area of general responsibility entrusted to him notwithstanding the fact that such acts are committed in violation of instructions issued by the company in good faith. . . ." Under the decentralization policy, distinguishing between an "innocent" corporation and its "guilty" executives would be tough, for Cordiner himself had given the general managers clear pricing powers.

The Cordiner position had another weakness: it was based on the assumption that GE was involved in only four cartels—at the most. Yet wider involvement could reasonably have been expected. That very month general counsel Luebbe (who retired on October 1, 1960) had been warned by one of the general managers who had confessed that collusion would be found to have spread across the whole company front. ("I tried to tell Luebbe to stop the investigation," reflected the general manager, "and try to make a deal with the government. I told him in

November 1959, that this thing would go right across the board. He just laughed at me. He said, 'You're an isolated case—only you fellows would be stupid enough to do it.'") Thus when wider involvement actually did come to light—the four cartels multiplied into nineteen and accounted for more than 10 percent of GE's total sales—the company found itself in the ludicrous position of continuing to proclaim its corporate innocence while its executives were being implicated by platoons. . . .

[In Philadelphia,] the first grand jury was looking into conspiracies in insulators, switchgear, circuit breakers, and several other products. The second grand jury was hearing four transformer cases and one on industrial controls. With a score of Justice men working on them, cases proliferated, and from December on lawyers began popping up trying to get immunity for their clients in return for testimony. Scarcely a week went by that Bicks and company didn't get information on at least two new cases. But what they still needed was decisive data that would break a case wide open. In January 1960, at just about the time Ralph Cordiner was making an important speech to GE's management corps ("every company and every industry—yes, and every country—that is operated on a basis of cartel systems is liquidating its present strength and future opportunities"), the trust busters hit the jackpot in switchgear.

"THE PHASES OF THE MOON"

Switchgear had been particularly baffling to the Antitrust Division, so much so that in trying to establish a cartel pattern in the jumble of switchgear prices the trust busters got the bright idea they might be in code. A cryptographer was brought in to puzzle over the figures and try to crack the secret of how a conspirator could tell what to bid and when he'd win. But the cryptographer was soon as flummoxed as everyone else. One of the government attorneys in the case, however, had made a point of dropping in on a college classmate who was the president of a small midwestern electrical-equipment company. This executive didn't have chapter and verse on the switchgear cartel but what he did have was enough for Justice to throw a scare into a bigger company, I-T-E Circuit Breaker. Indicating that subpoenas would follow, antitrust investigators asked I-T-E's general counsel, Franklyn Judson, to supply the names of sales managers in specific product lines. Judson decided to conduct an investigation of his own. When the subpoenas did come, a pink-cheeked blond young man named Nye Spencer, the company's sales manager for switchgear, was resolutely waiting—his arms loaded with data. He had decided he wasn't about to commit another crime by destroying the records so carefully laid away in his cellar.

There were pages on pages of notes taken during sessions of the switchgear conspiracy—incriminating entries like "Potomac Light & Power O.K. for GE" and "Before bidding on this, check with GE"; neat copies of the ground rules for meetings of the conspirators: no breakfasting together, no registering at the hotel with company names, no calls to the office, no papers to be left in hotel-room wastebaskets. Spencer, it seems, had been instructed to handle some of the secretarial work of the cartel and believed in doing it right; he'd hung onto the documents to help in training an assistant. But the most valuable windfall from the meticulous record keeper was a pile of copies of the "phases of the moon" pricing formula for as far back as May 1958.

Not much to look at—just sheets of paper, each containing a half-dozen columns of figures—they immediately resolved the enigma of switchgear prices in commercial contracts. One group of columns established the bidding order of the seven switchgear manufacturers—a different company, each with its own code number, phasing into the priority position every two weeks (hence "phases of the moon"). A second group of columns, keyed into the company code numbers, established how much each company was to knock off the agreed-upon book price. For example, if it were No. 1's (GE's) turn to be low bidder at a certain number of dollars off book, then all Westinghouse (No. 2), or Allis-Chalmers (No. 3) had to do was look for their code number in the second group of columns to find how many dollars they were to bid *above* No. 1. These bids would then be fuzzed up by having a little added to them or taken away by companies 2, 3, etc. Thus there was not even a hint that the winning bid had been collusively arrived at.

With this little device in hand, the trust busters found they could light up the whole conspiracy like a switchboard. The new evidence made an equally profound impression on the grand juries. On February 16 and 17, 1960, they handed down the first seven indictments. Forty companies and eighteen individuals were charged with fixing prices or dividing the market on seven electrical products. Switchgear led the list.[4]

A LEG UP FROM ALLIS-CHALMERS

These initial indictments brought about two major turning points in the investigation. The first was a decision by Allis-Chalmers to play ball with the government. This move came too late to save L. W. (Shorty) Long, an assistant general manager—he was one of the eighteen already indicted—but the trust busters were willing to go easier on Allis-Chalmers *if* the company came up with something solid. It did. Thousands upon thousands of documents were turned over to the government. Further, the testimony of Vice President J. W. McMullen, and others was so helpful (attorney Edward Mullinix had coached them many hours on the importance of backing up allegations with receipted hotel bills, expense-account items, memorandums, telephone logs, etc.) that a number of new cases were opened up. Only two of those first seven indictments retained their Justice Department classification as "major" cases. To them were added five new major indictments—power transformers, power switching equipment, industrial controls, turbine generators, and steam condensers—culled from thirteen to follow that spring and fall.

The second major turning point came through a decision in March by Chief Federal Judge J. Cullen Ganey, who was to try all the cases. That decision concerned whether the individuals and companies involved in the first seven indictments would be permitted to plead *nolo contendere* (no contest) to the charges. The matter was of vital importance to the companies, which might well be faced by treble-damage suits growing out of the conspiracies. (A GE lawyer had advised the Executive Office: "If a criminal case can be disposed of by a *nolo* plea, the prospective damage claimant is given no assistance in advancing a claim; it must be built from the ground up.") The matter was also of great

---

[4] The other six: oil circuit breakers, low-voltage power circuit breakers, insulators, open-fuse cutouts, lightning arresters, bushings. Each indictment covered one product and listed all the corporations and individuals charged with conspiracy to fix prices on that product.

importance to a determined Robert Bicks, who argued that *nolo* pleas would permit the defendants "the luxury of a 'Maybe we did it; maybe we didn't do it' posture. 'Oh, yes, technically before Judge Ganey we admitted this, but you know we weren't guilty. You know we didn't do this.' "

Actually, in the opinion of one veteran antitrust lawyer, everybody in the industry and 99 percent of the government thought the court would accept *nolos*. Indeed, the Justice Department was so worried about the matter, and so anxious to forfend such a development, that for the first time in the history of the department an attorney general sent a presiding judge an affidavit urging rejection of *nolos*.

"Acceptance of the *nolo* pleas tendered in these cases," William Rogers deposed to Judge Ganey, "would mean [that] . . . insistence on guilty pleas or guilty verdicts would never be appropriate in any antitrust case—no matter the predatory nature of the violation or the widespread adverse consequences to governmental purchasers. This result would neither foster respect for the law nor vindicate the public interest. These interests require, in the cases at bar here, either a trial on the issues or pleas of guilty."

But Judge Ganey didn't need to be impressed with the seriousness of the cases. He ruled that *nolo contendere* pleas were unacceptable (unless, of course, the Justice Department had no objections). The corporations and individuals would either have to plead guilty or stand trial. At the arraignment in April, Allis-Chalmers and its indicted employees promptly pleaded "guilty"; most others, including GE and its employees, pleaded "not guilty." They intended at that time to take their chances before a jury, no matter how bleak the prospects. . . .

A TALK WITH BICKS

The one thing nobody wanted was a trial where the dirty linen of the conspiracies would be washed every day in the public press. If one company, or even an employee of one company, chose to stand trial, everyone else might just as well too, for all the juicy details of their involvement would surely come out. But the problem of settling the case without trial was complicated by the fact that the companies involved were of different sizes and degrees of guilt. Five companies, for example, had had no part in any conspiracy save steam condensers; they were understandably opposed to any package deal on the twenty indictments that committed them to a guilty plea instead of the *nolo* plea they might otherwise have been allowed to make.

GE and Westinghouse, however, were both convinced by fall that rapid settlement was essential. GE's own hopes of a successful not-guilty plea had been trampled to death under the parade of grand-jury witnesses, and were interred by a decision in the Continental Baking case that summer.[5] Moreover, Bicks and company still had the grand juries going full blast; at the rate these were taking testimony any delay in settling might dump a half-dozen additional indictments on top of the twenty already handed down. Judge Ganey was certainly willing to speed up the proceedings and suggested all defendant companies have an exploratory talk with Robert Bicks.

On the thirty-first of October the lawyers of almost all the affected companies crowded into a Justice Department conference room and from nine in the morning till seven that night worked at hammering out a package of guilty and *nolo* pleas. On thirteen "minor" cases, where only corporations had been indicted, Bicks was willing to accept *nolos,* but he insisted on guilty pleas in the seven major cases. And he wanted pleas (guilty or *nolos*) on all twenty indictments at the same time. In December, GE pleaded "guilty" to all the major indictments against it, and with the government's consent, *nolo contendere* to the thirteen "minor" ones. The other major companies followed suit. The way thus cleared, judgment was swift in coming. On February 6, executives from every major manufacturer in the entire electrical equipment industry sat in a crowded courtroom and heard Judge Ganey declare: "What is really at stake here is the survival of the kind of economy under which this country has grown great, the free-enterprise system." Seven executives

---

[5] Said the U.S. Court of Appeals (Sixth Circuit): "The courts have held that so long as the criminal act is directly related to the performance of the duties which the officer or agent has the broad authority to perform, the corporate principal is liable for the criminal act also, and must be deemed to have 'authorized' the criminal act."

went off to a Pennsylvania prison; twenty-three others, given suspended jail sentences, were put on probation for five years; and fines totaling nearly $2 million were handed out. . . .

IS THE LESSON LEARNED?

So ended the incredible affair—a story of cynicism, arrogance, and irresponsibility. Plainly there was an egregious management failure. But there was also a failure to connect ordinary morals and business morals; the men involved apparently figured there was a difference.

The consent decrees hammered out by the Justice Department are partial insurance that bid rigging and price fixing won't happen again. Yet consent decrees are only deterrents, not cures. The fact is that the causes which underlay the electrical conspiracies are still as strong as they ever were. Chronic overcapacity continues to exert a strong downward pressure on prices. The industry's price problem—outgrowth of an inability to shift the buyer's attention from price to other selling points like higher quality, better service, improved design—could hardly be worse: many items of electrical equipment are currently selling for less than in the ruinous days of the "white sale." Corporate pressure is stronger than ever on executives, who must struggle to fulfill the conflicting demands of bigger gross sales on the one hand and more profit per dollar of net sales on the other. These are matters that require careful handling if conspiracy is not to take root again in the electrical-equipment industry.

The antitrust laws also confront the largest corporations with a special dilemma: how to compete without falling afoul of Section 2 of the Sherman Act, which makes it unlawful to "monopolize, or attempt to monopolize." It will take plenty of business statesmanship to handle this aspect of the law; one way, of course, is simply to refrain from going after every last piece of business. If GE were to drive for 50 percent of the market, even strong companies like I-T-E Circuit Breaker might be mortally injured.

Has the industry learned any lessons? "One thing I've learned out of all this," said one executive, "is to talk to only one other person, not to go to meetings where there are lots of other people." Many of the defendants *Fortune* interviewed both before and after sentencing looked on themselves as the fall guys of U.S. business. They protested that they should no more be held up to blame than many another American businessman, for conspiracy is just as much "a way of life" in other fields as it was in electrical equipment. "Why pick on us?" was the attitude. "Look at some of those other fellows."

This attitude becomes particularly disturbing when one considers that most of the men who pleaded guilty in Judge Ganey's court (to say nothing of the scores given immunity for testifying before the grand juries) are back at their old positions, holding down key sales and marketing jobs. Only GE cleaned house. . . . (Although the confessed conspirators at GE had been assured that the transfers, demotions, and pay cuts received earlier would be the end of their corporate punishment, this was not the case. In mid-March they were told they could either quit or be fired, and were given anywhere from a half hour to a few days to make their decision.)

DISJOINTED AUTHORITY, DISJOINTED MORALS

But top executive officers of the biggest companies, at least, have come out of their antitrust experience determined upon strict compliance programs and possessed now of enough insight into the workings of a cartel to make those programs effective. Allis-Chalmers has set up a special compliance section. GE and Westinghouse, without which cartels in the industry could never endure, are taking more elaborate preventive measures. Both are well aware that any repetition of these conspiracies would lay them open to political pressure for dismemberment; size has special responsibilities in our society, and giants are under a continuous obligation to demonstrate that they have not got so big as to lose control over their far-flung divisions.

This case has focused attention on American business practices as nothing else has in many years. Senator Kefauver said he intended to probe further into the question of conspiracy at the top levels of management. Said Attorney General Robert Kennedy in April 1961: "We are redoubling our efforts to convince anyone so minded that conspiracy as 'a way of life' must mean a short and unhappy one."

The problem for American business does not start and stop

with the scofflaws of the electrical industry or with antitrust. Much was made of the fact that GE operated under a system of disjointed authority, and this was one reason it got into trouble. A more significant factor, the disjointment of morals, is something for American executives to think about in all aspects of their relations with their companies, each other, and the community.

The Root of the FTC's Confusion* ————

HAROLD B. MEYERS

At the main entrances of the Federal Trade Commission building in Washington stand two massive granite dray horses, seventeen feet long and fifteen feet tall. Each horse is held back from murderous charge by a stalwart, bare-chested workman. Ever since the designs were chosen in 1938 there has been disagreement over just what is going on. "The sculpture is nonsymbolic," said the selection committee of art experts. Sculptor Michael Lantz disagreed. He saw something quite specific in his statues. "They are the symbol of the ability of man to govern tremendous power," Lantz declared. "The theory behind the design is that man controls trade. Trade is an enormous thing, like the horse in the design. But man by his intelligence controls the horse, as he controls trade."

However symbolic the taming of the horses really is, the confusion over their meaning is uncannily appropriate to the Federal Trade Commission. Uncertainty over what it should be and how it should perform its functions was present at the agency's birth in 1914, and the fog has never quite been dispelled. Established to celebrate and protect the benefits of free competition, the FTC has often seemed to view competition as desirable only if it could be had without losers—or winners. The FTC has been irrelevant to many of the dramatic economic changes that have occurred in its lifetime. It has been as much of a nuisance as an aid to busi-

* *August 1963*

ness, especially small business. Nor has it been a particularly effective white knight in protecting the basic interests of consumers.

To Chairman Paul Rand Dixon, these judgments seem unfair. A former Vanderbilt University quarterback who keeps his artfully bronzed old football shoes on an office bookshelf, Dixon is full of understandable zeal for the FTC. "Antitrust, as the enemy of monopoly, is a devoted friend and servant of the honest capitalist," Dixon fervently believes. He is puzzled no end by the alarm his messianic outlook causes among businessmen, and there are times when he can't help feeling that business just doesn't understand *him.* "The business community," he complained in 1963 to North Dakota law students, "provoked by its Socialist and Communist opponents, is becoming somewhat sensitive to criticism of almost every kind, sometimes without regard to its source or motives."

There is, of course, some justification for Dixon's sensitivity, though his North Dakota lament was rather farfetched. Under the pressure of legitimate government action, businessmen do sometimes fail to see that the enforcement of competition is a boon rather than a curse. And on more than one occasion the FTC has rendered valuable service. In the Forties, for instance, its pressure played a part in persuading the steel industry to abandon its obsolete basing-point system. As Commissioner Sigurd Anderson tartly observed, "If we abolished the FTC today, we should have to reconstruct it tomorrow."

Yet, valuable as it has sometimes been as a Socratic gadfly, asking questions about the economy that needed to be asked, the FTC has still failed to lay down the clear rules of the road that businessmen need from government. Further, the FTC often seems to be doing work that could just as well be left to other agencies, such as the Department of Justice's Antitrust Division. Some of the FTC's work even seems to contradict antitrust, in the sense that instead of promoting competition it penalizes price cutting.

A MONSTROSITY THAT SPELLS "ENIGMA"

The agency's confusions and defects trace back to the legislative intent of the statutes granting FTC's much too broad discretionary authority. In passing the Sherman Act in 1890, Congress declared war against "restraint of trade" and monopoly. By 1914 it was felt that something more was needed; enforcement of the antitrust law through the courts had proved both slow and difficult. Congress therefore passed the Clayton Act amending the Sherman Act and, for good measure, created the FTC to be competition's special guardian. Its charter gave the FTC power to delve into unfair methods of competition in commerce (including deceptive advertising) and to issue cease-and-desist orders against those practices it found to be against the public interest.

To this inclusive mandate Congress in 1936 added the Robinson-Patman Act. This law has been characterized by Washington antitrust lawyer Frederick M. Rowe as "a legal enigma whose mysteries are familiar to many but fathomed by few." In a scholarly book, *Price Discrimination Under the Robinson-Patman Act*, Rowe calls the act an "anti-antitrust" measure and says it was a legacy of the same depression-bred faith in combination, rather than competition, that produced the ill-fated Blue Eagle of the National Recovery Administration. Though supposedly aimed at "big buyers," such as chain stores, which used volume purchasing to gain unjustified price advantages, Robinson-Patman has been invoked most often against small firms for relatively insignificant violations. Rowe, in fact, proposed a Parkinson's law of FTC enforcement: "That Robinson-Patman proceedings proliferate with the ease of making a case."

This statutory underpinning gives the FTC more than enough to do—even with its $11,473,000 budget and 1,150 employees. And indeed, lack of activity has never been one of the agency's faults. In fiscal 1962 the FTC received 5,519 complaints involving deceptive practices and another 1,451 charging restraints of trade. Most of these complaints, it is important to note, were made by disadvantaged competitors: businessmen use the FTC as well as condemn it. The commission completed 1,677 investigations in 1962, approved 474 complaints, and issued 407 cease-and-desist orders (356 of them uncontested consent decrees).

The trouble is that amidst all this frenetic activity it is difficult to find a clear policy line on which businessmen can act. This difficulty is dramatically illustrated by the convolutions of the recent Sun Oil case. But it is also apparent in many other cases. Consider the following:

• *Deceptive practices*. In 1960 the FTC issued a complaint against the Quaker Oats Co. on the grounds that it misrepresented briquets as "charcoal" when they were actually made principally from the residue of corncobs. Quaker Oats fought back, arguing that there was no misrepresentation in calling its product "Chuck Wagon Charcoal Briquets." The FTC examiner who first heard the case agreed, citing evidence that nine dictionaries failed to limit "charcoal" to mean only the charred residue of wood. "In the face of these definitions," said the examiner, "it is difficult to see how a finding could properly be made that charcoal, even when restricted to fuel charcoal, can be made from no material other than wood, or that such is the understanding of the public." The FTC staff appealed the findings, and oral arguments were heard in 1963 by the full commission. Such a case seems hardly worth the time and money it has consumed. If charcoal means what the dictionary says, there was no misrepresentation, and if the product burned as well as wood charcoal and was not harmful, why should the government be concerned?

• *Discriminatory promotional allowances.* J. A. Folger Co. of Kansas City, second-largest coffee manufacturer in the nation, took part in "Foodaramas" sponsored in 1958 and 1959 by the Benner Tea Co., a small retail grocery chain with headquarters in Burlington, Iowa. The Foodaramas were open-house affairs at which samples of food were given away, but no sales were made. Folger paid Benner $150 each year for booths in which to promote its Folger brand. Other Folger customers, competing with Benner, protested to the FTC. The FTC brought a complaint against Folger under the Robinson-Patman Act, charging that Folger had failed to offer these other customers proportionally equal promotional allowances. Deciding the case last fall, the FTC said in its majority opinion: "It is this type of favoritism to a customer such as a chain organization, even in relatively small individual contributions, which the law exactly proscribes." Folger was ordered to stop discriminating among competing customers in paying promotional allowances—under all circumstances, not just at food fairs. Folger's appeal is pending in the Fifth Circuit Court of Appeals. In a minority opinion, Commissioner Philip Elman argued that the order against Folger was far too broad and should have been issued, if at all, only against the kind of food-fair activity complained of. Said Elman crisply: "If there were any violations here, they were marginal, isolated, and in an uncertain area of the law."

• *Anticompetitive and monopolistic practices, mergers.* Luria

Brothers Inc. of Philadelphia, largest iron and steel scrap dealer in the U.S., was charged by the FTC in 1954 with engaging in illegal and competition-damaging practices with a group of major U.S. and foreign steel producers. Luria and the mills, said the FTC, had entered into agreements whereby Luria became the principal source of scrap for them. The company increased its share of total U.S. scrap sales from 17.1 percent to 33.7 percent while its share of sales to the cited mills rose from 35.9 percent in 1947 to 78.5 percent in 1954. These "full supply arrangements" gave Luria the power to control prices received by other brokers and dealers, the FTC alleged, and the company reinforced its position by acquiring competing firms in 'at least two instances. Some 250 witnesses testified during 113 days of hearings, producing a transcript of more than 14,000 pages and introducing more than 1,300 exhibits. In February, nine years after the complaint was issued, the FTC concluded that the charges had been generally sustained. It issued an order against Luria and the steel producers, including Bethlehem, U.S. Steel, National Steel, and ten others. The order provided, among other things, that the cited mills must buy at least 50 percent of their annual scrap requirements from suppliers other than Luria for the next five years, so long as the other suppliers are competitive in price and quality. Luria was also told to divest itself of one competing scrap company it acquired in 1950; it cannot buy out any more dealers for five years without prior FTC approval.

The best criticism of the FTC's majority decision, which Luria has appealed, came in another thoughtful dissent by Commissioner Elman. He argued that it had not been shown that there was anything unlawful about the "exclusive patronage of Luria by each of the mill respondents." He added that the case "has little relevance to present conditions in the scrap market"—which, in the last decade, has changed from a sellers' to a buyers' market. A more useful proceeding, Elman suggested, would be a current investigation "to determine what corrective administrative action, if any, is required to maintain or re-establish healthy competition" in the scrap industry as it exists today. In effect, he accused his fellow commissioners of blindly beating a dead horse.

• *Discriminatory pricing.* The Borden Co. has been selling evaporated milk under its own well-known brand since 1892. About 1938 it entered the business of packing evaporated milk for sale under the private labels of purchasers. This private-label milk was sold at prices "consistently and substantially" lower than Borden-label milk of like grade and quality. The company justified the discrepancy in price on the grounds that its brand name, diligently promoted over many years, added to the salability, and hence the value, of the product. Smaller competitors, however, thought the lower price for private-label stock was intended to draw away their customers and drive them out of business, thus increasing Borden's already large share of the milk-packing market. At their behest, the FTC charged Borden in 1958 with a Robinson-Patman violation—unlawful price discrimination tending to lessen competition substantially. A hearing examiner filed an initial decision dismissing the complaint, but the commission reversed his finding and ordered Borden to cease discriminating in the price of *any* of its food products. Borden has appealed.

In reaching this decision, the commission (with Elman dissenting and two other members not participating) concluded that private-label buyers—generally larger retailers and chains—were given an unfair advantage over retailers that did not have enough volume to justify establishing their own brands. "The testimony from wholesalers as well as retailers disclosed the extremely low or nonexistent profit margins on evaporated milk," Chairman Dixon wrote, noting also that private-label milk was used as a loss leader to attract customers. Borden's actions, therefore, were found offensive by the FTC in two ways: (1) Small evaporated-milk producers were driven to the wall by Borden's competition, and this competition threatened the competitive situation in the industry; (2) the low prices forced on all private-label producers put a squeeze on wholesalers and retailers that were too small to have their own brands and were thus forced to stock the higher-priced brands. Nothing was said about possible benefit to consumers from the bitter competition in canned milk.

These cases—from *Quaker Oats* to *Borden*—suggest the FTC's extraordinary range of powers and problems. Nelson Gaskill, who served as a commissioner from 1920 to 1925, once wrote, in words that hold true today: "So far as I could learn, at no time during the Commission's existence prior to my appearance and certainly never during the five years of my service were there even the beginnings of a definite policy or the shadow of an established specific field of jurisdiction. . . . At least one result of this policy of no policy was that everything conceivable was tried at least once."

The "policy of no policy" still plagues the FTC, and the trouble is compounded by the fluctuating winds of politics. Even the staff is subject to rapid turnover and cronyism. In the Eisenhower Administration most of the principal staff directors were Republicans. Today, though the FTC claims to be a "bipartisan" agency, the six major bureaus are all headed by Democrats and no more than two of the twenty lesser divisions are directed by a Republican. Meanwhile the commissioners at the top come and go, and few bother to serve out their appointed seven-year term. At any point of time, the commission resembles a Congress more than a court, with its own built-in majority and minorities. . . .

WHEN YOU CAN'T TAKE ALL, TAKE SOME

Under Rand Dixon the commission has attempted various reforms. It has recognized, for instance, that cracking down on a single respondent for doing what all of his competitors are still free to do may be not only unfair but ineffective. The FTC has therefore placed new emphasis on what it calls "industry-wide actions." For a time in 1961 the issuance of new complaints in individual cases was suspended until broad surveys could be conducted to determine whether general practice was involved. One such "industry-wide" survey put the FTC in full cry after the wearing-apparel industry. In this dog-eat-dog business, cooperative advertising allowances from manufacturers to buyers have become a competitive element of great importance. Sending out questionnaires to 310 manufacturers, with replies required under threat of legal action, the commission decided that 248—or 80 percent—of the manufacturers were in violation of Robinson-Patman Act prohibitions against discriminatory advertising practices. The offenders were invited to accept the cease-and-desist orders entered against them by the FTC. Only 163 agreed. The other eighty-five are free to continue their complained-of and presumably profitable practices until the FTC can get around to taking action against them—which Dixon promises to do "in a hurry."

Commissioners Elman and Higgenbotham, in a caustic dissent

from the FTC's wearing-apparel action, pointed out that the number of clothing manufacturers in the U.S. has been estimated at 34,500. How industry-wide, then, is a survey of only 310? And how effective will action be against 248 if 80 percent of 34,500 are violators? The resources of the commission are inadequate to a true industry-wide crackdown using the case-by-case method, even when the number of cases is multiplied through the survey technique. Elman and Higgenbotham suggested an attempt at voluntary compliance—through a vigorous educational campaign to acquaint the manufacturers with the law, among other things—before embarking on wholesale prosecutions.

But voluntary compliance assumes that businessmen can count on how the law will be interpreted. One step in this direction has been emphasis on what are known as Trade Regulation Rules. Established on the basis of information developed in conferences with an industry's spokesmen, these rules set forth particular points that may be relied upon by the commission in future actions without further proof of the illegality of the practice involved (though the respondent may have a hearing on applicability of the rule). The FTC is now girding itself, for instance, to issue a rule stating that the use of the word "automatic" in relation to sewing machines is deceptive. In any future case the commission would "prove" the deception by simple citation of the rule, instead of by amassing voluminous fresh evidence that sewing machines, however versatile, cannot be "automatic."

THE DANGERS OF "GUIDANCE"

Another innovation by Dixon and his FTC followers—creation of a Bureau of Industry Guidance—breaks into more questionable ground. In setting up the new bureau in 1961 the commission proudly announced that it would offer an expanded advisory service for industry. Through it, businessmen can find out, privately and *in advance,* whether contemplated actions are acceptable to the commission. Such opinions had been available in the past, but they came from the staff only and were not binding on the commission. They promised nothing. Now the opinions are reviewed in advance by the commission. Once approved, an action in accord with an advisory opinion will draw no penalties.

even if the commission changes its mind, provided the action is then discontinued within a stated period.

One of these opinions, made public by its recipient, raised again the odd fact that the FTC often seems to hinder rather than help small business. The National Association of Retail Druggists asked the Bureau of Industry Guidance if a proposed cooperative advertising program by its members would be acceptable to the FTC. In replying, a majority of the commissioners ruled that any joint ad referring to price would be illegal, and a threat of jail for violators was implied. Commissioner Elman dissented with typical vigor. "It seems to me that the Commission, charged as it is with the duty to promote rather than discourage competition, and to strengthen rather than impair the ability of small business-men to survive, should take a more positive and encouraging at-titude toward programs for joint advertising by retailers," Elman wrote. He added: "The notion that small businessmen should be sent to jail for engaging in such a practice seems to me too fan-tastic to be taken seriously."

Quite aside from this kind of difficulty, knowledgeable at-torneys on the outside are skeptical of both the usefulness and the propriety of the advisory procedure. Of the first fifty opinions issued by the commission, only ten set forth a firm position. There is good reason for the apparent lack of decisiveness. The commission is not likely to commit itself unless the circumstances of a proposal are so clear, the legality or illegality so obvious, that even the veriest dolt of a country lawyer would see the proper course without guidance. The need for substantive interpretation comes in the gray area of the law, where an action might or might not get by. But it is on just such close questions that the commis-sion cannot be expected to commit itself without a full hearing. And even if it could, should it? To many, the whole procedure of specific guidance seems tainted with the poison of undue gov-ernment dabbling with private affairs. It enlarges without clarify-ing the FTC's already overinflated mandate.

It is obvious therefore that the "reforms" now being initiated by the commission will not really cure its failings. What would? One suggestion sometimes made is that everybody would be better off if the functions of the FTC were divided up among other agencies where jurisdiction is overlapping. In trying to protect the public from false advertising it treads on territory already policed, at least in part, by the Food and Drug Administration and the Federal Communications Commission. Even more serious is the overlap between the FTC and Justice's Antitrust Division. When the commission was first set up, it was thought that Antitrust needed buttressing. But as time passed, the Justice Department expanded its activity, and it is now hard to see a need for the FTC as an auxiliary trustbuster, the more so because in some areas the two agencies are actually at odds with each other.

THE TYRANNY OF DISCRETION

But while dividing up the functions of the FTC has something to be said for it from an administrative point of view, this would not in itself solve the legal problems at issue. For the recipient agencies would in their turn inherit all the present ambiguities of existing law. The more radical cure would be to repeal outright the Robinson-Patman Act, which is a fountainhead of trouble and which in some ways runs counter to the spirit of antitrust. Repeal would clear away much of the fog that now harasses the businessman. It would have the added advantage of greatly reducing the huge amount of discretionary authority the government exercises in seeking to maintain a competitive economy.

Such discretionary authority has been growing apace in the U.S. and perhaps cannot be wholly eliminated. Nevertheless, the whole moral of the FTC experience is that we should try to reduce not to expand the scope of administrative law. In his book, *The Language of Dissent,* former FTC Commissioner Lowell Mason warned: "Tyranny comes when the government agency operates under such a broad statutory command that it not only invents the means by which it carries on the duties Congress gave it, but can shape its methods to fit its own, rather than the public end." Another witness in this area, curiously enough, was Woodrow Wilson. In 1914, under the banner of the New Freedom, Wilson helped set up the FTC. But six years earlier, while president of Princeton University, he said: "Regulation by commission is not regulation by law, but control according to the discretion of government officials. . . . Such methods of regulation, it may safely be predicted, will sooner or later be completely discredited by experience."

The Strange Case of Sun Oil, which is damned if it does and damned if it doesn't* ─────

M. R. LEFKOE

The question of what constitutes a lawful pricing policy under the antitrust statutes as interpreted by the Federal Trade Commission and the courts has baffled businessmen for some time. But the six-year-old case of Sun Oil sets a new record in obfuscation.

Sun's dilemma began in 1955, when Gilbert McLean, one of its franchised dealers in Jacksonville, Florida, informed the company that he was being threatened with a price war by an independent-brand service station. McLean told Sun that a Super Test station across the street was undercutting him in price by as much as 8 cents per gallon, and requested some form of assistance. Continuing his pleas to Sun during the next four months and receiving no help, McLean finally warned the company that he would be forced out of business unless some price relief was granted immediately.

Sun had been concerned with the possible legal consequences of granting a price allowance to one dealer without making the same lower price available to all of its dealers. But a series of letters written by the director of the FTC's Bureau of Investigation had indicated that Sun's contemplated assistance to McLean was lawful. In one of the letters, the director had stated: "[A] seller is within his legal rights in confining his price reductions to dealers in the vicinity of the dealer or dealers whose competition he seeks to meet, even though such action results in injury to customers to whom similar reductions are not made available." Sun decided to rely upon this construction of a section of the Robinson-Patman Act that had not yet been interpreted by the courts, and came to McLean's rescue by granting him a discount

─────
* *August 1963*

just large enough to enable him to meet the competition from Super Test.

Learning of the price relief that Sun had granted McLean, several of Sun's other franchised dealers within a three-and-one-half-mile radius requested similar discounts. When Sun refused, the dealers complained to the FTC. After several months of deliberation the commission disregarded the assurances given by its own investigator. It issued a complaint against Sun, charging the company with price discrimination, a violation of Section 2 (a) of the Robinson-Patman Act.

In its defense, Sun invoked Section 2 (b) of the act, which permits a seller to rebut a prima-facie case of discrimination by "showing that his lower price . . . was made in good faith to meet an equally low price of a competitor. . . ." The commission pointed out that Sun had not attempted to meet a price cut originated by *its own* competition—another wholesale supplier; Sun had granted an allowance to one of its dealers to help him meet a price cut made by *his* competition—a competing service station. Consequently the FTC rejected Sun's use of the "good faith" proviso and issued a cease-and-desist order.

Sun appealed the commission's order to the Fifth Circuit Court of Appeals. Because of the difficulties inherent in making a strictly textual analysis of the Robinson-Patman Act, the court endeavored to ascertain the economic and legal consequences implicit in the interpretation of Section 2 (b) relied upon by Sun and the one advanced by the FTC. The court ruled unanimously in favor of Sun, pointing out that the commission's position "violates the policy of the Act that places emphasis on individual competitive situations; focuses on injury to competitors rather than on the health of the competitive process; . . . denies the realities of the marketplace in refusing to accept the undeniable fact that a supplier of gasoline competes with a supplier-retailer at the consumer level through filling station operators; tends to spread rather than localize price wars; and makes it impossible, as a practical matter, for a supplier to defend one of its filling stations, fighting for survival, or even to defend itself against destructive price raids of a supplier-retailer."

The FTC then appealed to the Supreme Court, which overruled the Appeals Court and denied Sun the right to use the "good faith" defense. In so doing, however, the Court stated that it had been forced to make two crucial assumptions because the record lacked certain relevant facts. Its decision, therefore, was based "on the assumption that Super Test was engaged solely in retail operations . . . [and that] Super Test was not the beneficiary of any enabling price cut from its own supplier." A footnote following this explanation stated: "Were it otherwise, i.e., if it had appeared that either Super Test were an integrated supplier-retailer, or that it had received a price cut from its own supplier—presumably a competitor of Sun—we would be presented with a different case, as to which we herein neither express nor intimate any opinion." Another footnote expressly reserved the right for Sun to reopen the case if either of the Court's two assumptions were invalid; but Justice Goldberg, who had written the Court's unanimous opinion, ordered this footnote deleted from the opinion the day following its release.

In fact, Super Test was a supplier-retailer, acting as a supplier in many instances in addition to owning and operating a chain of over sixty service stations. Moreover, according to affidavits collected by Sun after the Supreme Court decision, Super Test had received the bulk of its gasoline from Orange State Oil Co., then an affiliate of Cities Service Co. (a major integrated oil company that is a direct competitor of Sun). Finally, these affidavits indicate that Super Test had received an enabling "price break" from its own supplier. Armed with evidence that both of the Supreme Court's assumptions were invalid, Sun has moved to reopen the case with the lower court in order to introduce the new evidence. A decision by the court on the motion has yet to be handed down. Thus the Sun Oil case after six years of litigation is still up in the air.

To the rest of the petroleum industry, however, it is of secondary importance whether Sun is given permission to introduce new evidence, or whether Sun ultimately is exonerated on the basis of that evidence. The Supreme Court's ruling will still serve as the guiding interpretation of the law based upon a situation it assumed to be true—a situation in which an oil company's franchised dealer is caught in a price war because of a cut in the retail price made by one of the dealer's competitors. Since *this* situation occurs almost daily throughout the country, how are oil-company executives to handle the problem?

THE ILLUSORY GUIDES

Several "alternative" courses of action were proposed during the Sun case by the FTC examiner, the full commission, and the Supreme Court. Although each of the suggestions was offered specifically to Sun, they were meant to serve also as guideposts for the whole oil industry. Consider the "alternatives" offered:

1. The first "alternative" for the industry is implicit in the Supreme Court's statement that it had ruled only on the basis of the facts presented in the record. It might be possible for a supplier to cut its price to one of its dealers if that supplier could demonstrate that a competitor of his dealer (another service station) had been granted a price cut by *his* supplier.

The problem the marketing executive faces here, however, is twofold: Because he would have to be certain that a price allowance had been given his dealer's competitor, the act of obtaining and verifying such information might well open him to charges of price conspiracy under Section 1 of the Sherman Act. Unable to forget the jail sentences meted out by the Court in the recent electrical-equipment-industry price conspiracy, many oil-company attorneys have forbidden their clients to seek the information needed for a Section 2 (b) defense.

Moreover, recent interpretations of the 2 (b) proviso by the FTC indicate that a discriminatory price cut is lawful only if the price allowance being matched is itself lawful. Commenting upon the precarious position a company places itself in if it attempts to make use of the 2 (b) defense, Commissioner Elman argued in the American Oil Co. case: " 'Good faith' does not require businessmen to be put in the impossible dilemma of either (1) losing business by not meeting competitors' lower prices, or (2) meeting the competitive lower prices and running the risk that years later the Commission will find these 'third-party' prices to be unlawful, after complex and protracted proceedings whose outcome could not be confidently predicted even by legal experts specializing in the field of trade regulation." But Commissioner Elman was overruled by the full commission, and the "impossible dilemma" remains.

2. The oil industry's second "alternative," first suggested by the FTC examiner in the Sun hearings and later accepted by the full

commission, is that an oil company meet "competition at the dealer level by non-discriminatory reductions in price to all dealers."

The deficiency of this "alternative" was clearly identified by the lower court when it wrote: "In other words, to avoid the dilemma and to meet competition on the corner of 19th and Pearl Streets in Jacksonville, Sun, perhaps ruinously, would have to reduce its price to all of its dealers in the U.S. Or, assuming that the suggestion means 'all dealers' in Jacksonville . . . the Commission would have Sun enlarge the scale of the price war and risk a chain reaction that might set off price wars throughout Florida and Southeast U.S. In either case, other oil companies, majors and non-majors, would have to meet Sun's price cuts thereby spreading price wars and subjecting the margins of filling station operators to further compression."

To the lower court's analysis of this "alternative," one oil-company executive added bitterly: "Not only would following the commission's suggestion bankrupt our dealers, it would also be a good way to bankrupt the whole industry."

3. A third "alternative" offered the industry is the Supreme Court's suggestion that ". . . since Sunoco stations, though largely independently owned, operate under leasing, merchandising, advertising, and other policies set by Sun, other opportunities are available to Sun to strengthen its dealers in competing with other stations."

Precisely what the Court intended when it made this suggestion is not clear. If the Court meant that an oil company might consider granting special services or facilities only to those dealers engaged in a price war, then it would seem to be recommending the kind of price discrimination barred by the Robinson-Patman Act.

If, on the other hand, the Court meant that Sun could grant extra services or facilities to all its dealers throughout the country, then, in effect, it is recommending an act that is tantamount to a nationwide price cut. The cost to an oil company in providing these services or facilities would be as great as a price cut, and the same disastrous consequences already noted would result.

4. A fourth "alternative" for oil companies was proposed by the FTC examiner during the commission's hearings of the Sun case. The examiner suggested that Sun "could, if it chose to, meet

such competition at the dealer level by . . . operating its own stations and thus being [sic] in direct competition with other stations which reduce prices."

Interpreting this suggestion one way, oil companies might enter into consignment contracts with each of their dealers, whereby title to the gasoline would be retained by them. The dealers would then be acting only as agents, and the oil companies would be able to post any retail price they chose. But, almost concurrent with the FTC's suggestion that Sun could make use of this method, the commission found Sun guilty of an unfair trade practice because it attempted to set up consignment contracts with all of its dealers in the Norfolk, Virginia, area.

Interpreting this suggestion another way, the petroleum industry might change its system of distribution, integrate its retail outlets, and sell directly to motorists through stations the company owns and operates. But in offering the industry this "alternative," the FTC apparently chose to ignore the fundamental purpose of the Robinson-Patman Act: to promote local ownership, protect the small, independent merchant, and reduce the trend toward monopoly. Congressman Wright Patman, co-author of the act, has indicated that he would be totally opposed to vertical integration such as the commission proposed, in that his bill was "designed to accomplish what so far the Clayton Act has only weakly attempted, namely, to protect the independent merchant. . . ." Thus, it is unlikely that the oil industry could proceed very far in vertical integration before the FTC found some legal means to declare such action illegal.

5. A fifth possible "alternative" for oil-company executives can be found in the commission's statement during the Sun hearings that it would allow discriminatory price cuts if they were made to "all dealers in the competitive area." Justice Goldberg indicated that he also approved of this method by stating in his opinion that "carefully drawn sub-markets may be the proper measure of competitive impact among purchasers."

But this "alternative" is as illusory as the others, since the commission almost invariably challenges any company's definition of a "competitive area." In the present Sun case, the FTC ruled that one corner of a street was not large enough to be a competitive area, but gave no clear guidelines as to what would be. The literal impossibility of a company's determining the appro-

THE STRANGE CASE OF SUN OIL 147

priate "competitive area" was dramatized in the American Oil case when Commissioner Elman asked the FTC counsel how large an area American should have covered in granting its price concessions. The commission's counsel replied: "*I don't think that I am capable of answering that, I don't think you are, and I don't think anybody is capable of answering that question.*" (Italics added.)

6. As the industry's sixth, and final, "alternative," Justice Goldberg suggested that oil companies utilize "a so-called 'feathered' discount to its dealers, under which the amount of the price allowance diminishes as it reaches stations further away from the center of the price war. . . ." Here, however, an oil company has the same problem it has in deciding what constitutes a legal "competitive area." Even Justice Goldberg warned that "improperly designed or too sharply drawn 'feathering' gradations may produce precisely the same effect as no gradation at all, and consequently fall within the same ban as an outright illegal discrimination."

The above analysis shows that none of the so-called "alternatives" facing the industry are without peril. Justices Harlan and Stewart partially recognized this when they said in a separate memorandum to the Supreme Court ruling: "We leave unanswered as many questions as we have resolved." Donald C. O'Hara, general counsel of the National Petroleum Refiners Association, was more blunt. After reading the ruling he stated: "The Robinson-Patman Act has now been law for over twenty-five years and the Sun case alone has been in litigation for more than six years; yet, today, your lawyers cannot tell you when you can [legally] grant a discount to a dealer."

But an oil-company executive's problem of what constitutes a legal discount to a dealer under the Robinson-Patman Act is negligible compared to the problems faced by all businessmen owing to the fundamental contradiction between that act and the rest of the antitrust statutes. As John E. Swearingen, president of Standard Oil Co. (Indiana), observed: "With the Justice Department on one side, demanding harder competition under the Sherman Act, and the FTC on the other, trying to water down competition under the Robinson-Patman Act, the businessman is trapped in the middle, completely unsure as to the legality of any decision he makes."

part 3

FEDERAL REGULATION OF BUSINESS

REGULATION OF businesses by the national government is not confined to agencies concerned with enforcement of the antitrust laws. Many other departments and agencies are involved, especially the seven major independent administrative agencies. In addition, Congress frequently considers bills that would create new forms of regulation or promotion or alter existing laws. Many industries are controlled or encouraged in part by special legislation enacted to meet the problems of a particular field, and most American businessmen are uncomfortably aware of existing and possible federal legislation that would affect the conduct of their businesses. This section includes several widely publicized stories of companies and industries affected by events that led to government regulatory actions.

"Regulation by Elephant, Rabbit, and Lark" takes its title from the hybrid nature of the independent agencies. They were invented for an inherently difficult task, the laying down of practical rules for business without taking over the rightful functions of businessmen in a free enterprise economy. In the field of administrative law, the agencies are seeking a mixture that reconciles flexibility and certainty. However, the continuing effort to make administrative regulation work produces conflict with the classical doctrine of a free market. While there is a widespread desire for reform, it is not easy to change the agencies in the face of pressures from Congress, the President, influence peddlers, and the regulated industry.

One reason for business regulation lies in a search for ways to protect the interests of the consumer. The Federal Trade Commission, with a broad range of powers, not only administers the antitrust laws dealing with corporate power but also is concerned with deceptive practices that might injure the individual consumer. A recent case involved the effort of the FTC to order Colgate-Palmolive and its advertising agency to cease and desist using what the Commission regarded as a deceptive commercial. "The Great Sandpaper Shave" tells the story of the FTC's action and the long court fight that followed. The action was a matter of vital interest to people concerned with advertising, even though the difficulty of applying the rules and the further problem of fighting about them without looking foolish lent overtones of absurdity to the proceedings.

Two industries that have been affected by efforts at federal regulation of their practices in the interests of health and safety are the drug and cigarette industries. In each of these, a particular series of events involving tragic or dangerous effects on individuals suggested that if self-regulation does not clearly operate, government legislation will move in. In the case of the drug manufacturers, an imperfect system of clinical testing had gradually developed by 1962, but the thalidomide tragedy led to a new law and new Food and Drug Administration regulations on testing. These requirements almost entirely missed the main issue of getting more competent clinical investigators and improved techniques into the testing of new drugs. In the case of the tobacco industry, studies about possible links between smoking and cancer were followed by demands for laws restricting the sale and consumption of cigarettes and limiting cigarette advertising. The companies have been seeking a number of ways to live with the problem, including voluntary restrictions on advertising claims and modest research efforts.

Regulation by Elephant, Rabbit, and Lark*

GEORGE BOOKMAN

Chief Judge E. Barrett Prettyman, of the U.S. Circuit Court of Appeals for the District of Columbia, is not only a distinguished jurist but also one of that noble breed of Americans, a Virginia gentleman. As such, he is of course a good judge of corn whiskey and horseflesh, and also possesses that other mark of good breeding—a sprightly ability to express his thoughts in clear, pungent English. In the course of a lecture series appropriately titled "Trial by Agency," delivered at the University of Virginia Law School, Judge Prettyman summed up his impressions of government administrative agencies, after a lifetime of studying them as a practitioner and later as a judge. "To a purist in the theory of American government, an administrative agency is a hybrid, indeed a monstrosity," he observed. "It is part elephant, part jack rabbit, and part field lark."

Congress and the President are deeply concerned about the administrative agencies, whose loosely defined powers cut across the three principal governmental branches: legislative, executive, and judicial. The problem centers around the seven major agencies, designated as "independent" by Congress, which have such aggregate power over business that they have been called the "fourth branch of the government." Their writ runs into every facet of the economy, as their names imply: the Interstate Commerce Commission, Federal Trade Commission, Federal Communications Commission, Federal Power Commission, Securities and Exchange Commission, Civil Aeronautics Board, and National Labor Relations Board. Without the sanction of these agencies, no railroad, no airline, no interstate trucker, no pipeline or barge line may introduce a new service, discontinue an old service, or

* *June 1961*

set a rate; no radio or television station may operate; no gas producer may market his fuel or figure its price in interstate commerce; no interstate public utility may build a power plant; no sizable firm may market a new security, or safely plan a merger.

The agencies that administer these vast powers have been a problem to the President and Congress virtually since the first one, the ICC, was established in 1887. In fact, they constitute what Nicely-Nicely, the *Guys and Dolls* character, would probably have called the oldest established, permanent, floating mess in Washington.

HOW MUCH INDEPENDENCE IN A JUNGLE?

The built-in M (for mess) factor in the agencies is that they were invented for an inherently difficult task: to lay down practical rules for business, under broad policy statutes from Congress, without taking over from businessmen functions that are rightfully theirs in a free market place. Working in the fluid field of administrative law, the agencies were invented to make decisions that would be swift, sure, and expert both on events already past (i.e., adjudicating cases) and also in anticipating the future by making rules to cope with the ingenuity of businessmen and the effects of new discoveries in science and technology. The agencies were supposed to be as weighty and dispassionate as courts, yet not so rigid in procedures; as active as the executive branch, but not so political in outlook; as responsive to the public interest as Congress, yet able to dart quickly into the details of the changing industrial scene.

It was these conflicting functions that inspired Judge Prettyman's elephant-rabbit-lark metaphor. The conflicts are complicated by questions turning around the word "independent"—always a somewhat unrealistic concept in the Washington political jungle, where symbiosis is the rule. Congress, as Speaker Sam Rayburn never hesitated to point out, created the agencies and retains a jealous interest in them. But the President also has a great deal at stake. He appoints the agency members, names most of the chairmen, and reviews their budgets. Besides his constitutional duty to "take care that the laws be faithfully executed," he needs cooperation from the agencies for important parts of his economic program. For their part, many businessmen are sincerely convinced that the agencies should be responsive to business thinking. To encourage responsiveness businessmen sometimes use astute lawyers, political lobbyists, public-relations experts, and occasionally not so legitimate pressures.

Caught in these crosscurrents, the agencies have often sought safety in slowing their procedures to a crawl, avoiding decisions, and—when decisions were inevitable—diffusing the responsibility so that it would be hard to tell later who did what, why, and to whom. The supposedly clear-cut standards for making decisions have become increasingly blurred. Moreover, the agencies have fallen down badly on the job of developing new policies to meet new situations as they arose—e.g., the tough problem of deteriorating railroad commuter service in metropolitan areas. Worst of all, the quality of personnel and ethical standards in some agencies have deteriorated; in recent years there have been several charges of outright bribery.

TWO APPROACHES TO REFORM

Efforts to reform the agencies are almost as old as the agencies themselves. The reform effort has been a tug of war between those who thought the agencies should be judicialized (i.e., made more like courts) and those who believed the answer was to move in the opposite direction and assign the agencies' functions to regular executive departments, where at least there would be no hesitation in carrying out the Administration's policies. President Franklin D. Roosevelt (in whose Administration four of today's seven agencies were established) at one time despaired of ever making the agency concept work, and wanted to abolish them as independent units. Partly as a reaction to Roosevelt's slam-bang regulating, came the demand to judicialize the agencies, culminating in a code of procedures passed by Congress in 1946. Ex-President Hoover turned out two reports on government organization for Presidents Truman and Eisenhower. In his second report he recommended assigning all the adjudicatory work of the agencies to a special administrative court, an idea that the American Bar Association is still pushing. President Eisenhower sponsored self-help efforts to improve the agencies by establishing a conference on administrative procedures, an organization that President Kennedy reconstituted. In Congress, the emphasis of reformers lately has been on tougher ethical codes, as a result of revelations of the House Special Subcommittee on Legislative Oversight: e.g., the Bernard Goldfine-Sherman Adams scandals, rigged television quiz shows, payola and plugola. . . .

[President] Kennedy's modest proposals, aimed primarily at cutting down delay and fixing administrative responsibility, did not try to reach the heart of the problem. He asked Congress to clarify and strengthen the power of agency chairmen to administer agency staffs, and to delegate decision-making powers to panels of agency members and employees, subject to review by the full agency. Similar in purpose was Kennedy's proposal that the Federal Power Commission be enlarged from five to seven members. Kennedy's message was as notable for what it did not contain as for what it did. The President did not embrace [James M.] Landis' most controversial recommendation, which was that policy making in the agencies be supervised by an "overseer" in the White House, aided by "coordinators" in the field of transportation, communications, and energy policy. This idea was unceremoniously dropped when members of Congress raised strong objection. Senator Mike Monroney, for instance, has said the "overseer" plan sounded to him like setting up "a legalized Sherman Adams."

Nor did Kennedy take a stand in the controversy over how judicialized the agencies should be. He left that to be studied and reported on by the new Administrative Conference of the U.S. A close look at some sore spots in the agencies raises the question whether anything short of major surgery will restore the agencies to health.

HOW CONGRESS TAKES CARE OF ITS OWN

The first place to look at the problem is in Congress. For all its fond claims that the agencies are its legislative "arms," Congress actually treats them very shabbily. The worst feature of the relationship between Congress and the agencies, and the one least discussed publicly, is the right that many Congressmen feel they have to badger the agencies on behalf of private claimants.

The most outspoken man in Congress about using this kind of pressure—although not necessarily the worst pressurer—is Senator Everett Dirksen of Illinois, the minority leader, a veteran of twenty-eight years in Congress. Dirksen says that in the normal course of Washington life he meets many agency commissioners, particularly on the cocktail circuit. He sees nothing wrong in calling these gentlemen later on behalf of constituents.

"Meeting a commissioner at a cocktail party, you say, 'Hi, Joe,'" Dirksen recently explained. "You know him by his first name. You know something about his family."

Then when a constituent asks Dirksen to do him a favor, the Senator at least knows the procedure: "What is the natural thing to do? You say 'I will call up Joe Doak, I know him, I have seen him, I know all about him!'"

Dirksen explains: "I think that is a part of my job in a ponderous government with two and a half million people on the payroll, and agencies all over the lot, where the average citizen becomes thoroughly bewildered."

Most congressional badgering of regulatory agencies is motivated by the normal sort of "favor for a constituent" that has come to be tolerated in conventional Washington morality—i.e., making an appointment at a commission, inquiring into the status of a case. There is, however, an invisible and probably indefinable line between this "normal" sort of intervention and a more dangerous kind in which a phone call from Capitol Hill has more to do with the way a case is decided than the agency's own interpretation of law and public interest. Some Senators, notably Paul Douglas of Illinois, flatly refuse to contact the agencies on behalf of private claims by constituents. Douglas may lean too far backward in avoiding even the appearance of impropriety; but Dirksen is probably inclined too far the other way. Anyway, personal meddling at the agencies by Congressmen mocks the congressional doctrine that the agencies are "independent."

The other major respect in which Congress has not done right by the agencies is in the basic legislative task of defining their authority. Often the original laws creating the agencies were deliberately left vague, to be sharpened later in the light of experience. Unfortunately, later acts of Congress have frequently contained still vaguer policy guidance, and even conflicting directives, while Congress has been notoriously slow at modernizing legislation outmoded by changing conditions in industry.

The Federal Communications Commission, which has been scalded as much as any agency at congressional hearings, is a clear case in point. The only policy guidance that FCC has from Congress in awarding television channels is the broad instruction, in the original 1934 act (even before TV came on the scene), that a broadcast license should serve "the public interest, convenience or necessity." With so little to go on, the FCC has worked out its own list of criteria: are the applicants local people, do they participate in civic activities, have they broadcasting experience, and so on. In actual practice, what happens is that astute lawyers who specialize in obtaining TV channels for clients advise them how to "construct" applications to meet as many of these criteria as possible. The result often is that FCC has the well-nigh impossible job of choosing fairly between several applicants with seemingly equal claims to a license. Dilemmas like this lead FCC into trouble: at the very least, inconsistency in applying its own standards for awarding channels; at the worst, improper influences.

Congress has frequently been urged by the FCC and by others to enact more clear-cut standards for picking licensees. And former Attorney General Herbert Brownell suggests that where there are several applicants who meet the standards equally, the channel should be awarded on the basis of sealed bids, the license going to the highest bidder. Some educators suggest awarding the channel to the applicant, otherwise qualified, who agrees to devote the largest amount of broadcast time to programs of a public-service nature.

Other agencies are similarly hobbled. The FTC for years has been trying, without much success, to carry out conflicting instructions from Congress on business competition. Parts of the trade laws instruct FTC to encourage "hard" competition while other sections seek to soften the impact of the competition. As for the FPC, ever since the Supreme Court in its 1954 Phillips case decision declared that the agency should set rates for thousands of independent gas producers, Congress has been unable either to resolve the dispute over whether the law should be changed to exempt them, or to give FPC clear authority to use short-cut methods in disposing of its huge load of cases arising under this decision. The FPC Chairman has estimated it would take thirteen years to dispose of all these cases under the present time-consuming procedures.

President Kennedy, in his special message on the regulatory agencies, sensibly recommended that Congress cut this knot by exempting from regulation the thousands of small gas producers so that FPC can concentrate on regulating the 270 large ones that account for 90 percent of the production. Perhaps the backing of a Democratic President may persuade Congress, at long last, to take this common-sense step.

In the transportation field, the original concept that ICC should foster the most efficient means of transportation has been buried under an avalanche of special legislation to protect various interests: shippers, railroad unions, farmers, barge operators, local communities, and so forth. Conflicts in the laws in this field have become so flagrant that ICC Commissioner Tuggle complains: "Congress tries to please everybody. They call in the railroads, and the waterways, and everybody adds a sentence here and a sentence there and at the end you can't tell what they had in mind." Many agencies could make a similar complaint. The two main defects in the relationship between Congress and the agencies are: (1) Congress in its constitutional lawmaking capacity gives the agencies too little guidance; (2) Congressmen as individuals meddle too much with the workings of the agencies.

THE WHITE TELEPHONE

The history of White House relations with the independent agencies shows similar defects from time to time. In earlier days, the regulatory agencies were frequently given strong guidance from the White House on policy matters, and perhaps this was an element of their initial success. President Hoover, for instance, used to issue statements to let the ICC—and simultaneously the public—know his views on railroad matters. President Roosevelt's relation with some of the agencies was much closer. A white telephone was installed on the desk of SEC Chairman Joseph P. Kennedy; over a direct line to the White House calls in both directions were frequent. President Eisenhower on at least one occasion did not hesitate to send the FPC commissioners his views on a matter he considered vital: he let them know he favored swift approval of the power project on the St. Lawrence Seaway, and they complied.

But in general there was little direct contact between the President and the independent agencies during the Eisenhower Administration. For example, Sinclair Armstrong, who was an

SEC commissioner from 1953 to 1957, says his agency, an "orphan" in the Washington wilderness, did not get badly needed White House support for more money, a more adequate staff, and legislation to plug loopholes in the securities laws.

It is not easy to draw the dividing line between proper White House influence of the general kind, which Armstrong desired, and improper pressure of the sort attributed to Sherman Adams. Guideposts, however, are clear.

There is little dispute about the laws that give the President important controls over personnel, money, and some policies of the agencies. A clash of philosophy between an agency and the President cannot last very long because, as terms of commissioners expire, the President can remake the agency more to his liking. Furthermore, the President's power of the purse is clear-cut: the spending plans of the agencies and new legislation they wish to propose are screened by the Budget Bureau, a part of the Executive Office. In addition, the President specifically has the right— for reasons of foreign policy—to review decisions of the Civil Aeronautics Board involving international routes, and he has frequently used it to reverse CAB decisions. Thus there are important legal exceptions to the "independence" of the agencies from the White House.

On the other hand, when President Roosevelt fired an FTC commissioner, William E. Humphrey, simply because "your mind and my mind do not go along together," the Supreme Court ruled that commissioners can be fired only for causes specified by law. Furthermore, it is clear that the White House is not supposed to interfere (either by "white telephone" or more publicly) when an agency is performing its judicial function of deciding a specific case or is getting set to punish a violator of its rules.

What is needed is for the White House to show constructive interest in what the agencies are doing, to provide them with broad policy leadership and support, but without tampering with individual case decisions. The facts of political life in Washington are that if a regulatory agency does not get guidance and support from the White House, it gravitates toward its "clients," that is, toward the industry it is supposed to regulate or toward some sections of that industry. At first, the agency may use industry for political help on Capitol Hill—for example, to push appropriations or certain legislation. But this may all too easily lead to undue industry influence on the policy thinking of the agencies.

An agency that lacks both a strong sense of its judicial character and a clear sense of its public purpose can slip into the kind of morass in which the Legislative Oversight subcommittee found the FTC and the FCC in the matter of rigged TV shows and other broadcasting malpractices. According to the subcommittee, the two agencies knew of the practices and had legal authority to take action; yet, despite complaints, they did nothing decisive to stop them. Said the subcommittee reprimand: "Where a commission takes a passive view of its role, it is clear that the public interest suffers by default." Policy leadership from the President can be an effective tonic for administrative passivity.

THE BLANDISHMENTS OF THE REGULATED

But the worst drubbing of all for the public interest comes when an agency slips into the tender traps of Washington influence peddlers. Vying for the valuable favors the agencies can dispense, such as TV channels and airline routes, companies in a regulated industry can beguile tractable commissioners with an array of blandishments, including expense-account entertainment and the promise of jobs after they leave government. One Washington lawyer, William C. Burt, who specializes in CAB cases, says: "It is almost inconceivable the pressure that can be on a board member. When they are appointed, I think they sort of start living in a different world. You might say that they are somewhat akin to Marilyn Monroe after their appointment [in the sense] that everybody who sees them from then on has something in mind." In recent years there has been considerable publicity given to allegations of improper contacts between commissioners and business representatives. For example, federal courts during 1958 and 1959 remanded to the FCC an unprecedented number of cases citing improper outside influences: these included decisions on TV channels in Boston, Miami, and Springfield, Illinois. Company representatives and commissioners are sometimes found to be in close personal relationships. Former FCC Chairman John Doerfer, for instance, admitted accepting a free vacation aboard the yacht of a broadcasting executive, but he argued that there was nothing improper about his excursion because the yacht did not venture far from the dock while he was aboard. This led the Baltimore *Sun* to invent "Doerfer's Law," which holds that the extent to which a public official can be influenced improperly aboard a yacht varies inversely with the shallowness of the water.

Then there are the insistent arguments made to commissioners in private by able, adept lawyers, such as Thomas G. Corcoran, the New Deal's "Tommy the Cork," who got into congressional hot water last year when it was found he had made visits and telephone calls to FPC commissioners on behalf of Midwestern Gas Transmission Co., which had an important case pending before the commission.

To control this kind of thing in the regulatory agencies and elsewhere in government, President Kennedy sent Congress a message proposing legislative changes and announcing new executive rules. Under existing law, the President pointed out, a Cabinet officer could try to influence an FCC commissioner on behalf of a business associate who had applied for a TV license; then the Cabinet officer might legally share in the profits of the TV station. Kennedy also asked that each agency be required to promulgate rules prohibiting off-the-record contacts between agency officials and interested parties in pending cases. (In the same message he reactivated the Administrative Conference and later named Judge Prettyman as chairman of its council; this body will study the procedures of the agencies with a view to harmonizing their elephant, rabbit, and lark functions.)

DOES FAMILIARITY BREED AFFECTION?

The most difficult pressure of all to define, and especially to control, is the perfectly legitimate pressure by regulated industry to influence the general philosophy of the commissioners. Landis says that many honest, capable agency members are affected by what he calls "the daily machine-gun-like impact" of industry representation. The agencies are frequently accused of having been "taken over" by industry—i.e., "the regulated become the regulators."

It is quite true that regulated industry is very resourceful at impressing its viewpoint, in perfectly legitimate ways, on the regulators. For example, on the eve of congressional hearings on pay-TV in 1958, affiliates of the Columbia Broadcasting System, which opposed pay-TV, put on a dinner in Washington with entertainment provided by television stars. "My God," said one Washington lawyer who attended, "there were more Congressmen present than for the State of the Union Message." On hand as invited guests were commissioners of the FCC, presumably to be impressed by the big turnout from Capitol Hill.

Up to a point it is certainly desirable that the commissioners become familiar with the industries they regulate. The question is—how familiar? Part of the basic idea of the agencies is that they are supposed to apply "expertise" in deciding practical business problems. How are commissioners to acquire the expertise if they do not rub shoulders with industry? It is lamentable, for example, that FPC Chairman Kuykendall, in charge of regulating the gas industry, has never seen an oil well being drilled. Nelson Lee Smith, a former FPC chairman, says the commissioners must not just sit passively in their offices waiting for cases to be brought to them, but rather should "keep thoroughly informed as to conditions in the industries with which they are concerned. . . ." Practically speaking, that cannot be done without informal contact with industry sources.

Finally, any thorough look at the troubles of the agencies must turn from the broad matters of their relations with Congress, the White House, and industry to such operational questions as the agencies' huge work loads, cumbersome procedures, and inadequate staffs.

Much has been made of the matter of work loads, and indeed they are preposterously heavy. At the ICC a commissioner found he had to make a decision on the average of every five minutes of his working day. Commissioner Frederick Stueck of FPC testified last November that in five years he shared in the responsibility for 18,000 decisions at the commission level, a burden that left little time for broad policy planning. At the staff level, work loads have increased faster than budgets. The SEC, for example, given a niggardly appropriation by Congress, in 1960 had 10 percent fewer employees than ten years ago, but handled three times as many security registration statements.

WHO BUILT BLEAK HOUSE?

All efforts to do something basic about the work loads, however, always run into the tangled procedures used by the agencies. Procedures have become so involved, so time-consuming and costly to the public, that they make a mockery of the original idea that administrative agencies would be better suited to handle business regulation than the courts.

It would be a serious error, however, to think that all one needs to simplify procedures is a pair of scissors for cutting red tape. There is much more to it than that. In fact, most of today's elaborate procedures have been imposed on the commissions by law or by court decisions and are designed for the laudable purpose of protecting individual rights from arbitrary action at the hands of administrative lawmakers.

Most of today's procedural complexities go back to a sweeping Administrative Procedures Act, passed by Congress in 1946, at the urging of many lawyers and jurists. This law emphasized the rights of private litigants as against the government agencies. It spelled out detailed legal procedures the agencies must follow and required clear separation between commissioners, acting as judges, and their staffs, acting as prosecutors.

The result has been that the agencies now have full-fledged adversary proceedings, complete with cross-examination of witnesses, rebuttals, rules of evidence, technical objections, etc.—a catalogue of legal weapons worthy of Jarndyce and Jarndyce, the interminable Chancery Court case in Dickens' *Bleak House*. Agencies are required to give a hearing to anyone who claims to be affected by a proceeding, which leads to such spectacles as the parade of seven airlines, forty-seven cities, and sixty-six "intervenors" appearing before the CAB in the Seven States case involving local air service for states of the upper Midwest. Another requirement is that commissioners must state in writing their detailed reasons for every element of a decision, and for the disposition they make of every exception that has been filed. One former commissioner says that a man being denied an application before the FCC actually gets more due process of law than a man being tried for murder.

These requirements are really what causes the interminable delays and huge loads of paper work. Records get so bulky that commissioners have no time to read them, and must rely on subordinates to tell them what went on at the hearings and to write their legal opinions. One of the worst features of the long delays are the many opportunities presented for behind-the-scenes influence on the commissioners by interested parties. At the CAB, for example, an indecent gap of as much as a year sometimes elapses between the time the board hears oral arguments in a case and the time it issues its decision and opinion. A gap of this kind invites lobbyists to work in private to influence the eventual decision.

FLEXIBILITY VS. CERTAINTY

Further judicializing of the independent agencies, as proposed by the American Bar Association, would of course make them less flexible instruments for carrying out policy. But it is precisely because practical business problems were deemed to require a flexible approach that Congress created the agencies in the first place. Roscoe Pound of Harvard has put the case for the flexible approach:

"The moment you begin to make hard-and-fast rules, you begin really to depart from the whole purpose of committing a subject to administration, because legislation can deal with matter easily enough if it is just a matter of rules. It is because rules aren't adequate to the situation that something is committed to an administrative commission."

This, of course, gets to the heart of the conflict. Classically, free enterprise makes its decisions bound only by a framework of general law, enforceable by courts. The free-enterprise theory makes no provision for subjecting business decisions to direction from government administrators who act according to their own interpretation of "the public interest." On the other hand, when Pound says that general rules of law are not always adequate for the regulation of business, he expresses an American conviction, based on experience, with which many businessmen, particularly in the last two generations, have agreed. Certainly, the U.S. is not going to abandon its effort to make administrative regulation work, even if it conflicts with the classical doctrine of a free-enterprise economy. Thus there is no "solution" to the basic problem of the regulatory agencies. One group of critics will continue to demand that the agencies conform to legal norms and another group will demand that they be flexible administrators of expedient policy. In practical terms, the problem is not to decide which group is right (both are), but to bring about a relatively wise mixture of the two contradictory tendencies. Precisely because it involves this fundamental conflict, the function of the agencies is inherently more difficult than the normal functions of courts, or of lawmakers, or of administrators.

In recent years neither the commissioners nor their staffs, in general, have lived up to the very high standards required. Since World War II the agencies have found it increasingly difficult to attract and hold good people. Landis suggests that the jobs be made financially more attractive, with better salaries, longer terms, pensions and expense allowances for commissioners, who now get $20,000 a year for terms of five to seven years. Quality of agency personnel has also suffered from the practice of both parties in recent Administrations of using agency appointments to pay off political debts. Needed most are independent-minded commissioners who can tell the difference between one Congressman and the voice of Congress, between one telephone call from a White House aide and the proclaimed policies of the President.

But better commissioners and bigger staffs will never wholly resolve the elephant-rabbit-lark incompatibility that lies at the root of the difficulties. In the long run, what is needed most is the continuing development of statutory law and clear agency rules that will enable businessmen to know in advance what they can and cannot do.

THE FTC PRESENTS:

The Great Sandpaper Shave * _____

DANIEL SELIGMAN

Almost anyone who was watching much television in 1959 is apt to remember something about a commercial message that is involved in a case before the U.S. Supreme Court in 1965. The commercial's central theme was the wonderful effectiveness of Rapid Shave, an aerosol shaving cream manufactured by the

* *December 1964*

Colgate-Palmolive Co., on tough "sandpaper beard." Two men presumed to have tough beards, football stars Kyle Rote and Frank Gifford, were shown shaving contentedly with Rapid Shave. But the clincher was a demonstration in which real sandpaper was shaved smoothly and easily after Rapid Shave had been applied to it. At least, the viewer thought he was seeing real sandpaper. Actually, as the Federal Trade Commission later established, he was seeing a "mock-up," in which plexiglass overlaid with sand substituted for sandpaper. Charging a deception of the public, the FTC ordered Colgate-Palmolive and its advertising agency, Ted Bates & Co., to take the commercial off the air.

This may seem like a laughable matter for the Supreme Court to be concerned about, and in one sense it *is* laughable. There is always an element of the absurd in situations that oblige persons of high seriousness to concern themselves with frivolous themes, and the shaving of sandpaper would seem to qualify as a frivolous theme. Unfortunately for the FTC, it is quite regularly entrapped in such absurd postures. Preventing deceptive advertising is one of its permanent assignments, and a great deal of advertising copy is frivolous in the extreme; at the same time, the commission is perhaps excessively serious and devoid of humor. This is a large shortcoming for regulators on the advertising beat.

Despite those overtones of absurdity, the outcome of the "sandpaper case" is a matter of considerable interest to people concerned with advertising, and for good reasons. The FTC has been acting against deceptive advertising for almost half a century, but its understanding of the problem is not entirely clear to many big advertisers. Many of its orders to advertisers are rather peremptory. In the sandpaper case, however, the commission has made a fairly detailed statement of the principles it believes to be involved; and since so many *are* involved, the statement affords a pretty good summary of the rules of the game as the FTC would now like to apply them. Some of the rules are new: Commissioner Philip Elman, who has been delivering the FTC's views in the case, has made it the occasion for propounding a doctrine that delineates, in detail, the techniques to be permitted advertisers in tests and demonstrations.

It is principally this new doctrine that has kept the case in the courts for so long. When it was initially stated, and again after it was modified, the doctrine on demonstrations was challenged as unreasonable by the U.S. Court of Appeals. Both Elman and Judge Bailey Aldrich of the First Circuit seem to be men of spirit and ingenuity; their long-running argument has been consistently fascinating and occasionally very funny. The reasonableness of this new doctrine is now the main point at issue before the Supreme Court—although it may, of course, go far beyond that issue and tackle the FTC's basic rules for advertising.[1] Meanwhile, the legal profession's special fascination with the sandpaper case has been evidenced recently by lengthy articles in the Yale, Columbia, Notre Dame, and UCLA law reviews. Those who are neither lawyers nor advertising men may also find the case irresistible because of the manner in which it has, insidiously, drawn the government of the U.S. into a confrontation with some ancient philosophical questions about perception and knowledge.

FOILING THE COMPETITION

Congress did not at first intend the FTC to enforce truthfulness in advertising; it was set up, in 1914, only to prevent restraint of trade, and its rather ponderous regulatory apparatus, with elaborate provision for preliminary hearings, appeals to a full commission, and judicial review, still seems more suitable to large antitrust cases than to thwarting purveyors of white lies and weasel words. The FTC almost immediately began pushing into advertising because, it found, deceptive claims sometimes had serious competitive effects and might, in themselves, tend to restrain trade. Later the FTC asserted (and was upheld in an opinion written by Justice Brandeis) a right to protect consumers from deceptive advertising even when no restraint of trade was involved. In 1938, Congress passed the Wheeler-Lea Act, which formally affirmed the commission's power to act against "deceptive acts or practices." However, this still left the assignment in the hands of men who were apt to be antitrust specialists. In the *Columbia Law Review* article Ira M. Millstein of the American Bar Association's committee on the FTC observed that the commissioners "are not chosen for their expertise in ascertaining the meaning of advertisements, or for some general intuitive knowl-

---

[1] The Supreme Court upheld the FTC's finding of a material deceptive practice on April 5, 1965. [*Editor's Note*]

edge of the public's understanding of sights and sounds." Commissioners tend to have legal and political backgrounds. The present chairman is Paul Rand Dixon, formerly counsel to Senator Estes Kefauver's antitrust and monopoly subcommittee; Commissioner Elman is a former assistant solicitor general. In sum, the regulation of advertising is ordinarily in the hands of commissioners with no special expertise, wielding an administrative apparatus of no special suitability.

The commissioners' amateur standing would not be so great a problem if the law they were administering provided them with some objective standards. But the nature of "deceptive acts or practices" is, inevitably, elusive. And some creators of advertising copy can be artful.

There are some ads whose deceptiveness would seem to be noncontroversial. Advertisers and/or their agencies occasionally make statements that are explicit, significant, and demonstrably false. They sometimes "rig" performance tests and mislabel photographs. A while back, Alcoa and the Ketchum, MacLeod & Grove agency were assailed by the commission for a television commercial in which "New Super-Strength Alcoa Wrap" was contrasted visually with an "ordinary" household aluminum foil. A photograph showed the relative condition of two pieces of foil, allegedly after each had been wrapped and unwrapped the same number of times; there seemed to be no doubt that the Alcoa foil had held up better. The complaint charged (and the agency did not deny) that the "ordinary wrap" had been deliberately torn and wrinkled before the two samples were photographed.

THE CASE OF THE VANISHING LATHER

Another case of deception that would seem to be clear-cut involved a television commercial for Rise shaving cream, manufactured by Carter Products. Carter's advertising agency, Sullivan, Stauffer, Colwell & Bayles, Inc., had devised an ad in which a man was first shown shaving, in obvious discomfort, with an "ordinary" lather that had dried out on his face almost immediately after application; later he was shown shaving happily with Rise. The commission established that the "ordinary" lather used in the film was not, in fact, a shaving cream, but a solution called "ultra-wet 60L," which had been specially formulated so that it would come out of the can in one good puff and then disappear rapidly.

Advertisements resting on gross falsehoods are not very numerous, however, and probably not very effective either. The real problem in trying to prevent deception is the half-truth—the advertisement that is ambiguous. A great deal of advertising copy, and especially copy for mass-marketed consumer products, consists of words whose import is not altogether clear. They are suggestive rather than explicit; alternatively, they assert an explicit claim at one point but hedge or even contradict it at another. The problem of ambiguity is especially great on television, where words may be spoken rapidly and with odd emphases, and where, moreover, they are used in conjunction with photographs that are themselves often ambiguous—in part because special effects may be created by shooting from angles and with special lenses, and in part, because sequences of pictures may be used suggestively. A lot of the FTC's toughest advertising cases in recent years have involved television commercials.

Unfortunately for both consumers and advertising men, the commission seems badly overmatched. It is unable to protect consumers very meaningfully because it moves so slowly and is not staffed to handle many cases. At the same time, advertisers may justifiably complain about the commission's rules. Whether it is even possible to write rules that will cover the infinite varieties of deception is an interesting theoretical question to which the answer is not entirely clear. It is clear, however, that the rules the commission regards as crucial are in some respects as ambiguous as the ads they are intended to govern. It is also clear that the rules have been applied unevenly.

THE MEANING OF PEPSODENT

One of the commission's repeatedly cited "ground rules" says that when an ad is susceptible of two different interpretations, and one of these entails a false claim, then the ad is illegal—no less so than an ad in which a false claim is put forth unambiguously. This doctrine sounds useful and was upheld by the Supreme Court forty years ago.[2] In practice, however, the doctrine is often

---

[2] *United States v. 95 Barrels of Vinegar.* The point at issue was whether a product labeled "Apple Cider Vinegar" could be made of dried or evaporated apples—i.e., instead of fresh apples. Justice Butler, attacking "statements, designs and devices which . . . are ambiguous and liable to mislead," said the product was misbranded.

not applied. Consider what happened when the commission took up a television commercial for Pepsodent toothpaste, a product of Lever Brothers.

The central theme of the commercial, which was prepared by the Foote, Cone & Belding agency, was the toothpaste's effectiveness against cigarette stains. It began with an announcer saying, "Pepsodent is the toothpaste that cleans away yellow smoke stains, as well as stains caused by many foods." Then a white-smocked laboratory technician took over: "I'd like to prove that to you right now. This is a cigarette-smoking machine. It deposits yellow smoke stains on enamel like the hard surface of your teeth. (HAND RAPS ON ENAMEL) With the Pepsodent we brush across the stain. Then rinse with plain water. (WATER EFFECT) See? The smoke stain is gone—where we used Pepsodent." At that point the announcer came back: "Yes, Pepsodent removed even yellow smoke stain, perhaps the hardest of all stains to remove. In fact, Pepsodent cleans your teeth more *effectively*, polishes more protectively than any other leading toothpaste."

The commercial was ambiguous in several different respects, but the commission's main question about it was this: Would it suggest to a viewer that Pepsodent could brush away tobacco stains accumulated over years—or only the more superficial stains incurred in smoking three or four cigarettes? If it was suggesting the former, the claim was surely false, for no toothpaste can remove accumulated tobacco stains with a single brushing, and it is not even clear that repeated applications of toothpaste can remove them: some expert witnesses at the commission's hearing on this case indicated a belief that accumulated stains cannot be removed without special abrasive compounds. On the other hand, if the commercial conveyed only the idea that Pepsodent would remove superficial stains, then it was probably truthful; most of the expert witnesses said that a toothpaste like Pepsodent would indeed remove such stains.

Well, what *did* the commercial claim? A majority of the commission concluded, as had the hearing examiner, that the commercial made only the modest and truthful claim—i.e., that Pepsodent would brush away superficial stains. In reaching this conclusion, the hearing examiner observed, "The stains are referred to as yellow smoke stains, which is the usual color of a fresh tobacco stain, instead of the brown or black color usually associated with accumulated stain." Unless one "injected novel meanings" into the commercial, he suggested, it could not be taken as a claim that Pepsodent removes accumulated stains. However, two members of the commission, including Chairman Dixon, dissented from this finding. They argued that the distinction between superficial (yellow) and accumulated (brown) smoking stains is one not ordinarily made by the public, which might therefore conclude that Pepsodent could remove all smoke stains; in addition, the minority pointed out, the reference to yellow stains as "perhaps the hardest of all stains to remove" would inhibit the viewer from relating yellowness to superficiality. They added, "The most charitable interpretation of this commercial is that it is ambiguous."

One might suppose that when commissioners themselves disagree about the meaning of a commercial the commission would have to conclude that it was susceptible of different interpretations. But things don't seem to work that way. Instead, there is a tendency for the majority, however slender, to assert that its own interpretation is the only reasonable one. In practice, then, the problem of ads with two meanings is often not recognized as such by the commission, which instead proceeds on the curious assumption that research and argument will ultimately lay bare the one true meaning.

WALL-TO-WALL REASONING

The assumption is especially curious because it collides head on with another of the commission's ground rules. This is that the commission will not judge advertisements only by the standards of the sophisticated and intelligent; it will also protect the trusting, the casual, and the naive. An advertisement may be literally true, but if it is worded so that a careless or naive reader would be led to believe something that was false, then the commission will outlaw the ad. There are limits to this protection; some consumers' innocence borders on the unreasonable, and the FTC does receive a considerable number of complaints from unreasonable people. Montgomery Ward uses the "Satisfaction Guaranteed" slogan in its advertising, and every once in a while someone who bought a Montgomery Ward carpet (say) fifteen years ago, and lately burned a cigarette hole in it, and then found that Ward will not take it back and return his money, complains to the FTC that he has been deceived. His position is simple: he was guaranteed satisfaction, and now Ward refuses to satisfy him. The commission rejects such complaints.

The FTC is resolved, then, to protect the innocent, but not to overdo it. At what level of intelligence should it draw the line? Its answer to this question has varied considerably. In the Pepsodent case it approved a commercial that its own chairman believed was making a false claim; in its rendering of that case, it was manifestly drawing the intelligence line pretty high. In general, however, it has drawn the line low—i.e., it has outlawed ads that would deceive no one but a near-moron. Ira Millstein of the Bar Association's FTC committee believes that the record low was probably set in a 1941 case, which involved a claim that a product "could color hair permanently." Pondering these words, the commission got to worrying about some naive persons who might read them to mean that the product would color, not only the hair to which is was applied, but hair *still ungrown* at the time; the ad was ordered withdrawn.

Related to the commission's intelligence standards is a rule that says the public is entitled to get the product it thinks it is getting, even if its reasons for wanting the product are not entirely valid. An advertiser cannot represent a plastic product to be made of rubber, even if the plastic's performance is equal (or superior, for that matter) to the rubber's. The underlying rule about these matters is surely reasonable. However, the cases that come before the commission are not always as clear-cut as rubber vs. plastic; too often there is a real uncertainty as to what the public thinks it is getting. Which again leaves the commission all tangled up, and looking a bit absurd, trying to figure out who thinks what.

A few years ago, for example, the FTC got itself impaled on a question about the public's understanding of charcoal. The Quaker Oats Co. was offering "charcoal briquets," which were mostly made of a corncob residue; and this, said the commission staff, was deceptive, for "the public generally understands and believes that a product described as 'charcoal' is made from wood. . . ." The relative merit of briquets made from wood and from corncob was not at issue; the FTC's interest was centered, as usual, on a narrower question—whether the product was what the advertising represented it to be. But when a charge of misrepresentation hinges on the public's understanding, how can the charge be substantiated? Dictionary definitions are useful but inconclusive as to the public's understanding. Polling the public seems impractical. In the Quaker Oats case the commission called expert witnesses and individual consumers to the stand, and the company called both kinds of witnesses too. But, of course, the understanding of such carefully selected witnesses is not necessarily that of the general public either, as the hearing examiner pointed out in dismissing the complaint. (Only one of the experts, in any event, had taken the position that charcoal *had* to be made of wood.) The commission upheld the examiner; but the persistent wobbliness of its intelligence standards is evident in a one-sentence dissent by two of the commissioners. They objected to the ruling on the ground that it afforded no protection to "those persons who believe that charcoal is made from wood." The minority, it would appear, was trying to shelter consumers against "misrepresentations" that arise, not out of the advertising itself, but out of the consumers' own misconceptions.

THE MEANING OF DEALING AND PUFFING

Advertising—at least, hard-sell advertising—necessarily involves a certain amount of hokum, or blarney; and the line between acceptable blarney and outright deceit is faint at many points. The courts have, in fact, been trying to draw this line more clearly for quite a few decades. In the nineteenth century, when there was no FTC and charges of deceit were more likely to concern individual salesmen than published advertisements, the law of torts made this distinction: what was then called "dealing talk" was a natural and permissible ingredient of business in America; what was impermissible was any accompanying suggestion of material falsehood or suppression of material fact.

The distinction sounded plausible, but it was frequently hard to relate to the facts of any one transaction. In part it was hard because of the subjective fog that has always enveloped the word "material"—a problem in many branches of the law. In addition, there just may be an ineradicable trace of deceit buried in the concept of "dealing talk"; the salesman might not lie, but the purpose and effect of all his wheedling, flattery, and arm-twisting was often to smother any instinct the prospect might have to think clearly about the proposition at hand.

These difficulties still get in the FTC's way when it tries to regulate mass advertising today. The modern equivalent of "dealing talk" is what the commission calls "puffing," and another of its major ground rules involves a distinction between puffing and deception. Puffing, which is permissible, consists of expressions of enthusiasm not meant to be taken as factual claims. A Wrigley's chewing-gum slogan, "The biggest little treat in all the land," is one clear example of puffing. But many examples are not so clear —i.e., it is not clear whether the advertiser is saying something specific or just blarneying away. In the Quaker Oats case, one subsidiary question (which was never resolved) concerned the use in the company's ads of the phrase "real Hickory Flavor!" Was that an example of puffing, or did it constitute a specific assertion that the briquets were made of hickory wood? Again, it will be observed, the answer depends on what the public thinks—or, rather, on what the FTC thinks the public thinks. The FTC may not be the most lovable agency in Washington, but you have to feel some sympathy for anybody who spends so much time trying to figure out how ambiguous messages of uncertain importance will be construed by viewers of limited intelligence. You also have to sympathize with anybody obliged to figure out what the commission's rules mean in practice.

SHAVING IN THE COURTROOM

The difficulty of applying those rules, and the further difficulty of fighting about them without looking foolish, were endlessly illustrated in the sandpaper case. Viewers of the commercial back in 1959 might well have resisted the notion that it was Supreme Court material. Yet it soon became clear that the commercial had a litigious destiny. Complaints about it began arriving at the FTC almost immediately after it went on the air. Oddly enough, they had nothing to do with the complainants' own whiskers; instead, they were almost unanimous in expressing indignation that *they* weren't able to shave sandpaper with Rapid Shave, the way the man was doing it on television.

The commercial showed a football player, either Frank Gifford or Kyle Rote of the New York Giants (there were different versions of the commercial), who was proclaimed by an unseen announcer to be "a man with a problem just like yours . . . a beard as tough as sandpaper . . . a beard that needs PALMOLIVE RAPID SHAVE . . . super-moisturized for the fastest, smoothest shave possible." A few seconds later the viewer saw some Rapid Shave lather spread upon sandpaper, and immediately afterward a hand appeared with a razor and shaved a clean path through the lather and the gritty surface of the sandpaper; during this action the announcer was saying, "To prove RAPID SHAVE's super-moisturizing power, we put it right from the can onto this tough dry sandpaper. It was apply . . . soak . . . and off in a stroke." A little later, a "split screen" showed Rapid Shave again being applied to sandpaper while Gifford or Rote applied some to his own face; and immediately afterward the viewer saw razors easily shave both the sandpaper and the face. The commercial ended conventionally, with Gifford or Rote looking pleased with himself and an off-camera male chorus singing a rousing jingle about Rapid Shave. All of this took exactly sixty seconds.

On January 8, 1960, after its investigators had established that the "sandpaper" used in this commercial was in fact plexiglass and sand, the FTC issued a formal complaint against Ted Bates and Colgate-Palmolive. The proceedings began with hearings before an FTC examiner, William L. Pack; these took place in October 1960, and again in February and April 1961. The spirit of the proceedings was naturally somewhat argumentative, but they are a treasure trove of information about sandpaper and shaving.

Sandpaper, the hearings made clear, is a rather more varied commodity than many of us realize. There are 37,000 different grades of it—that, at least, was the figure supplied by expert witness Joseph R. O'Neil, who is an engineer with the Carborundum Co. and the author of numerous monographs on sandpaper. ("I have also written some lighter things," he noted.) O'Neil testified that the commercial seemed to depict an "extra coarse" grade of sandpaper, and that any such grade would be extremely difficult to shave. His own efforts to do so in court helped to prove this point, and so did those of Kyle Rote. The transcript suggests that Rote's appearance afforded a moment of high drama:

Mr. Downs (the FTC attorney): Let the record show that Mr. Rote has applied the Rapid Shave to the sandpaper and he is now wiping it off his hand.

Q: Is that the stroke you would use on your face, Mr. Rote?

A: Not at all.

Q: Is that heavier than you would use on your face?

A: Yes, sir.

Q: Will you now apply as much pressure as you can in an attempt to shave off this rough surface of this sandpaper?

A: Yes, sir [complying].

Mr. Downs: Let the record show that Mr. Rote has used both hands on it.

Q: Were you able to shave this sandpaper clean in that attempt?

A: I wouldn't say it would be clean, no.

The record showed, however, that finer grades of sandpaper could be shaved. Bates's principal witness, Brantz M. Bryan Jr., an account executive, seems to have gone to some lengths to establish this point. Under cross-examination, it emerged that Bryan had been shaving sandpaper on a table in his own office, and *was still shaving it in his car* on the morning he drove to the hearing. His experiments showed that medium-coarse grades of sandpaper could be shaved if they were soaked for periods of twenty to eighty minutes; some finer grades could be shaved if they were soaked for as little as a minute. Unfortunately, Bryan pointed out, the agency could not use a fine sandpaper in filming the commercial, because the television camera would make it look like ordinary wrapping paper.

Attorneys for Bates and Colgate defended the commercial in several different ways. It said you could shave sandpaper with Rapid Shave, and you can. To be sure, prolonged soaking was necessary, but that was implied in the wording of the commercial. (The implication was allegedly in the phrase "apply . . . soak . . . and off in a stroke." Colgate's attorney cited a dictionary to the effect that "soak" means "wet thoroughly, saturate. . . .") The distinction between fine and coarse sandpaper was one that could not possibly interest the public. Finally, the commercial had been mere "puffing"; no reasonable viewer would regard it as a serious demonstration. "If I may get into the realm of common sense," said Colgate's attorney, "it is inconceivable to me how this particular advertisement could have misled anybody anyway because it was clearly just a fanciful kind of thing. . . ."

Hearing examiner Pack agreed, and dismissed the complaint.

REALITY IN ICE CREAM

This ruling seems to have disturbed the FTC considerably. It agreed to hear an appeal, and in January 1962, it unanimously reversed the hearing examiner. Commissioner Elman's lengthy opinion argued that Colgate had seriously represented the ability of Rapid Shave to do something it could not do. It had shown the cream enabling someone to shave sandpaper smoothly and easily, whereas in fact the sandpaper depicted could not be shaved at all, and other grades could be shaved only after long periods of soaking. The opinion brushed aside the "technical quibbles" about the meaning of the word "soak"; and it insisted that the commercial taken as a whole was deceptive, especially in light of the commission's concern for "the trusting as well as the suspicious." It rejected the contention that the commercial could be construed as harmless puffing. Serious "factual representations" had been made, and these were false.

The opinion suggested that the conventional distinctions between puffing and deception needed some reformulating in the television age. A detailed statement of principles on the use of mock-ups began with the rule that any representation as to what the viewer is witnessing must be truthful. Television's technical limitations, said the opinion, may sometimes require an actor to wear a blue shirt when the script calls for white (a shirt that was really white would reflect too much light), but if the viewer's attention is in any way directed to the shirt's whiteness, and especially if the whiteness is offered as evidence for an advertising claim, then the shirt must be white—really white. Shirts and sandpaper were not the only products involved in this new doctrine. Orange juice and iced tea seem to lose their natural colors on television, and have generally been simulated by colored water. Some products would melt rapidly if they were exposed to the hot lights in TV studios: ice cream, for example, is usually represented by mashed potatoes. The "head" on a real glass of beer doesn't last long enough for directors, and so a specially formulated foam is used. All these substitutions, in Commissioner Elman's view, would now have to end. In fact, he observed, the use of plexiglass in the Colgate commercial would have violated the law *even if Rapid Shave did enable you to shave sandpaper smoothly and easily.*

Colgate and Bates appealed, and the next stop for the sandpaper case was the U.S. Court of Appeals. Three judges in the First Circuit (Boston) heard arguments on it in the fall of 1962, and seem to have regarded it as a rather amusing trifle; Judge Bailey Aldrich, who wrote the opinion, said the case was "rather trivial," and the petitions "noteworthy principally because of the extremes [to which they had] led the parties." There were, indeed, signs that the people involved were getting mad. In the circuit court, when Colgate and Bates again argued that the sandpaper demonstration had been mere puffing, and that no serious person would believe it proved anything about human shaving, the FTC attorney put forth a new thought—that in making this argument the companies were acknowledging a *further* misrepresentation, i.e., their commercial had led viewers to believe an ability to shave sandpaper was relevant to the problems of human shaving. Judge Aldrich said he found this thought interesting; however, he did not implement it. His opinion upheld the finding that Colgate and Bates were guilty of deception. On the nature of reality, however, his views appeared to differ from the commission's.

A STUDY IN TEA AND MILK

The viewer's reality, he said in effect, is what he sees on the screen; he is not brought any closer to the truth by requiring the producer to bring the real thing into the filming studio. During the proceedings, Judge Aldrich put the following case to the FTC counsel: "Suppose a prominent person is photographed saying, 'I love Lipsom's iced tea,' while apparently, he drinks a glass of iced tea. In truth the individual does like Lipsom's tea, and frequently drinks it, but for . . . technical reasons is then drinking colored water. What the viewer sees on the screen looks exactly as Lipsom's iced tea does in fact look." On the new FTC doctrine, was this use of colored water a deception of the public? The commission's counsel replied that it was indeed—that the public thought it was seeing iced tea, when in fact it was not. Judge Aldrich then tried out an even tougher one on the counsel. Suppose, he asked, we were dealing with a product that, unlike iced tea, looked *better* on television than at first hand—e.g., a milk product that somehow photographed creamier than it really was. How would the FTC's new insistence on photographing "the real thing" apply in that case? The counsel somehow managed to avoid a direct answer, and Judge Aldrich commented that "his client has left him without one." The judge sent the case back to the FTC for a more reasonable statement of principles.

His criticisms inspired the commission to reconsider the entire case and to formulate a new order. This order still found the commercial to be deceptive and illegal. However, there were some new mock-up rules, written by Commissioner Elman in light of the judge's "various suggestions." Mock-ups were permissible in cases where the appearance of the product was only "an incidental aspect of the commercial," as in the Lipsom's tea example. They were impermissible when the advertiser was trying to *prove* something by showing you a test or demonstration of his product; then he had to show the real thing. Actually, the commission went on to suggest, this was the distinction it had been making from the beginning. The commissioners said one reason for the misunderstanding might be the "extreme arguments" made by counsel in the hearings before the Court of Appeals. They never did explain what their counsel should have said about the product that photographed extra-creamy.

Whether they were moved by heartfelt conviction or mere masochism is unclear, but it is a fact that Colgate and Bates once again appealed from the FTC's ruling, and in mid-1963 the First Circuit had the sandpaper case back. The judges heard arguments on the revised rules, and once again asked the FTC counsel some searching questions; this time they also thought to inquire whether the counsel's answers had been cleared by the commission (they had). The opinion Judge Aldrich eventually wrote, in December 1963, contains several indications that he was now getting mad himself. He tartly observed, for example, that he had not given the commission "various suggestions," but rather had reached conclusions that it "was not free to disregard." And he again found the proposed rules to be unsatisfactory. He wrote: "In spite of the Commission's belief that it has resolved all ambiguities, we envisage great difficulty in determining any dividing line between what is and what is not a test or experiment." If a detergent manufacturer exhibits a bed sheet that is actually blue but photographs white, might it not be assumed that he is depicting his own product's cleaning power—even if there is no mention of a test or demonstration? Such difficulties, said Judge Aldrich, suggest that the proposed rules would bog down in a quicksand of ambiguity, and, accordingly, violated "the principle that an order must be capable of practical interpretation." He added, "The relative insignificance of the issue before us makes it particularly unwarranted to offend this principle." Of all those entangled in the sandpaper case, Judge Aldrich appears to be the only one who never wavered in his views about its significance.

WHAT WOULD THE BISHOP SAY?

Beyond the problem of ambiguity, the Judge persisted in quarreling with the commission's concept of reality. He suggested that there was nothing wrong with using mock-ups in a test, so long as they represented "faithfully a test which has been actually performed." The reality that the FTC should be concerned about, he insisted, is what the viewer sees, not what the producer has in the studio. In its concern with the latter, "the Commission sometimes loses sight of the difference between a mock-up which presents an accurate portrayal and one, like Colgate's, that effects a basic deception. . . ."

Students of philosophy may detect in this dialogue echoes of an argument that throughout history has engaged the attention of many great minds. The argument has to do, essentially, with the existence of an objective reality. One strand in the history of philosophy is identified with those who have held, in various ways, that "man is the measure" of reality, i.e., what is real to him is what he perceives with his own senses, and since different men perceive things differently, there are different realities—and no one reality that can be called objective. This view can be traced back to Protagoras, who lived in the fifth century B.C., but it has been embraced in varying forms by many other philosophers; Bishop Berkeley, who lived in the eighteenth century, went so far as to argue that material objects do not exist at all except through being perceived. The Bishop, presumably, would have had no objection to mock-ups. Many other philosophers have opposed any such relativism, arguing that there *was* an objective reality (although not agreeing among themselves as to its nature). To the extent that it has stood for "the real thing," as opposed to mock-ups, the commission seems to have identified itself with this position.

The discourse in the sandpaper case has not always been on a philosophic plane, but the Supreme Court now has an opportunity to put it there. The FTC appealed the verdict of the First Circuit, complaining that the judges were improperly poaching on its own administrative preserves. It is quite possible, of course, that the Court will issue only a perfunctory ruling; what with civil rights, reapportionment, and school prayers, it may have no time left this year to enlarge our comprehension of reality. That would be a pity—though it would be hard to quarrel with any ruling that brought the sandpaper case to an end.

Laws Alone Can't Make Drugs Safe* ____

LAWRENCE LESSING

In the wake of the thalidomide tragedy that hit headlines in the summer of 1962, with its pitiful legacy of deformed babies, the U.S. enacted a whole new set of laws and regulations for the stricter control of drugs. Whatever its other virtues and defects, this legislation is hardly likely by itself to avert the recurrence of such tragedies. And it may impose such costs and burdens on pharmaceutical companies as to slow down the development of life-prolonging new products. Indeed, no set of regulations can get around the great dilemma that confronts medical science, the industry, and government in the testing and introduction of new drugs. It is impossible to determine definitely whether a drug is free from harmful effects unless it is tried widely on humans—and that inevitably means risking lives.

The dilemma is nowhere more clearly seen than in the case of thalidomide itself. This compound was first synthesized by the

* *March 1963*

small West German firm of Chemie Grünenthal GmbH in 1953. It was built on one of the natural amino acids found in all protein synthesis, glutamic acid, and it early showed promise as a sedative. After three years of tests on animals and humans, it was released to the market in West Germany in 1957, and soon after to other countries in Western Europe. Thalidomide was an almost immediate success, for it had some unique properties. Unlike the common barbiturate sleeping pills, it had no apparent troublesome side effects, was non-habit-forming, and nonlethal even in large doses. The importance of the latter is underlined by the fact that in the U.S. some 1,500 deaths a year are caused by overdoses of barbiturates. Within a short time thalidomide was selling at the rate of some 20 million tablets a month in West Germany alone.

In 1958, U.S. license rights to thalidomide were acquired by the Wm. S. Merrell Co., division of Richardson-Merrell Inc. Merrell began animal and clinical testing of its own, later including distribution for experimental use of some 2,500,000 tablets to 1,267 selected U.S. doctors. On the basis of a year and a half of these tests and of nearly three years of widespread use in Europe, with no known unfavorable effects, Merrell in September 1960, made application to the U.S. Food and Drug Administration for approval to market the drug.

Then disturbing reports came in from Europe of peripheral neuritis or a tingling in fingers and toes of a few long-term takers of thalidomide. And late in 1961, after nearly five years in which many thousands of patients had used the drug without apparent serious incident, came the first reports suspiciously linking thalidomide with a rising number of deformed births. The drug was pulled off the West German market in November 1961, similar action in Britain followed closely, and Merrell promptly notified the FDA. Then, as the terrifying evidence mounted in 1962, Merrell and the FDA worked around the clock to recall all test supplies.

Birth defects caused by certain drugs have not been unknown in the past. For instance, quinine has been found to harm the human embryo, and morphine used to allay labor pains can cause severe respiratory failure in the newborn. But never before in medical history had a drug apparently triggered so massive an eruption of deformities of so peculiar a type as did thalidomide, in which the hands, feet, or whole limbs of infants failed to form at all. By the end of 1962 at least 3,000 such malformed babies were estimated to have been born in West Germany alone. And hundreds more were spread over Europe, Japan, Canada, and South America, where the drug was also widely sold. In the U.S., owing to the wariness of the FDA and a single worker, Dr. Frances O. Kelsey, approval of the drug for marketing was held up, and the toll was kept to a handful of possible cases linked to thalidomide. All together, it was one of the major medical disasters of recent times.

"SOMEBODY HAS TO BE FIRST"

Could such a disaster have been prevented? Generally, European laws controlling the introduction and sale of new drugs are laxer than those of the U.S. Presumably some closer, faster checking up and reporting of the drug's effects on people might have lessened the world-wide tragedy. And perhaps Merrell was leaning too heavily on the European experience in its early, stepped-up distribution of experimental tablets to doctors. But all this is hindsight. The fact is that thalidomide, long before it came a cropper, had met all the testing procedures under which hundreds of new drugs are released each year. It had first passed the usual tests for safety in animals. These did not include tests on pregnant animals. So far these have been almost wholly unsatisfactory in predicting effects in humans. Indeed, on the evidence of the usual animal tests alone, a number of U.S. drug houses had earlier turned down thalidomide because it showed so little activity— sedative or otherwise.

The animal tests did prove the drug reasonably safe to try on humans. And here thalidomide passed all the usual clinical tests for safety and effectiveness. But there were no formal tests on pregnant women. Doctors generally are reluctant to give new drugs to them because of all the unknowns and the fragility of the human embryo. Hence thalidomide came only gradually into widespread use as a relaxing, anti-nausea drug in pregnancy. Then recognition of its effect was further delayed by the fact that once the deformed births began to appear—of a rare type known as phocomelia—it took a long search among all possible causes to pin suspicion on thalidomide. To confuse things still more, many mothers taking the drug gave birth to entirely normal babies. Thus it took a massive rise in phocomelia cases for the effect to be recognized at all.

As researchers dug in to find out what had gone wrong, the chances of earlier discovery narrowed even further. It appeared that thalidomide has its baleful effect in only one short period of early pregnancy—not more than about two weeks and possibly as little as a few hours long—when limb buds are forming on the embryo. One speculation is that the drug's unnatural form of glutamic acid blocks some critical organizing or protein-forming process at this crucial juncture. Taken only briefly before this period or after it, thalidomide appeared to have no ill effects, thus accounting for the many normal births. Nothing like it had ever been observed before.

Most medical, clinical, and drug authorities now believe that the thalidomide case shows up certain deficiencies in clinical testing procedures, which will be examined later in this article. But they also believe that the tragic thalidomide effect was almost wholly unpredictable and therefore largely unpreventable in the present state of knowledge. No series of control tests yet devised can uncover all the possible and unexpected side effects of new drugs in the complex human body. And every new drug presents a risk and a danger, for at some point the first humans must take it to discover whether it works—and this is the heart of the dilemma. It is not resolved by political charges, such as rose at the height of the thalidomide fright, that drug companies are using human beings as guinea pigs. "We must face up to the fact," says one eminent clinician, "that somebody has to be first, or we could have no new drugs."

THE UPRUSHING PROBLEM

The best hope of reducing the risks is the continued improvement of scientific clinical testing or clinical pharmacology, a relatively new and far from fully developed branch of medicine. In the not remote past, drugs still came into use slowly by the historical trial-and-error method that sometimes produced disasters rivaling thalidomide's, in horror if not in scope. As science began to penetrate medicine, less than a century ago, the development and initial testing of new drugs became the province of the individual scientific investigator of a disease, mainly in the universities, and most of the basic discoveries continue to come from this source. But then, starting with the sulfa drugs in the Thirties, came the great chemical-pharmaceutical industrial revolution, building on and extending these discoveries through research into mass production. The introduction of efficacious new drugs—antibiotics, antimalarials, anticoagulants, antihypertensives, tranquilizers, diuretics, steroids, polio vaccines, to name but a few—rose to a flood.

Today over 400 new drug applications are filed with the FDA each year. About 90 percent of all prescriptions written today are for drugs that were unknown to therapeutics some fifteen years ago. Formerly the pharmaceutical industry made only what the doctor prescribed; now the doctor prescribes what the industry makes. In the last thirty years or so, medicine has encompassed more advances than in the preceding five hundred. In countries practicing modern medicine, these have made possible the control of nearly all infectious diseases and the spectacular rise of life expectancy in this century from an average of about fifty years to close to seventy.

The sheer volume of new drugs, however, poses an immense problem in clinical testing. It is lessened only somewhat by the fact that of the more than 400 new drugs each year perhaps only forty are entirely new chemical entities; the rest are new formulations, new dosage forms, or slight molecular modifications of existing products. Since even the slightest change in a chemical compound often markedly alters its biological or therapeutic effect, the modifications must generally be tested with all the care of entirely new drugs. The problem is heightened as research turns to attack the more deep-seated degenerative diseases, such as cancer and heart disease, by the emergence of ever more powerful and more toxic new drugs. And with the rapid distribution of new drugs—the very success of the pharmaceutical revolution—the problem and risks are widened still further.

THE DESIGN OF A CALCULATED RISK

From conception through all the intricacies of research and development, the odds on developing a new, safe, and efficacious drug have been estimated at about one to 30,000. To test the flood of new compounds adequately, swiftly, and safely, the pharmaceutical industry long ago had to work out, by necessity and later by law, a system for clinical testing. Indeed, organization of clinical pharmacology as a separate discipline has been more a commercial art than a science up to now. It is a system still developing, still imperfect and chaotic, open to abuse and to criticism. But the leading reputable pharmaceutical companies, large and small, generally have pursued high standards. In fact, their research and production techniques have set most of the quality and control standards there are.

In pursuit of a research lead suggesting a new drug for a specific disease, a pharmaceutical company's chemical laboratories may synthesize and study thousands of new compounds. These are first run through rapid, highly organized screening tests in mice or rats to discover which compounds have some biological activity. With luck, a handful will. The most promising are then put through the major preclinical stage of testing on laboratory animals. This has two parts. First, the compounds are tested to find out which, if any, have the desired pharmacological effect. Then, if a sufficiently active compound is found, it is put through more elaborate, more expensive tests to detect toxicity and measure it. All together, these preclinical tests may take up to two or three years.

The most critical and difficult of the tests are those for toxicity. Some compounds, of course, are so highly poisonous in any amounts that they must immediately be discarded. But all substances are toxic in some amounts, even pure water, and all drugs, designed to kill or block diseases, are toxic in large measure. An overdose of aspirin can kill. Hence the prime purpose of toxicity tests is to determine the dosage that will produce the greatest desired effect with a minimum of harmful side effects.

Adding to the complexities is the fact that no two animal species react to drugs in exactly the same way—morphine depresses the dog, excites the cat—so that tests must be performed on at least two species to cover the possible variables. And the gap between animals and man is even wider. Some drugs are highly toxic in dogs but not in men, and vice versa. No strict correlation of drug effects has been established between animal and man, though some valuable guidelines have been gained by long experience. The best that animal tests can do is to forestall most of the grosser accidents and suggest some of the possible effects in men.

IT'S SAFEST TO AVOID THEM ALL

After the thalidomide case, toxicity tests on pregnant animals, despite their shortcomings, will probably be required for all drugs that might be used by pregnant women. Researchers working diligently after the event have now succeeded in producing thalidomide's effect in some pregnant rabbits, rats, and mice, at fantastically high dosage levels, and the hope is that this will open the way to new understanding of birth anomalies. But there is no certainty that other drugs will work in a similar way or that pregnant animals will show their hidden effects. "Unfortunately," writes Dr. John T. Litchfield Jr., who heads Lederle Laboratories' large animal-testing facilities, "a negative finding in an animal test predicts very little as far as human hazard is concerned. It is only after the fact that it is known whether or not the test conditions were appropriate. In this special area of drug effects on fetal and newborn animals the test conditions are extremely critical and not well defined at present." Knowledge is so meager in this area that a seminar on birth defects at the University of Michigan last fall concluded that the only safe procedure is to avoid all pills and drugs, from aspirin on up, in early pregnancy, except where the health or life of the mother is clearly at stake.

At the conclusion of animal testing, after statistically analyzing the data from hundreds of blood, liver, kidney, and other histological studies, weighing species differences, balancing off good against bad effects, extrapolating data and dosages from mice to men, and searching the soul, the pharmaceutical company's medical director must make the momentous decision whether the new compound is safe enough to try on a man. In one recent year, it is estimated, the industry examined some 114,000 new compounds, of which only about 1,900 were considered safe and active enough to test on human beings, only about forty proved worthy of marketing, and possibly only three or four will eventually be judged real contributions to medicine.

THE CLINICAL BARRIER

For initial clinical tests on humans, a pharmaceutical house must generally go outside its own laboratories to find medical investigators or specialists, attached to universities, hospitals, clinics, or other institutions, willing to take on the job as part of their research. As will be seen later, finding the right clinical investigators to carry on this work has become a major problem itself, one that is intensified by the flood of new drugs to be tested.

Testing on humans is cautiously approached in two phases, which are the reverse of those in animal testing, i.e., safety is tested before pharmacological effect. Both are usually performed on healthy human volunteers—to try a new drug immediately on the ill would be too dangerous. Volunteers are almost always available among medical students and prison inmates, who are rewarded with a small fee and a sense of serving society. In the first phase a small group is generally fed the drug in tiny, gradually increased amounts to test its toxicity. As an added precaution, one volunteer may be given 30 percent more in each dose than the rest of the group, so that if a level of undue toxicity is suddenly reached there will be only one sick man to treat rather than half a dozen. If all goes well, the drug is tested for the desired pharmacological effect on another small group of volunteers; since they are healthy, the effect can be observed and measured only by delicate systemic studies. Occasionally drugs are tried on near-terminal cases that have nothing to lose by experiment. In these two phases of testing on humans, a large percentage of new compounds that have shown promise in animals are generally eliminated, because they are too toxic or inactive in man.

If a drug is designed for some chronic disease, meaning that it must be taken over an extended period, it must go back into animal testing for a period of six months to a year or more so that its long-term effects can be explored. These may be quite different from, and more dangerous than, those exhibited in short-term trials.

The drug that passes muster moves on, in larger and larger test samples, to the patients for whom it is designed. This is the final stage of human testing, which also has two phases. In the first, the drug is given experimentally to a limited, controlled group of patients in a hospital, clinic, or other institution, where its effects can be closely watched and studied. Duplicate tests must be run in more than one institution to make the results as objective as possible. Care is taken to balance the test groups as to age, sex, and condition, and to design the experiment in suitable statistical form. A common one is the blind test, in which the conductor administers, unknown to the patients, either the drug or a harmless, inactive placebo, which acts as control. For pain-relieving or sedative drugs, in which subjective reactions can confuse the issue, the double-blind test is used, in which both the conductor and the patients are kept in the dark as to which is the drug and which the placebo. Variations are numerous, including the testing of a new drug against an old one to measure any gain in effect.

In the final phase, large experimental amounts of the drug are distributed to complying specialists and physicians for judicious testing on patients to discover, if possible, the aberrant effect or side effect that usually shows up only after it has been administered to a large sampling of people. The clinical tests up to this point may have taken another two or three years. Only after all the data is in, showing no serious or catastrophic side effects, is an application filed for FDA release of the drug to the market. Since 1938 pharmaceutical firms have been required to submit to the FDA all relevant test data, often amounting to a five-foot stack, proving the safety and, by inference, effectiveness of a drug before marketing. And in the usual course of events the agency holds up the application a number of times with requests for additional information or testing.

SURPRISES, PLEASANT AND UNPLEASANT

This long course of development is necessarily expensive. Costs have run into the millions of dollars in developing and testing such major new drugs as Upjohn's Orinase tolbutamide, an oral antidiabetic that frees many patients from daily insulin injections, and Merck's Diuril chlorothiazide, an agent used in the control and even, in some cases, the remission of essential and usually fatal hypertension.

No matter how costly and careful the development is, however, totally unexpected incidents and effects will often still crop up, long after a drug has been approved for marketing. Only a short time before it was hit by the thalidomide blow, the Merrell company was suddenly forced to recall an approved drug, MER/29 triparanol, an anticholesterol used in hundreds of thousands of arteriosclerosis cases, when it was suspected of causing eye cataracts and other adverse side effects in some long-time users. The inventory loss alone was close to $2 million. Much less seriously, Lederle's Declomycin, a tetracycline-type antibiotic, was widely used as a treatment for a broad spectrum of infections, mainly throat and pulmonary, before it was discovered that it caused an unusual susceptibility to sunburn in some patients. None of the usual tests, conducted indoors, could have uncovered this.

Occasionally, a drug developed for one purpose turns out to have another, quite different one. Lederle's Diamox, acetazolamide, a new diuretic used in the treatment of congestive heart diseases, was unexpectedly found useful in the treatment of glaucoma, another eye disease.

It is now axiomatic in medical circles that in the normal course of marketing a new drug "the favorable reports will always appear before the unfavorable." The history of the so-called "wonder drugs" bears this out. The reason is not only that the pharmacist, investigator, and physician are always optimistically hopeful of new cures, but also that, given the complex and intransigent nature of patients, all the possible effects of a new drug are slow to appear.

The only way this situation can be improved is by a better fundamental understanding of the mechanisms of the human body and disease, and of the biological actions of drugs on both, so that nasty jolts can be foreseen and forestalled. There are still large gaps in knowledge of drug action and of the body's complex reactions and interactions. Even if all reactions were fully known and coded into a giant computer, it would still be impossible to predict every chance effect or disaster. For the human is a highly mixed breed, genetically. No two individuals ever respond in exactly the same way to a drug, and a joker or two is always lurking somewhere in the genetic deck. In truth, the giving of a drug, old or new, is always an experiment. In this immensely complex situation more knowledge, rather than more politics or regulation, is urgently needed.

THE BURDEN OF PROOF

Nevertheless, new amendments to the food-and-drug law were passed in October 1962 on the crest of the thalidomide panic. Often in the past an uncommonly aroused public has spurred useful and needed reforms. It took long exposés of the horrifying effects of noxious patent medicines and Upton Sinclair's *The Jungle,* painting disgusting conditions in the meatpacking industry, to get the first Pure Food and Drugs Act passed in 1906. So far as drugs were concerned, this law only mildly required that medicines be honestly labeled as to content. And the first major strengthening of the law came in 1938, only after a careless manufacturer mixed an "Elixir of Sulfanilimide," using diethylene glycol (related to permanent-type antifreeze) as a solvent, which killed over 100 people. Up to then there was no legal requirement that a drug had to be tested or approved as safe before marketing. The pharmaceutical industry now agrees, after some early opposition, that the 1938 amendments put a firm base under the last twenty-five years of spectacular drug development. But the new legislation that grew out of the thalidomide case is something quite different.

For nearly three years before thalidomide's toxicity was heard of, Senator Estes Kefauver and his antitrust subcommittee had been fishing in pharmaceutical waters, spreading the bait for new legislation aimed mainly at curbing drug prices and profits, excessive numbers of brand names for essentially similar products, and other commercial practices. Kefauver also incorporated in his proposals some long-considered provisions from an omnibus bill designed to strengthen the 1938 law, mainly in the area of drug effectiveness. Conservative Congressmen, responding to industry opposition, had practically emasculated the Kefauver bill by the time the thalidomide story broke. Using that as a lever, Administration forces proceeded to reinvigorate the bill. None of Kefauver's key commercial strictures were restored, but some old regulatory ideas were revived and some new provisions were rushed in from the White House, ostensibly to meet the thalidomide situation. Congress quickly passed the salvaged measure.

The main provision of the new law is an extension of the old, requiring a new drug to be proved not only safe but also, by "substantial evidence," effective against the disease it claims to treat. Since reputable ethical-drug firms have been doing this all along, they object only to the redundant bureaucratic detail involved. Mainly, the new provision seems to be aimed at eliminating such things as questionable cancer "cures" and cutting down the 20 percent or so of new drugs that the American Medical Association's Council on Drugs found had been slipping by without sufficient clinical data to support their claims. The only substantive change is that henceforth the burden of proof of a drug's effectiveness will be on the manufacturer, whereas heretofore it fell to the FDA to prove that a drug was ineffective in order to remove it from the market. Needless to say, nothing in this would prevent another thalidomide, which was shown to be effective and safe as a sedative and still remains so in all instances except early pregnancy. Indeed, thalidomide has been returned to restricted use in Britain at the request of doctors.

Other provisions of the new law give the FDA authority to inspect and control manufacturing procedures, quality, and standards more closely; to consider a new drug application initially for 180 days (previously, clearance was automatic if the FDA did not act in sixty days); to designate "official" generic names for new drugs and require them to be printed on all labeling in type at least half as large as that of brand names (a vestige of the curb Kefauver wanted to put on brand names); and to withdraw a cleared drug from market if substantial question arises as to safety and effectiveness or if it shows signs of being an imminent hazard (a power that the FDA has in effect exercised all along). Another provision requires all package leaflets to contain a full disclosure, and all prescription-drug advertising a brief summary, of known hazards, side effects, and contraindications. About the only new provision bearing on the thalidomide problem is explicit authority to monitor and control the clinical testing of experimental drugs, including the required reporting of clinical experience as it emerges. This power had been implicit in the old law but never used.

Nothing in these provisions would ensure that a hidden side effect like thalidomide's would be detected any faster than it was. For nothing in the standard clinical tests required by the FDA is likely to reveal such far-out anomalies, and nothing is so dangerous as a false sense of security. It is simply impossible to regulate or prevent with any certainty what is not yet known.

A PAPER MONUMENT

In August 1962, even before the new law was passed, the FDA rushed out a set of new regulations under the old law to govern the clinical testing and investigational use of new drugs. The medical profession and pharmaceutical industry were given sixty days to file comments or objections. Almost all the comments were mixed or hostile. Early this year the regulations, revised somewhat in response to objections, went into effect.

A pharmaceutical company is required to notify the FDA of each new drug it proposes to test. Each notification must contain complete data on the drug's composition, sources, purposes, and manufacturing procedures; data and evidence from preclinical chemical and animal tests to prove reasonable safety, with names and qualifications of the preclinical investigators; an outline of the plan for clinically testing the drug, by phases, and the names and qualifications of all investigators, with certification that they are "suitable experts." The clinical investigator will have to supply the drug's sponsor with full data on his training, qualifications, and facilities, keep "adequate" records and case histories, transmit periodic reports to the sponsor, and certify that consent of patients has been obtained to use the drug, except where this is not feasible or in his professional judgment is contrary to the best interests of patients. In each clinical phase the company will be required to make progress reports to the FDA at intervals not exceeding a year, and promptly notify it of any changes in plans, any alarming side effects discovered, or any decisions to discontinue tests, with the reasons therefor. At any point the FDA may step in to review the program, examine records, and halt trials if they are not conforming to plan or regulations.

On each of the thousands of experimental drugs clinically tested each year, this will produce a monumental pile of papers, details, and investigational lines to follow, with endless opportunity for controversy. In addition to the massive data accompanying every application for release of a new drug to market, a pharmaceutical firm will now have to file reports from the moment it begins clinically testing a new compound, on all the quirks and turns of its testing, even on all the compounds that lead nowhere. All together, it is estimated, the number of required reports flooding in on the FDA each year will run between 300,000 and 500,000.

Many in the industry concede that some check over the mushroom growth of clinical testing has been needed, and that some curb was long due on such abuses as insufficient clinical testing or excessive promotional use of the final phase of this testing, in which the still experimental drug is widely distributed to doctors. But they are also certain that the new regulations will greatly increase costs and prices, slow down the introduction of new drugs, and, if arbitrarily administered, constrict in endless red tape the experimental advance of medicine. At an extreme, this new experiment in regulation might be more devastating than any experimentation with the drugs themselves.

STOPPING THE VIVICOSMIC DISC IS NOT ENOUGH

Seriously at question, first of all, is the FDA's capacity to enforce the highly complex new regulations. . . . In the autumn of 1962 a distinguished citizens advisory committee appointed by former Secretary of Health, Education, and Welfare Abraham Ribicoff came in from a year-long study with a flat recommendation that the FDA be completely reorganized. It should be reoriented, in the committee's view, away from its punitive policing role, toward a more strongly based scientific, cooperative agency, aimed primarily at educating the consumer and gaining voluntary industry compliance.

Conceived as an agency to crack down on the more outrageous patent nostrums and adulterated foods flourishing at the turn of the century, the FDA is still heavily at it. Only last November, for instance, it reported the seizure of some apparatus called the Vivicosmic Disc, the Radiant Life Meter, and the Household Analysis Set, shipped by Radiant Laboratories out of Tum Tum, Washington. While such frauds still bulk large, they are now a relatively minor backwoods problem compared with the highly subtle ones posed by the enormous growth of modern drugs. "The statistics of FDA's enforcement activity," concluded the Kefauver committee report in 1961, "indicate that most of its effort is focused elsewhere than on the quality of ethical drugs." At the time of the thalidomide crisis, only a little over one-fourth of FDA's staff of 3,000 worked on drugs, and it is estimated that an additional 470 will be needed to handle the new drug regulations. But getting them is something else again. When a supplemental $2,600,000 was requested in 1962 for additional staff, Congress, which had just made a heroic play in voting the new law, turned down the request to implement it. And even if its budget were increased, FDA would still have difficulty getting the right kind of men. Its heavy quasi-legal cast and low federal pay have never made it attractive to outstanding medical men.

"IF THEY COME LIKE POLICE"

Seriously at question, too, is whether legislators and the FDA are competent to regulate in this new experimental area at all. One of the original proposals in Congress, which was revised in the final bill, was that all patients must be informed and their permission secured before a new drug could be tried on them. This proposal might seem a reasonable protection against using people as guinea pigs, but it not only would have violated the ancient discretionary rules of medical practice but also would have ruled out all scientific "blind" testing. Another regulation, in its original form, would have required clinical investigators to provide "complete" plans of their testing programs beforehand and to keep and make available to the FDA on request "complete" reports of their progress. Not only would this have put a straitjacket on experimentation, but it would have snowed investigators in report writing, leaving less and less time for research. After wide protest, "complete" was changed to "adequate," and other flexibilities introduced. But the final wording still allows the agency too much leeway in intervening in the long-sacrosanct, confidential, and confidence-building relationship between physician and patient.

What dismays a leading clinician like Dr. Irvine H. Page of the Cleveland Clinic Foundation, noted pioneer in the study and control of hypertension and associated heart diseases, is that the FDA made no effort to mobilize interested medical and scientific people before it put out the first-draft regulations. Only later were meetings held. Says Dr. Page: "Some of the regulations are unsophisticated and show little understanding of how clinical research works. If you're going to legislate these matters, you have to have firsthand knowledge of clinical testing—which means have you *done* any? What we need to have is a sufficiently knowledgeable group of men at the FDA, so that when something occurs they along with the clinical investigator can study the problem together, rather than turn it over to the political panic boys."

The major interest of most competent clinical investigators is research into the basic mechanism of a disease, and clinical testing of new drugs is only a part, a necessary but pedestrian part, of this research. Too close or officious administration of the new regulations will put off the competent men from clinical testing, leaving only the pedestrians. "If they start coming around like police," says Page, a blunt-spoken man, "they know what they can do with it."

THE MUDDLE AT THE HUB

The new law and FDA's new regulations almost entirely miss the main issue: how to get more competent clinical investigators and improved techniques into the testing of new drugs. This cannot be done by rote or by regulatory supervision. The best chance of catching the earliest subtle signs of harmful side effects, as well as leads to the improvement of drugs or techniques, is to have the clinical testing done by the best independent investigators in a field, men who have special background in a disease and expertise in testing. In this aspect of the situation, much is left to be desired.

The drug companies rely on a rather haphazard system of clinical testing, grown up over the years, into which they have so far put much less efficiency and money than into their chemical-pharmacological research and development. Of some $248 million spent all told by the industry on research and development last year, only $25 million went to research "outside the firms," i.e., mainly clinical testing. Most of this was in grants to hospital clinics, medical-research institutes, and universities. The doctor, who must be sought out to do the clinical testing because he has medical access to patients, is a more or less free agent attached to such an institution. He usually gets nothing directly out of the drug company's grant to his institution. In fact, he is given little incentive for doing this vital investigating job. Generally, since the drug is passed out to a number of investigators for testing simultaneously, he can expect little professional glory. And the whole matter of payment is an uneasy muddle, ranging from nothing at all to a luncheon, a check passed under the table, or a fee openly paid if his institution permits. The hunt for competent investigators willing to do testing under these conditions becomes feverish and open to abuse, with the jobs often going to the not-so-competent.

A MEETING OF MINDS LONG OVERDUE

In 1962 the Committee on Public Health of the New York Academy of Medicine issued a report calling for a strengthening of the whole clinical-testing system. It found that some drug companies seemed to regard mere possession of an M.D. or Ph.D. degree as sufficient to qualify a man as an expert in testing. It cited an AMA attempt, as long ago as 1946, to bring together qualified investigators and drug companies through its Council on Pharmacy and Chemistry, an attempt that quickly faded for lack of industry interest. It noted that to date no official or professional body has set or applied any professional standards for clinical testers. (In fact, it is only in recent years that clinical testing has begun to be taught as a separate discipline in some medical schools.) The new FDA regulations sidestep this issue because, quite properly, the FDA wanted to avoid interfering in medical practice by putting all responsibility for selecting "suitable experts" on the industry. But this leaves everything as before, with nothing to raise the standards of testing.

Page believes that two measures, if adopted by drug firms, could go far to get more competent testers. First, a clinical investigator should be given some priority in testing a new drug, particularly in the initial clinical phases. As he explains, a scientist not in industrial research generally gets his main reward and reputation from being first in a development; he finds no charm in doing what half a dozen other investigators are doing at the same time, under industry pressure to get quick and often superficial results. Second, an investigator should get some regular form of payment. Most top clinicians don't want to accept money from a company to test a drug, because they feel it would tie their hands as to objectivity, and because it wouldn't look objective to the outside world or to the profession. This stigma, Page suggests, might be removed by having the drug companies pay periodic sums into a general fund administered by the AMA, which would then pay investigators for this necessary work, with no specific company strings attached. But, ultimately, the whole final responsibility for testing new drugs rests on the medical profession, which must soon set some standards and find more efficient ways of using the available supply of competent clinical investigators.

So far there has been little meeting of minds between the medical profession and the pharmaceutical industry on clinical testing or on other great problems caused by the proliferation of modern drugs. An exchange of views among thoughtful leaders and the establishment of a common policy is long overdue. Where self-regulation does not clearly operate, government legislation, often bad legislation, moves in. Indeed, in this current attempt to carry regulation for the first time back into the intricate, uncertain by-paths of scientific experimentation and freedom of research, fraught as it is with matters of life and death, the benefits of the past may well be dissipated and those of the future jeopardized.

Embattled Tobacco's New Strategy* ───────

For 1962, stockholders of the R. J. Reynolds Tobacco Co., the largest U.S. cigarette maker, received an earning report quite unlike the reports they had grown accustomed to. From 1952 to 1961, Reynolds' earnings had improved every year. The stock had been split twice during the decade, the dividend had been increased eight different times, and Reynolds was established as one of the most dependable growth companies anywhere, in any industry. But in 1962, the report showed, earnings had declined slightly for the first nine months. Like its competitors, Reynolds

───────

* *January 1963*

is talking in a tone of concern these days. Its executive vice president, Spencer B. Hanes, in a recent address to a group of tobacco men, said grimly: "Fate has conspired to make this particular moment a testing time for tobacco. The industry is being ganged by many problems."

Observers in the investment community seem to agree. In July 1962, Bache & Co. recommended four leading tobacco stocks (American Tobacco, Lorillard, Philip Morris, and Reynolds) as good bets to outperform the market as a whole in the following twelve months. But in September, Bache reversed itself and said that their intermediate-term prospects had dimmed. A few weeks later, another Bache report rated the *long-term* prospects down too. Like many others, the cigarette stocks fell by 40 or 50 percent; but unlike many, they have scarcely recovered from their lows.

The chief reason for investors' lack of enthusiasm is obviously the steadily increasing attack on cigarette smoking (which accounts for nearly 90 percent of U.S. tobacco consumption) as a cause of lung cancer and other diseases. As Hanes suggested, the industry—on which Americans in 1962 spent nearly $8 billion— has other problems too, but none of them are as potentially devastating or as difficult to grapple with.

The problem in its present form dates from the early 1950's when studies correlating smoking and lung cancer first attracted nationwide attention. The latest round of troubles for cigarette manufacturers began in London in March 1962, when the Royal College of Physicians issued a report called "Smoking and Health." In its summary the report said: "Cigarette smoking is a cause of lung cancer, and bronchitis, and probably contributes to the development of coronary heart disease and various other less common diseases." The British Ministries of Health and Education followed this up with an intensive educational campaign against smoking, directed especially at young people. In the first several months of the campaign, sales of cigarettes in England dropped by an estimated 10 percent, though later a good part of the loss was recovered. There were echoes of the British action elsewhere in Europe. The Italian Government banned all cigarette advertising. A Danish commission issued a report linking smoking and cancer, and recommended restrictions on cigarette advertising.

BAD NEWS FROM LANCASTER

In the U.S. the industry was jolted badly in early October 1962 by an Air Force ruling that prohibited the free distribution of cigarettes to patients in its hospitals and clinics, and eliminated cigarettes from flight lunch boxes. In issuing his order, the Air Force Surgeon General declared that the "overwhelming evidence" linking cigarette smoking and lung cancer, pulmonary and cardio-vascular diseases could "no longer be ignored."

This would appear to be only the beginning, and the industry is now bracing itself for criticism from two other directions. The U.S. Surgeon General, with the President's approval, named an Advisory Committee on Smoking and Health. In an interview shortly after he was appointed, Executive Director Dr. Herman B. Kraybill told a reporter for his home-town newspaper in Pennsylvania that he believed current information "definitely suggests tobacco is a health hazard." This obscure interview in the Lancaster *Intelligencer Journal* was noted anxiously by cigarette executives all over the U.S. They are also on notice that the American Medical Association, after staying above the battle thus far, has commissioned a definitive study of smoking and health, and is preparing to take an official stand on the issue. When the U.S. and AMA studies are completed, the industry fears, they may become the basis for new federal laws or administrative regulations on the sale of cigarettes.

The industry's official view, as expressed through the Tobacco Industry Research Committee, is that tobacco's responsibility for lung cancer and other diseases has not been proved—that the evidence from statistical associations is suggestive only, and that as long as science has not yet discovered the actual causes of cancer, the public should not single out cigarettes for blame among the many possibilities under study. Joseph F. Cullman III, president of Philip Morris Inc., argued recently, "The cigarette habit is showing sustained growth. While I do not minimize the health question, I think that eventually cigarettes will be exonerated." The industry's viewpoint received a setback in November, however, when a federal district-court jury ruled in an important test case that Chesterfield cigarettes, made by Liggett & Myers

Tobacco Co., had been "one of the causes" of the lung cancer of a Pittsburgh carpenter. It was some consolation to the industry that the jury found the manufacturer not liable for damages, holding that the smoker, Otto Pritchard, had knowingly assumed the risk of injury by his heavy smoking.

PUFFING HARD FOR PROFITS

Meanwhile, there is no doubt that the health controversy is having an adverse effect on sales. After the industry recovered from the first cancer scare of 1953–54, unit sales of cigarettes in the U.S. (the figures include sales to U.S. forces overseas) increased around 3 or 4 percent a year through 1961. Last year, however, according to a preliminary estimate by the U.S. Department of Agriculture, the gain was only 1.8 percent, to a total of almost 512 billion cigarettes.

Profits have been hit even harder by the antismoking campaigns, for they have forced the companies to adopt some costly counterstrategies. This can be seen in an analysis of the five publicly owned cigarette companies: Reynolds, American, Lorillard, Liggett & Myers, Philip Morris. Taken together, on the basis of preliminary estimates for 1962, they show a combined *fall* in profits of at least 1 percent, despite a 2.5 percent increase in dollar sales, and also despite the cumulative effect of some important economies on the production line. The industry as a whole has increased its cigarette output 27 percent in the last ten years while the production work force has remained about the same size. There have also been new economies in tobacco utilization, which are important because leaf costs are the biggest single item of cost in manufacturing cigarettes. (Reynolds attributed its decline in profits to higher leaf costs, but this must have been a special and temporary problem, for average prices at auction in 1962 were lower than in 1961.) Some of the new economies are associated with the increased market for filter cigarettes, which now command 55 percent of the market. Filters obviously use less tobacco than non-filters of the same length, and the saving on the tobacco more than offsets the cost of the filter itself. Less obvious to the smoker, perhaps, filters sometimes use cheaper grades of leaf, which have a stronger taste, so that the smoker will get more flavor despite the filter. In addition, in making many types of cigarettes, manufacturers now are equipped to use parts of the tobacco leaf that once were considered waste. All told, and despite the increased popularity of the king size, manufacturers today need about 15 percent less tobacco for an average cigarette than they did a decade ago.

It is the bigger outlays for advertising that have bitten most deeply into profits. A lot of these outlays have been made to promote new brands that the companies brought out in the wake of the health scare: the six major manufacturers, which offered twenty-five brands in 1953, now offer thirty-six. The cost of establishing the new brands, and devising new marketing strategies for the old ones, has been considerable. In 1961 the industry spent some $171 million for advertising of all tobacco products, according to an estimate by the Television Bureau of Advertising. Preliminary estimates indicate that the advertising bill for 1962 will show an increase of 5 to 10 percent over 1961—i.e., a lot more than the rise in unit sales. Hence the "per carton" cost of advertising, which has averaged around 6 cents for several years, according to *Advertising Age,* is rising.

"NOBODY YOUNG WORRIES MUCH"

Before going further into the special sales problems that arise out of the present climate of criticism, it will pay to have a glance at the market's potentialities. There is one area, at least, in which the industry can apparently look forward to a substantial increase. This is among the teenagers.

There has not been a national census of smoking habits since 1955, but several regional studies show that teenagers have not been much impressed by any anti-smoking campaigns. Dr. Daniel Horn, consultant to the American Cancer Society, who has made special studies of teenage smoking, says that one high-school student in three is now a regular cigarette smoker, and that by graduation 44 percent of seniors smoke regularly—i.e., they are not far behind the percentage for the entire population. According to Gilbert Youth Research, Inc., smoking by teenagers in general (all those thirteen through nineteen) has risen sharply in the past two years, from 25 percent two years ago to 35 percent last year. Their prevailing view about the health issue is epitomized in the comment of one Oregon high-school student: "Nobody young worrries much about some disease they might get forty or fifty years from now."[1]

In the period 1960–65, the total smoking-age population—i.e., all those fifteen and over—is rising by a little more than 8 percent. At present, just about half of this over-fifteen group (60 percent of the men, 38 percent of the women) smoke cigarettes, with an average consumption of just over one pack a day. Applying these rates to the 1965 smoking-age population suggests unit sales then of over 540 billion; extending the calculation to 1970 gets the figure up to 585 billion. That would mean a 1.8 percent annual growth rate for the rest of the decade.

Actually, the rate might be higher than that, and indeed the industry expects it to be: it is counting on something like 555 billion cigarettes by 1965 and 650 billion by 1970. For one thing, the over-fifteen population will be more heavily weighted than it is now with men and women at the younger end of the age band, who tend to smoke most. Teenagers themselves ordinarily start off as light smokers, but they step up their consumption considerably when they get into their twenties. Between 1960 and 1970 the population aged twenty to twenty-nine will rise by 39 percent.

In addition to these demographic factors, the industry also appears to be counting on a resumption of the long-term increase in smoking per capita. But here there may be trouble; for if the teenagers seem unimpressed by the health scare, it is plain that some older consumers are worried plenty and have, in fact, cut their smoking down—or out. Their concern is shown in numerous samplings, not to mention the evidence of everyday life. A survey of Massachusetts doctors showed that over a recent five-year period there was a sharp increase in the number who did not smoke, from 34 percent in 1954 to 45 percent in 1959; the trend away from cigarettes was particularly marked among doctors who smoked a pack a day or more. The American Cancer Society, in a national sampling of over 43,000 people in 1959–60, found

---

[1] But in New York City the Cancer Society reported some success for its education efforts among high-school students. Almost half of several hundred student smokers polled at Morris High School said that a film and recording on cancer danger had impressed them and that they would consider abandoning cigarettes.

that those of higher education and those in professions (teachers, lawyers, doctors, dentists, veterinarians, and clergymen) are more likely to have quit smoking than other groups. For instance, among men thirty to thirty-nine the survey found that 23 percent of college graduates had quit smoking, vs. 16 percent of those who had no high-school education; among men fifty to fifty-nine, 38 percent of college graduates were ex-smokers, vs. 27 percent of those who did not attend high school.

A clear indication that *some* sizable groups are cutting out smoking lies in the fact that last year the estimated proportion of smokers among those over fifteen years of age was unchanged from 1961. This was the first time since the cancer scare of the early 1950's that the proportion did not rise. The fact that it evidently remained stationary, at a time when the smoking-age population was becoming more heavily weighted with younger groups, is a bad sign for the industry.

Another of its concerns these days is that some of those younger groups, even if unworried about health, might have their smoking restricted by new laws—or new enforcement of old laws. Most states have laws banning the sale of cigarettes to minors, with age limits beginning at fifteen, but these laws are largely unenforced. The cigarette industry admits to no responsibility for backing up law enforcement in this respect, taking the position that manufacturers have no control over what happens to their product after it gets into wholesale and retail channels, and that smoking by minors is a matter to be handled by family discipline and local law-enforcement officials. Meanwhile, cigarette ads often portray and seem to be pitched directly at young people.

Enforcing the age rule on cigarette sales would, of course, be just about impossible while so many sales are made via vending machines in unsupervised locations. In Britain, one tobacco company has voluntarily withdrawn vending machines from unsupervised spots. In this country, no one has shown much concern about the problem; Chicago is one of the few cities that have banned unsupervised machines.

Several threats of broader kinds of regulation also hang over the industry. Bills have been offered in Congress that would, among other things, impose restrictions on cigarette advertising or require the tar and nicotine content of cigarettes to be specified by the manufacturer on the label. The Federal Trade Commission is studying these propositions, but will probably not act until it has at least seen the report of the Surgeon General's committee.

THREE FRAGMENTS OF A MARKET

With the boundaries of the market no longer growing so fast, at least temporarily, and some danger of increased regulation, the cigarette companies have been obliged to step up the pace of their marketing efforts and alter the tone of their sales pitch. Yet in a very real way the men who plan all this expensive new marketing must operate in the dark, for they are dealing with taste, in its nature hard to foresee and frequently shifting; and dealing with fears that are immeasurable and often unadmitted. The smoking public wants a pleasurable taste and also wants safety, but its ideas about the cigarettes that can deliver these are endlessly various. To make matters worse, there seems to be a kind of intrinsic conflict between safety and taste—i.e., the better the taste the more tar and nicotine the cigarette is apt to deliver. Which way, then, will consumers turn?

The not very surprising answer is that they have turned in several different directions; and the companies' effort to keep up with them is what has fragmented the market. Essentially, it is divided today into three parts.

• Filter-tip cigarettes, presumably appealing to the smokers most concerned about health, now have 55 percent of unit sales (vs. only 1.4 percent ten years ago). More than 35 million smokers have *switched* to filters. Within the filter market, there has been a rising demand for mentholated cigarettes; for many customers, apparently, the menthol taste supplies the "kick" that would otherwise be lost in the filtering. About a quarter of the filter market—and a seventh of the entire market—is taken up by mentholated cigarettes. Reynolds' Salem today dominates this market with 16 percent of all filter sales—i.e., it has 62 percent of all mentholated sales. Among the unmentholated filters, the sales leaders have been Reynolds' Winston (22 percent of all filter sales) and Lorillard's Kent (13 percent).

• The second major market created in recent years is for non-filter king-sized cigarettes, which now have some 20 percent of all sales. Some customers may be attracted to kings by their apparent economy; but the kings' basic appeal seems to be to smokers who are concerned about health, and are therefore receptive to the argument that tobacco itself filters the smoke if the cigarette is long enough. But many of these smokers then lose the filtration afforded by the extra length when they smoke the king down to the butt. This argument has been most effectively employed by American Tobacco's Pall Mall, which overwhelmingly dominates the non-filter-king market, with 72 percent of its sales (it is the single most popular brand of any kind). Said an executive of Philip Morris, which has had little success with its Commander king, "We thought there was a king-size market; it turned out to be only a Pall Mall market." It is significant that Pall Mall's greatest growth has been since the early 1950's, when the health scares began.

• The third market today is for the "regulars"—so called because they once accounted for virtually all cigarette sales, and as recently as 1952 for 80 percent. Today they have 25 percent. The market is dominated by Reynolds' Camels, with 52 percent of "regular" sales.

In the new, fragmented market, the manufacturers must ordinarily pinpoint the customers they are going after, and the recent records show that there have been a lot of expensive misses. (The special promotion cost involved in launching a new brand usually run around $10 million.) Among the more spectacular casualties: Riviera, American's 1959 bid for an entry in the menthol market; Hit Parade, its 1956 effort to crack the non-menthol filter market; and Kentucky Kings, a 1960 effort by Brown & Williamson in the non-filter-king market.

Occasionally, it appears, a new brand can edge its way into an already crowded market by cleverly promoting a gimmick. Marlboro was helped to success by its flip-top hard box, now widely imitated in the trade; and Brown & Williamson now has a clutch of packaging gimmicks—notably a slide-top box and a "flat fifties" package for Viceroy and an aluminum-foil package for its new king-size Coronet.

A QUESTION OF TASTE

While they are trying to pinpoint the individual targets of their advertising campaigns, the manufacturers also seem agreed on certain basic themes that the industry as a whole should—and should not—be striking these days. Partly by inclination, and partly because of government pressure, the cigarette companies have recently dropped just about all health claims from their advertising. Nowadays the dominant theme in all advertising is "the pleasure of smoking." No attempt is being made to meet the medical charges made against cigarettes. Gone from the ads are those doctors in white coats lecturing gravely on the protection of the T-zone, or comparing droplets of tar from the sponsor's cigarettes with jugfuls of sticky stuff from "Brand X." The filter tips got their start with a rash of such hard-sell advertising (e.g., "they're just what the doctor ordered"). But then, it appears, the manufacturers slowly realized that they were impugning their own product. Herbert Leggett, in one of his widely read commentaries for the Valley National Bank of Phoenix, Arizona, jolted many cigarette executives when he wrote of the so-called "tar derby": "Never before has an industry spent so much money trying to talk itself out of business. The 'commercials' keep reminding us that tobacco contains tars, resins, and other bronchial abrasives. Smokers are quite obviously committing slow suicide, but each brand claims that its own product is somewhat *less lethal* than other brands." In 1955 the Federal Trade Commission issued "guides" for advertising, which banned any filter claims not supported by scientific proof. The "tar derby" broke out again, however, when several companies brought out brands that were "proved" to have "ultra high filtration." In 1960 the FTC ended the argument by telling all manufacturers flatly: "There will be no more tar and nicotine claims in cigarette advertising." The brand hardest hit by the edict was Brown & Williamson's Life, which had especially stirred the FTC's ire with ads implying that its claims for filter efficiency were based on government figures. Perhaps because of the publicity given the FTC assault on this claim, Life has been lifeless ever since.

Nowadays, all allusions to the health question are models of indirection. Lorillard, for example, has developed a new type of filter and has claimed in press releases that it will remove from tobacco smoke up to 90 percent of the phenols, which are among the cancer suspects. Yet nothing has ever been said of this in ads for Kents, which endlessly urge you to "Treat your taste kindly with Kent . . . new Micronite filter" (never explaining what is new about it). Newport "refreshes while you smoke," Winston "tastes good," L & M gives you "lots more," Marlboro has "the unfiltered taste," Viceroy the "taste that's right." Luckies still taste "great," Camels are a "real" cigarette, and Parliaments give you "extra margin," though of what is not too clear. Tareyton has a dual filter, but no special claim is made for it, and the emphasis is on "flavor you never thought you'd get." Reynolds' new Brandon has an equally mysterious filter; its cigarette "tastes so mild you think it *has* a filter—tastes so rich you know it *doesn't*." Chesterfield provides only "twenty wonderful smokes." . . .

IN SEARCH OF AN ARGUMENT

All the companies' approaches to the cigarette market today suggest that they are trying, though with varied success, to "live with" the new problems created by the health issue. In one way or another, they are trying to gain positions in the expanding filter and king-size markets while shoring up as best they can the older "regular" market. However, the companies have not as yet tried any of several more ambitious approaches that appear to be open to them.

In 1954, after health first became a big issue, tobacco manufacturers, growers, and warehousemen set up the Tobacco Industry Research Committee to finance scientific studies of the links, if any, between smoking and various illnesses, especially lung cancer and heart disease. TIRC retained Dr. Clarence Cook Little, a leading geneticist, as its scientific director, appointed a scientific advisory board of other distinguished specialists, and also provided funds for research grants—a total of $5,450,000 through 1962—as the industry's contribution to the broad national effort in this field. After eight years, TIRC's official position on the health issue, as summarized in the latest annual report by Dr. Little, is this: "The origin of lung cancer is complex and still obscure. There probably are many contributing factors."

The renewed pressure on the health issue has inevitably spawned some criticism of the modest scope of the industry's research effort. The research funds provided for TIRC represent less than 1 percent of the industry's $170-million annual advertising expenditures. TIRC's $800,000 appropriation for 1963 is about half of what the much smaller German cigarette industry is spending currently on cancer research. Is the U.S. industry spending enough? Dr. Little says that the problem is not money, but finding relevant new leads to pursue. On the other hand, several leaders of the industry think it might be wise to double the funds for cancer research. Some of them also think that the industry should be facing the health problem more directly. For example, Philip Morris' Cullman would acknowledge the health danger but argue that there are offsetting advantages, "pharmacological and psychological," to smoking.

Another proposal, heard more outside the industry than in it, is that the FTC ban on health claims in cigarette advertising be scrapped, in order to encourage cigarette companies to develop more efficient ways of reducing the tar and nicotine content in cigarettes. As it is now, even if a company should develop the world's most efficient filter it would not be allowed to say so in its advertising. One way or another, it seems likely that the industry will be publicly taking more notice of its largest problem.

part 4

DEFENSE AND SPACE: THE
BIGGEST BUSINESSES OF ALL

GOVERNMENT IS not only regulator and promoter; its original and continuing purpose is that of protector against outside enemies. Today in the United States more than half the national government budget, and about 10 percent of the gross national product, is devoted to the task of providing for defense. A growing effort is also found in the space program, with its mission combining defense and peace. These two massive programs provide major markets for much of what American industry produces; at the same time the scientific effort brings about changes in industrial technology and organization. In the semi-free markets in which contractors deal with government procurement officers, the ground rules of competition do not apply, nor are the old divisions into public and private spheres useful ways to classify what is being done in the economy and in society.

"No Business Like Defense Business" makes clear in a few words why private and public standards of efficiency are not comparable. However, Defense Secretary McNamara has been carrying out a revolution in defense procurement, using many techniques of the professional manager. He has been working to reduce waste by utilizing programs of cost effectiveness and commonality, while cutting back on sole source buying. In dealing with McNamara's department, the contractor's powers of innovation are stretched to the utmost, while he is offered a greatly expanded horizon of profitability.

209

A President's attitudes on defense concepts and strategies determine his views toward defense spending. While President Johnson took a hard-line stand on U.S. military power before taking office, his views on defense are still emerging. President Eisenhower chose to invest on the side of strategic technological advantage, while President Kennedy prepared heavily for conventional warfare. The costly Kennedy buildup of conventional forces, which resulted in increasingly cautious investment in the more speculative military technologies, is re-examined in "The Desperate Drive to Cut Defense Spending."

"The Defense Industry Is Facing Trouble" with the continuing downturn in procurement and its impact on major contractors. There are no new massive programs looking toward further experiment, invention, and production taking shape. There is anxiety over how to hold together the unique bodies of engineering and scientific talents the military prime contractors began to assemble a decade or so ago when the tide of technological innovation was on the rise. Not all experts are sure that we have reached a plateau in our invention and development of weapons, or that we can afford to relinquish the lead in space and military technologies, yet clearly changes in the structure of the defense industry will affect the nation's capacity for action.

Space exploration, meanwhile, is experiencing the greatest mobilization of scientific knowledge and effort, and the results are tremendously fruitful both industrially and socially. The cost is stupendous, but the outflow of ideas is also very great. The immediate effect has been to change the pattern of business profoundly. This is the first paramilitary effort in history not accompanied by a demand for heavy hardware and mass-produced materials. Its great demand is for hard-to-find professional people, and in the long run this will be a prime force in increasing the U.S. scientific and professional population. It will also accelerate greatly the tendency of U.S. business to depend more and more on research and development, and eventually change the organizational structure of industry.

*No Business Like Defense Business**   _____

EDITORIAL NOTE

The notorious inefficiency of the Defense Department has become, over the years, the despair of budget-balancers, and almost a staple of humor among businessmen thrown into contact with the department. Why is it so hard to cut the Pentagon's fat away? One interesting answer is supplied by Herman Kahn, who is a consultant to the Defense Department on a wide range of strategic problems, and who is the author of a volume called *On Thermonuclear War,* published by Princeton University Press. In one of many arresting passages, Kahn argues the case for inefficiency in Defense—or rather, the case that the department's standards of efficiency cannot fairly be compared to those of a private business. He invites the department's critics to imagine themselves in this position:

"They are made responsible for the operation of all aspects of a business and must make all the decisions; but they are to make them in a curious environment. They are told in only the most approximate and casual way what things cost and when they will be available, often by people who are actually trying to mislead them; in any case, nobody really knows. They are not told what items 'sell' [i.e., what items will please their purchasers when put to use]. They are not told what items will cause extreme dissatisfaction among customers. They have to deduce these things by reading records of what similar stores sold ten or twenty years ago and by making some general and purely theoretical calculations . . . Nevertheless, they have to order merchandise years in advance. . . .

"Finally, this business makes most of its money on a sale day which occurs once every decade or two at a time unknown to the management. The management does have a signal on the

_____

* *February 1961*

morning of the sale that *this is the day*. This helpful signal consists of leading competitors coming into the store, breaking up all
the equipment, shooting most of the help and generally causing
as much damage as they can.

"In the circumstances under which this business is operated,
it is quite likely that there will be some minor inefficiencies. . . ."

In Defense of the Defense Secretary* _____

EDITORIAL

If anything was predictable when Defense Secretary McNamara
shot down the military's unanimous decision in the award of the
potential $7-billion contract for the TFX bi-service fighter,[1] it was
that *his* decision would run into political flak from Capitol Hill.
And understandably so. Nobody knows better than Senators and
Congressmen that politics and big defense projects frequently fly
wing to wing in the cold-war epoch of permanent mobilization,
and it behooves Congress to have its radar working all the time.
But Secretary McNamara's anguished protestations are understandable, too. Nothing less than a revolution is afoot in defense
procurement, and prolonged debate over a particular contract,
even the biggest one in history, misses the fundamental point.

The revolution springs from the plain fact that modern weaponry requires vast commitments of U.S. resources. The corollary,
of course, is that mistaken commitments impose staggering penalties, which impair the economy and weaken national security. The
main force compelling change in outlook and procedure is rapidly
advancing technology. Weapons now must be designed, and
commitments made, on the basis of projected future environments,
materials, and techniques beyond the exclusive purview of any
single service. The development of an atomic airplane, at a cost
of more than a billion dollars, and the air-launched Skybolt missile,
at a cost of $500 million, were undertaken on the basis of short-

_____
* *April 1963*
[1] Subsequently renamed the F-111. [*Editor's Note*]

sighted assumptions about the future of manned aircraft. The cancellation of these weapons underscores the need for a new order of prescience and a new set of disciplines in defense procurement.

Despite the Defense Secretary's deserved reputation as a mover and shaker, he is actually steering the inevitable. How far he will go and what system he will finally erect are legitimate subjects for informed debate. But his direction has been foreordained by mounting pressures and the weight of experience. His guiding concept of "cost effectiveness" merely asserts the lesson of Skybolt and other costly errors of judgment: given the pace of change and the scope of commitments, the costs of weapons and their military effectiveness are interdependent. His evolving techniques of management and control, while arguable in degree and emphasis, recognize the need to overhaul a system clearly in danger of going out of control.

The traditional system of defense procurement is founded on separate budgeting of separate and competing military services. Companies and even entire industries came to draw close to individual services, and from the collaboration of civilian and military experts flowed a stream of weapons that won major wars and preserved the peace. This relationship, at the working levels, should be preserved for the impressive accomplishments it produces. But a harmful byproduct of such collaboration has been the aggressive pursuit of parochial goals. Enlisting powerful political support, the military and their industrial partners sometimes have sought new weapon systems more to enhance service prestige and win contracts than to protect U.S. security. President Eisenhower will not soon forget the hurtful "missile gap" propaganda, which got a big boost from a contract-hungry manufacturer with an obsolescent missile to sell. The painful and corrosive influence of the military-industrial alliance, in the absence of an effective countervailing force, moved Eisenhower to sound his remarkable farewell warning: "We must never let the weight of this combination endanger our liberties or democratic processes."

THE NON-SYSTEM

On taking office, Secretary McNamara and his civilian aides were unimpressed by the monolithic potential of the military-industrial complex, which seemed more apparent than real because of internal stresses and divisions. But they *were* impressed by the demonstrated capacity for waste. Interservice rivalry had produced alarming proliferation of smaller weapons and duplicate installations. In practice, the prevailing system was a non-system. The individual services were buying weapons on the traditional criterion of improved performance (i.e., the biggest, the fastest, the most destructive), and alert contractors, heeding the time-honored rules, were prospering by selling better performance at steeply rising costs. A contractor with a feasible-looking idea had little difficulty "buying into" a service budget with an attractively low bid. His understated costs were routinely made up on overruns, which routinely ran as high as *ten* times the original cost.

In 1962, McNamara launched a five-year cost-reduction program, aiming at a saving of $3 billion annually in logistical costs. His first step was to impose on the services (and the contractors) a rounded concept of defense, in which missions were defined without regard for cherished but inefficient service prerogatives.

Under the gun of "cost effectiveness" duplicate weapons are being thinned out. Fewer, larger weapon systems, subject to close top-level supervision, are coming in. New emphasis is being given to what McNamara calls "the pencil stage" of weapon development, in which the military must define with unprecedented precision what they seek and why. A key tenet of the Secretary's "cost effectiveness" program is the design of weapons with a high degree of "commonality," which meet the *minimum* specifications of more than one of the services.

As in the design of the bi-service TFX, cost becomes critical only *after* the minimum specifications of a major new weapon have been hammered out; then the pounding is unmerciful. Improvements in the performance of weapons that satisfy service taste, beyond essential requirements, come under the McNamara heading of "gold-plating." Taking a jet fighter's specifications to illustrate his point, McNamara notes than an improvement from mach 2 to mach 2.1 is a gain of 5 percent in improvement, but it may boost costs 20 percent. Evidence of the success of McNamara's economy drive thus far is the fact that operating and hardware expenditures are currently running some $2 billion below early estimates.

"BREAKING OUT" THE PARTS

The Secretary believes that competition as a spur to economy has not been given sufficient scope. Some esoteric components must necessarily be purchased from the few companies making them, but McNamara is cutting back the use of "sole source" buying. Instead of automatically reordering common but expensive components from the producer of an assembled device, the procurement officers are "breaking out" the parts and seeking competitive bids. The part, purchased separately, commonly costs 25 to 50 percent less than it did in the assembled package. By 1965, says the Secretary, almost $2 billion is to be shifted from sole source to competitive buying, at an annual saving of $500 million.

Perhaps the most dramatic move in McNamara's ambitious program is away from cost-plus-fixed-fee contracts, in which the contractor's profit is fixed in advance and is unaffected by his performance. On McNamara's arrival, cost-plus contracts accounted for 37 percent of all new prime contracts; the proportion is currently under 27 percent, and the goal of the five-year program is 12.3 percent, which will cover mainly advanced research and development projects. A rough but conservative estimate by the department places the saving in the change-over from cost-plus to incentive contracts at 10 percent. Hence the planned shift of $6 billion by fiscal 1965 is expected to yield an annual saving of at least $600 million.

PEERING OVER SHOULDERS

To realize economies of this magnitude, McNamara has taken giant steps toward a new managerial capability for the Pentagon, and here is the heart of the revolution in procurement. The TFX competition illustrated the new demands "cost effectiveness" will make on the military and the contractors. First came the military's agony of agreement on the minimum specifications; then the exhaustive analysis-in-depth of cost and engineering data submitted by would-be contractors, and finally the brain-twisting runoff between two leaders. All these exertions came in *advance,* as opposed to the former system in which feasibility was sufficient to flash the green light. Backup programs, as in the use of the Titan missile as a backup for the Atlas, are now an impossible luxury. New weapons must work well the first time.

Unprecedented preplanning of weapons is succeeded by close surveillance of every stage of a contract's fulfillment. Using the PERT system and other controls, the Pentagon will peer over the contractor's shoulder at every step, keeping tabs on production and costs. So profound is the impact of this new scrutiny than an executive at General Dynamics/Astronautics has proposed a reorganization of management around the key decision points on the PERT chart. He reasons that the pyramidical organization structure, originally inherited from the military, is in conflict with the whole PERT theory. It is a symbolic observation.

Yet if McNamara's managerial controls force the contractor to stretch his powers of innovation to the utmost to deliver advanced, reliable weapons at firm costs, the new system also expands his horizon of profitability. For the Defense Department, following up a movement begun late in the Eisenhower Administration, is using incentive contracts with new boldness. These contracts vary in detail, but mainly call for either lump-sum (fixed fee) payment, or a sliding scale of payments (or penalties) adjusted to performance. Before a contract is signed, weeks and even months will be spent in a contractor's plant or one of the Defense Department's seventy-eight major procurement offices, analyzing cost projections, weighing past performance, and negotiating the terms of payment. The Navy and Newport News Shipbuilding Co. required nine months, in which a team from the Bureau of Ships bore down on 4,500 "cost centers," to work out the final contract for the nuclear-powered aircraft carrier *Enterprise*. Now undergoing final trials, the *Enterprise* is expected to come in well under the target price of $209 million (which in turn was well under the original estimated cost), and that means maximum profit for Newport News.

The range of profit potential in incentive contracts formerly was unexciting; a very good job or a very poor one caused relatively little fluctuation in the contractor's return. In contrast, consider the contract recently awarded to Space Technology Laboratories, Inc., of Redondo Beach, California, which calls for ten satellites to monitor nuclear explosions in space. The target fee (or profit) for the $13,900,000 project is 7.75 percent, but depending on STL's cost control, performance, and time of delivery, the fee can nose-dive to 0.55 percent or soar to 14.95 percent. As novel as the wide profit swing is the use of an incentive contract on a project of this sort: although the end result sought is new, many of the components are not, and a departure from the customary cost-plus deal promised a better job.

THE NEED FOR COUNTERPRESSURE

Contractors are understandably chary of some of McNamara's changes, and in some sectors will probably have to find ways to counter his pressures if this is to be a system they can live with. For one thing they fear that unrealistically low cost targets may make adequate returns a mirage. Under the present system aircraft manufacturers, for example, have no way of knowing whether overzealous Defense Department negotiators are driving them far below competitors' bids. To build up a counterforce, the Aerospace Industries Association has commissioned Stanford Research Institute to assemble industry cost data for use in contract negotiations. A deeper problem lies in the transition of the defense industry from hardware production to emphasis on design. How shall profits be measured? Measurement as a percentage of invested capital or sales is outmoded when companies are applying more and more brainpower to less and less hardware. A new yardstick should be devised to relate profits to the industry's investment in creative capability.

In the most extreme formulation of the industry's new problems, the changing environment seems destined to imprison contractors. An executive of an aerospace corporation reflects: "It is apparent we are a captive industry. We can only retain the old customer relationship in a few areas, for example, when something brand-new turns up and the entrepreneur is able to take the risk. But most weapons are so expensive that we cannot risk our own funds in their development." The projected development cost of the TFX, a fantastic $1.1 billion, appears to seal the gloomy prospect.

Revolutions have a way of making former days look better than they ever were, until the possibilities of change are grasped. Secretary McNamara cannot begin to develop the in-house capability to make the defense industry truly captive. Nor can he sensibly attempt to stifle competition in weapon concepts, both among the services and individual corporate technical staffs or combinations thereof. A key weapon in the Secretary's own strategic design—the Polaris missile—might not have been developed if the Navy had not married its unique experience to new technology. In terms of technical experience and capability, both the military and the defense industry will remain superior to the Pentagon's civilian chiefs. Where they must catch up, and they are doing so, is in the area of advanced management techniques.

It remains for McNamara to demonstrate beyond doubt that the disciplines he is imposing are not arbitrary. The revolution he is guiding has brought predictable outcries that he is downrating military advice, which the TFX investigation has amplified to an angry roar. The Secretary may safely dismiss the particular occasion of these outbursts if he observes the general proposition that war remains a professional's calling. McNamara is a manager by profession, and a superb one. And he will keep the nation's respect so long as his judgments reflect full awareness that the purpose of the world's biggest business is not mainly to procure, but to protect.

The Desperate Drive to Cut Defense Spending*

CHARLES J. V. MURPHY

Ever since President Johnson proclaimed thrift and frugality as the watchwords of his Administration, the Pentagon has been ablaze with light well into the midnight watch. In the past such a glow along the Potomac has been interpreted by Washingtonians as a signal that international trouble was brewing. This time, however, the emergency was of an entirely different kind. It was, as they say there, "an in-house flap" produced by the President's rapid decision to halt the prolonged upsurge in defense costs.

The total fiscal outlook had become a matter of special concern

* *January 1964*

to Johnson immediately after his succession to office. Since defense in the aggregate (including nuclear weaponry) is taking 60 percent of the entire federal revenue, and since the volume of defense spending has been rising faster than have outlays in the civilian sectors of the budget (excluding space), it was obvious to him that any significant curtailment of government expenditures had to begin with a rollback at the Pentagon.

Unlike Presidents Kennedy and Eisenhower at the outset of their administrations, Johnson needed no introduction to his Secretary of Defense. In past months Johnson had listened respectfully, even admiringly, while Robert S. McNamara ran through the countdown of the now famous cost-reduction programs, incentive contracts, and the techniques of systems analysis that he has put in train throughout his vast department. Johnson has also long been familiar with the Secretary's impressive tables and graphs testifying to his persistent efforts to extract an ever higher military content from every dollar of the billions that flow through his hands. Yet, when seen in the perspective of the spending rate itself, all the charts and all the careful projections were in fact little more than evidence of McNamara's desperate struggle against a rising tide of costs that had begun to engulf him, as in the past it engulfed his predecessors. . . .

Here it is important to note that the confrontations of Johnson and the defense budget was more than a passing encounter between a personality and columns of figures. The new President was actually taking a closer look at defense concepts and strategies that did not necessarily express his own views. Thus these views were likely to be as influential in setting the guidelines for his programs of defense spending—and cuts—as his better-advertised commitment to frugality.

A RESPECT FOR PROFESSIONALS

There has never been any question about Johnson's stand where U.S. military power is concerned. He has steadily been for and continues to be for—as he emphatically reiterated in his November 1963 address to Congress—"military strength second to none." Practically everybody is for that, of course. Still, when Johnson uses the term, he means something beyond the timeworn platitude. By strength second to none he means strength that the

professional military leadership—and not only the civilian planners in the Pentagon—will certify as such. He has entered the
White House, moreover, after an education in the political ends
of high strategy and the means and doctrines of force that no
other President in the twentieth century, save General Dwight
Eisenhower and, in a much simpler world, Theodore Roosevelt,
even began to match.

As a Senator, he was a member of the Armed Services Committee and chairman of the influential Senate Preparedness Subcommittee that was created, during the Korean war, to act as
watchdog over the military procurement process. As Vice President, he was outranked only by Kennedy on the National Security
Council and he presided over the National Aeronautics and Space
Council. By reason of these overlapping experiences and responsibilities, he was already very much at home, before he moved into
the White House, with the highly specialized, highly secret matters that bear so heavily on the national security. In fact, valuing
as he does experience in the management of forces, his visible
respect and liking for the military professionals has at times sur-
passed his enthusiasm for the procession of Defense Secretaries—
there have been seven all together, not counting McNamara—
who passed before his legislative eye.

Johnson has not always felt at home with the policies, let alone
the policy makers, that he now commands. In the New Frontier's
remarkable three-year encounter with world affairs, the policy
advisers ranged around President Kennedy were divided into
several contending factions. One consisted of the hard-nosed,
skeptical individuals of conservative bent, who were opposed, by
and large, to attempting business with the Soviet Union unless
the terms were brassbound and copper-riveted. Another faction
was made up of self-styled "rationalists." By and large, they were
convinced that a *détente* with Russia could be brought off with
mollifying, even though somewhat hazardous, concessions in the
power position of the West. Somewhere in between were the
real decision makers, grouped around Kennedy himself, who
called themselves pragmatists. They thought of action in the world
struggle as a sequence of limited chess moves, and their action
words were "flexibility," "options," "wider choice," and a U.S.
response to challenge that would be "measured," or "controlled,"
or "graduated." Among these factions Lyndon Johnson was known
as a hard-liner.

WHEN JOHNSON STOOD FIRM

His position came dramatically into view during the historic debate around Kennedy over the course of action to be taken after the discovery of Soviet rockets in Cuba in October 1962. The debate went on for nearly a week, and Johnson, on a campaigning assignment in Hawaii during the first day of discussion, was late getting into it. When he was made privy to the gravity of the Soviet action, he spoke up for a decisive response. Not only the rockets, but the Soviet troops as well, had to be removed, and by force if necessary—so ran Johnson's advice. The American people, he argued, would never accept anything less. But the rationalists pulled harder, for a while, on Kennedy than was generally appreciated. There was serious deliberation over the question of a *quid pro quo* with Khrushchev. Should the demand for his retreat from Cuba be linked with an offer to open political talks on other matters at issue, including Berlin? Wouldn't the U.S. have a better case before world opinion if, in return for the withdrawal of Soviet rockets from Cuba, American rockets were pulled out of Italy and Turkey?

Gradually, the middle-course counsel of the men who stayed on as Johnson's principal instruments in the struggle with Soviet power—most conspicuously Secretary of State Dean Rusk and Defense Secretary McNamara—shaped the decision. The practical consequence of the decision was the partial blockade of Cuba, combined with a great show of force as for the invasion of Cuba, and Kennedy's own partly stern, partly conciliatory private diplomacy with Premier Khrushchev.

For his part, Johnson never wavered from his original conviction. The apprehensions among some of Kennedy's closest advisers that Russia would counter a U.S. blow against Cuba with a salvo of rockets against the U.S. seemed to him to be groundless. His confidence in the American capacity for decisive and salutary action—a confidence that was based on his direct knowledge of the forces in being—remained unshaken. By his lights, the migration of Soviet military power into the Western Hemisphere could not be tolerated. Johnson took his stand on the historic meaning of the Monroe Doctrine, holding that its breaching, if condoned, would undermine the new Alliance for Progress and damage U.S. prestige throughout the world. And he was further troubled by a settlement that would leave Fidel Castro in unscathed command of Cuba.

Johnson was not alone in believing these things. Although General Maxwell Taylor, the Chairman of the Joint Chiefs of Staff, was inclined to the McNamara-Rusk middle course, the other service chiefs saw eye to eye with Johnson. So did the director of the Central Intelligence Agency, John A. McCone. They were a minority, however, and after the die had been cast for the middle course, one of the Kennedy men, in an aside directed at the Johnson position, made a cold remark that sensitive memories have tended to blur since the change at the White House. According to one who was within earshot, it was to the effect that, in the rational shaping of policy, "Courage is no substitute for intelligence." This was the kind of gliding, epigrammatic half-insult that Johnson is ill equipped to parry. When he heard of it, he froze.

Johnson's attitude in the October crisis is, today, significant. His courage under pressure has been certified, and his sense of power relationships made clear. While agreeing that an exit had to be provided through which Khrushchev could back out of Cuba without a fight, nevertheless he was insisting that the U.S. government should make sure that Khrushchev was maneuvered toward an exit that would close behind him. As matters turned out, the supposed exit became a revolving door; Soviet forces continue to come and go in Cuba and the Castro-inspired terror has continued to reach into Latin America, most deeply (and recently) into Venezuela. As for the rockets in Italy and Turkey, they were presently dismantled and withdrawn. True, these particular weapons were somewhat obsolescent in comparison with what they might have been replaced with, but they were not replaced. Instead Washington announced that U.S. Polaris submarines had been assigned to the Mediterranean. As regards the intermediate-range capability of the allied forces in Europe, however, the departure of the land-based missiles represented a net loss to the NATO order of battle.

It is no secret that the Kennedy men, and most noticeably the inner group of political and social scientists at State and Defense who were closely linked to the White House, were then indifferent to, even scornful of, Johnson's competence in their fields of expertise. The truth is that he was all but a stranger to many of them during the three years that the direction of national security policies and actions was being gathered into the White House. Drawn into Kennedy's centripetalism and exhilarated by the intimacy of the connection, the Kennedy men, for the most part, had little time for Johnson.

Secretary Rusk was one exception. Perhaps because he, too, was at times a lonely man, but also because he valued Johnson's knowledge of the ways of Congress, Rusk remained amiable, attentive, and informative. He was solicitous in his briefing of Johnson on political matters before Johnson set out on his foreign excursions, and was faithful in sounding out Johnson's views afterward. McNamara also got along well with Johnson, without ever achieving quite the same degree of warmness. McNamara was punctilious about keeping Johnson informed of the Defense Department's actions and contingency plans during periods of tension, and he made a practice of seeking the Vice President's counsel whenever he faced a difficult test with Congress. . . .

THE KENNEDY-McNAMARA WATERSHED

The military budget for fiscal 1965 is the fourth and the last to bear a clear Kennedy imprint. It is a crystallization of the Kennedy Administration's judgment relating to military forces and strategical doctrines, and both in dollar terms and in the new balance and composition of forces it modifies certain concepts developed by Dwight Eisenhower. In this respect, the budget for fiscal 1965 represents a watershed in the postwar evolution of U.S. military forces and policies.

Measured simply in money terms, the watershed is a high one. The total Kennedy drafts on the defense account kept rising every year. By the end of fiscal 1963, the Kennedy-McNamara defense expenditures (including foreign military assistance) had risen to about $50 billion, an increase of some $6.3 billion over the level of cost that Eisenhower had come to, with great reluctance, in his last year in office, fiscal 1961.

For the 1964 fiscal year, McNamara originally asked Congress for $53.7 billion in new money. Added to the carry-over of unexpended balances from the previous year's appropriations, this sum would have given him a total obligational authority of $55.2 billion for his needs through fiscal 1964, and for the funding of programs the full impact of which would not be felt until later years. Congress, however, struck some $1.8 billion from his main money bill. . . . As recently as the summer of 1963, before the Pentagon felt the chill winds from Capitol Hill, indications were strong that the momentum of his programs would carry spending close to $55 billion a year. An outlay of that magnitude was needed to bring to a rapid climax his long-range programs for restructuring the military forces. The $55-billion level would, for example, have just about completed the capital funding of the huge new strategic nuclear systems (notably the Polaris fleet and the Minuteman rocket force) that were started in Eisenhower's administration. The additional infusion was calculated to bring the Army within striking distance of the huge reserves of battle stocks it would need for major conventional campaigns.

Once these major investments were largely behind him, McNamara was confident that between then and 1968–69 the annual running costs of the military establishment could be reduced by at least 10 percent. His ultimate goal, in other words, was *gradually* to bend the military spending curve downward to a plateau represented by an annual cost on the order of $50 billion, perhaps even a little less. Instead, circumstances have forced upon him an immediate leveling off between $51 billion and $52 billion annually.

THE BASIC KENNEDY PROPOSITION

. . . When McNamara went to Washington from the presidency of the Ford Motor Co., he was almost as innocent of experience in the issues relating to strategy as was his much-abused predecessor from Detroit, "Engine Charlie" Wilson, Eisenhower's first Defense Secretary. The strategical premises were constructed in large measure by Kennedy and his advisers during the preparations for the presidency. The main point of departure between the governing strategic concepts of the Eisenhower Administration and those of the Kennedy advisers—the one that has had the utmost influence on the military economics—was the Kennedy challenge to certain basic assumptions about the value of nuclear weaponry in war deterrence and war waging.

The Kennedy proposition, in simplified terms, went something like this: The emergence of Soviet Russia as a nuclear power, well equipped with warheads for both general and limited wars, had produced a nuclear stalemate or, in any event, a balance in the capacity for thermonuclear retaliation so close that one side could not rationally expect to introduce such weapons without inviting from the other a catastrophic blow—to which it could respond only by extending catastrophe. An exchange of nuclear rockets between the U.S. and the U.S.S.R. had therefore ceased to be a "credible" assumption in the planning of forces. Concurrently, as the Kennedy advisers saw it, the Eisenhower plan for the nuclear defense of Europe had lost validity, inasmuch as even a relatively small-scale nuclear action there would in all probability escalate uncontrollably into full-scale war.

On this reasoning, then, the Kennedy men concluded that a major Soviet military aggression, if and when undertaken, would revert to conventional warfare of the World War II standard, utilizing masses of infantry, armor, and tactical aircraft. Restoring the American capability of the TNT side of the equation inevitably led to a substantial expansion of the Army and the tactical Air Force, along with their supporting apparatus.

This was a thoroughly respectable proposition. For many Americans, perhaps even a majority, the mere thought of resorting again to nuclear weapons had become morally repugnant. The pervasive uneasiness might well inhibit the American will to act whenever the nuclear risk might seem high. The proposition was also politically attractive to many in Europe. Finally, it was given plausibility by Khrushchev's famous disquisition on strategy in January 1961, the month Kennedy came into power. The Russian leader announced that the Kremlin was ruling out nuclear warfare as an instrument of policy. He proclaimed the Communist expansion would proceed by means of "wars of liberation" —through civil warfare, that is, rather than the clash of nations.

WHY EISENHOWER REDUCED THE FORCE LEVELS

Eisenhower had not been ignorant of, or indifferent to, the moral and political disabilities attaching to a nuclear strategy. Indeed, on a number of occasions he said that general nuclear war was unthinkable. Yet his judgment of the considerations bearing on the world balance of power led him to a rather different line of policy from Kennedy's. During the Korean war, the U.S. military forces were swelled until they numbered nearly 3,700,000 men and women. After that challenge subsided, Eisenhower was faced with the problem of reshaping this huge establishment for a prolonged test of endurance.

Before long the rising impact of the revolution in military technologies that had started under Truman forced Eisenhower into a series of decisions regarding capital allocations that radically altered the traditional roles and missions of the services. The invention of the thermonuclear weapon gave rise first to the B-52 and B-58 jet bomber forces, then the Atlas and Titan intercontinental rockets, then the Polaris fleet, then the Minuteman force, and then the B-70 concept. Each system required in its turn huge outlays for research and development, for hardware, and for training of specialists in unprecedented numbers. The same technological advances opened equally revolutionary possibilities on the side of the defense—enormous electronic systems for warning, surveillance, and command, as well as costly air-defense systems utilizing both supersonic interceptors and rockets. And then in 1957, three years before Eisenhower left the White House, the Soviet space successes called for programs of a whole new order. By Eisenhower's last year, the capital allocations for R. and D. had risen in four years from about $2 billion a year to about $6 billion; and for procurement, chiefly in the form of advanced weapon systems for the Air Force and Navy, the figure was approaching $12 billion annually.

In pursuit of the technological advantage, Eisenhower was progressively compelled, in the allocation of capital, to throw his weight against the doctrines in which he had been bred and from the application of which had come his fame. The Korea-swollen Army consisted of 1,500,000 men and twenty divisions when he became President. When he left, it was down to fourteen divisions and about 900,000 men. He brought the Air Force Tactical Air Command down from fifty-five wings, organized to support the Army in battle, to only thirty-two. All together, Eisenhower reduced the uniformed strength by nearly one-third, from 3,600,000 persons to less than 2,500,000. It is no secret that he wanted to cut even deeper. If he had had his way, the Army's ready strength would have been still further diluted by the withdrawal and disbanding of at least two of the five divisions and four regiments deployed in Europe, and the Navy would have been limited to perhaps twelve attack carriers instead of fifteen.

As Eisenhower read the future, the military advantage in a trial of endurance would rest with the side that held the technological upper hand. To him, this meant a *contest between the American supply of capital and technical skills and the Soviet supply.* Rather than strain American human and capital resources by trying to maintain two different kinds of military establishments simultaneously, one equipped predominantly for conventional warfare and the other shaped around the nuclear technology, he chose to concentrate the investment on the side of strategic technological advantage. He believed that this would prove to be the surest deterrent to war.

By no means did this mean that he was limiting his options to "massive retaliation" alone. Right down to his last year in office, upwards of two-thirds of the budget was being devoted to the support of an Army, Navy, and Air Force whose essential function was to fight "brush-fire" or "limited" campaigns in conventional style. It was Eisenhower's firm conviction that fourteen Army divisions (three of which were training divisions), plus three Marine divisions, plus their supporting tactical air forces, were quite enough to cope with any limited war that it might be in the American interest to fight. He rejected the idea that the U.S. would ever again send great armies abroad to fight wars of attrition. He reasoned that superior military technologies, broadly based on tactical nuclear capabilities, would enable the U.S. to control the ground battle, if one were to develop on a serious scale. His insistence on this point led in 1959 to the breach between him and the then Army Chief of Staff, General Maxwell Taylor, who reemerged in the Kennedy Administration as the senior military adviser to the President.

Eisenhower protected the nation with much more foresight and imagination than is generally realized. The great new systems, offensive and defensive, were all well in hand when he left Washington. It is also a matter of historical record that he weathered the Red Chinese threat at Quemoy and Matsu, and menacing Soviet moves at Berlin and in the Middle East without having to call up the reserves.

THE ECONOMIC CONSEQUENCES

When it fell to McNamara to reverse the investment priorities, he was inevitably drawn into the money bind that Eisenhower had tried to evade. The Kennedy thesis that the nuclear retaliatory power had lost credibility as a prime factor in a deterrent strategy was at least an arguable proposition. But once believed it carried with it a costly corollary: to be certain that the Russians, too, would believe in the nuclear stalemate U.S. nuclear power must be made strong enough to withstand a Soviet surprise first blow. To the Kennedy advisers this meant that the American strategic retaliatory forces must be converted at all possible speed to "second strike" posture.

Thus before McNamara was even well launched on the business of rebuilding the conventional forces, he was compelled to enlarge the ready strategic nuclear forces at a pace considerably faster than Eisenhower had deemed necessary. Among other actions, he more than doubled the output of Polaris submarines (from five to twelve a year), doubled the output of the Minuteman (from thirty missiles to sixty a month), set about positioning the Titan missiles in hardened sites at all possible speed, and increased the fraction of the Strategic Air Command in round-the-clock air alert.

The stepped-up outlays on the strategic side, however, represent only between a quarter and a third of the total dollar increase in the Kennedy-McNamara budgets. The rest is accounted for chiefly by the much heavier investment in conventional forces, especially the Army. The Army has been raised to sixteen divisions, two more than before; of these the three divisions that previously had functioned merely as grinding mills for trainees have been transformed, at no mean cost, into ready forces. Also, various specialized battle groups have been reinforced and brought to a high degree of readiness, and something quite new has been added—the Special Forces created for coping with guerrilla warfare.

To support the Army in conventional warfare, the number of fighter-bomber wings in the Tactical Air Command has been raised from sixteen to twenty-two; the troop-carrier wings have been fleshed out; and more than half a billion dollars worth of non-nuclear munitions have been stockpiled, over and above previous requirements. Six divisions in the Army Reserve are in the process of being manned and equipped for rapid deployment overseas. The airlift capacity has also been doubled, as was dramatized by the Big Lift operation in October 1963. And there are 15,000 more men in the Marine Corps than Eisenhower allowed. One of the fundamental Kennedy premises was that the U.S. should be able to cope with two large-scale conventional wars of the Korean type simultaneously in different parts of the world. This concept was, of course, one that Eisenhower rejected.

By reason of the intense preoccupation with conventional means of warfare, the number of people in uniform exceeded 2,800,000 at one point in the Kennedy-McNamara buildup, nearly 335,000 more than Eisenhower tolerated. The number now stands at about 2,700,000. The funds allocated to the "general-purpose forces" category—i.e., conventional—had risen from $14.5 billion annually under Eisenhower to $18.1 billion in fiscal 1963 and still are rising.

THE DEVOURING FACTOR

This is only part of the continuing investment in conventional means, however. The annual cost of the air-sea lift, represented largely by capital outlays for faster and bigger air transports, is $500 million more than it was. The yearly costs charged to "general support" of the entire military establishment also are $2 billion higher, and the larger part of this increase must be charged to the conventional side of the military ledger. It appears that between $5 billion and $6 billion of the $8 billion that the Kennedy-McNamara strategy had added to the annual cost of defense is represented by the search for more non-nuclear options.

What old soldier Eisenhower knew all along, and what the newcomers to military economics first brushed aside, was that the devouring factor in a military organization is not hardware but "bodies"—the people and their dependents who must be housed, fed, clothed, trained, paid, moved about, and cared for when ill. At present the annual outlays for R. and D., military construction, and the procurement of weapons and other equipment add up to about $24 billion. But the upkeep of the forces, including family housing and retired pay, runs to about $26 billion a year. This averages out at about $10,000 a year for each man, apart from the cost of putting a weapon in his hand or giving him a truck to drive. It is the additional bodies McNamara has "taken aboard" (as they say at the Pentagon) that have helped to inflate defense costs so fast and that will become by far the major element in future costs.

The total effect looks like this: The Kennedy military budgets add up to a total spending of about $202 billion for four years. This compares with a total of about $172 billion for the last four Eisenhower years. These figures, incidentally, do not include the cost of developing and manufacturing nuclear weapons. The Atomic Energy Commission bears this cost, which is on the order of $2 billion a year.

A NEW AUDIT OF FORCES AND STRATEGY?

The hauling and pulling in Congress over the fiscal 1964 budget, while leading to temporary stretch-outs and deferments rather than to major amputations of program, nevertheless signaled a rising skepticism about the high level of defense spending. It was to mollify this mood of questioning that President Johnson encouraged McNamara to proclaim a number of long-evaded shutdowns, such as the suspension of the Air Force's Dynasoar space program (McNamara had been gunning for that for more than a year) and the closing down of inefficient and worthless bases, shipyards, and the like. McNamara believes that upwards of $5 billion a year can be trimmed from defense spending simply through subjecting the forces and the Pentagon's own contracting procedures to sterner managerial disciplines.

So far so good, but is not a far more serious audit of forces and strategy justified, considering the basic causes of recent increases in defense expenditures? McNamara himself seemed to invite just such a national questioning in November 1963 when, only a few days before Kennedy's death, he addressed the Economic Club of New York on the topic, among other matters, of the U.S. power position. He was extraordinarily explicit. He certified the clear superiority of our strategic nuclear forces over those of the Soviet Union. He held that the conventional forces already in being in the West could be a match for the like forces that Russia was presently capable of deploying in Europe. This advantageous situation, he all but guaranteed, should last through the next decade.

The inference was clear enough: McNamara, on the strength of his analysis of the U.S. intelligence estimates of the Soviet potential, was ruling out the possibility of any effective major military action by the U.S.S.R. in the foreseeable future. This was how Eisenhower had read the future, too, in a period when Senator Kennedy, in a famous and melancholy speech in 1958, was casting our country in the role of underdog, its peril being likened to that of Britain in the sixteenth century, after the loss of its continental stronghold at Calais.

No doubt McNamara's new confidence is as well founded as was Eisenhower's. Ever since the U-2's started to operate over the U.S.S.R. and Red China nearly a decade ago, the U.S. has been able to track, with a precision never before available to intelligence techniques, the physical evidence of Soviet deployments of forces and machines. The reconnaissance airplane has been succeeded by the reconnaissance space machine, and its photographic gleanings are being amplified by a steady flow of intelligence from other sources—cryptography, economic analysis, electronic eavesdropping, radar tracking, and (one assumes) plain, ordinary espionage.

It is widely agreed that the capabilities of the Soviet strategic forces in being have been established with reasonable exactitude. Little mystery attaches to the deployments of the greater part of the Soviet air and rocket forces; a good deal appears to be known about their separate rates of growth, and from this and other information it is possible to form certain persuasive deductions about the rate, scale, and nature of the Soviet capital allocations to the military.

One could wonder, on the face of his November analysis, whether McNamara, on long second thought, has come privately to agree with Eisenhower—and, incidentally, with President Charles de Gaulle—that the outcome of the struggle for military advantage is being governed by the relative technological positions, and here the pace has taxed the adversary. In any event, the expected reconstruction of the Soviet military machine around conventional means has simply failed to materialize. On the contrary, the ready front-line strength of the Red Army, although being continuously modernized, remains between sixty and eighty divisions, a range of estimates that goes back nearly a decade. In the meantime, the major Soviet capital investments on the military account have been methodically plowed, through the Kennedy years as in the Eisenhower, into strategic and tactical rocket systems, into air and missile defenses, and into the advanced electronic systems that are required by both.

AN OVERDONE BUILDUP

While the evidence is convincing that the existing Soviet strategic forces, both rocket and bomber, are markedly inferior to our own, the same evidence also strongly suggests that the Russians are proceeding toward an ICBM force that will eventually number many hundreds of weapons. It is further well established that the hundreds of medium-range rockets that they have already deployed in the direction of Europe leave the Continent itself, apart from the distant U.S. strategic power, in hostage to close-in Soviet power.

There is no way of proving the statement, but it does seem, in the absence of proof to the contrary, that the intense, costly buildup of the U.S. conventional forces was probably overdone. The supposed "conventional gap," as an index of a critical deficiency in the American capacity for effective action, appears to have been as much a product of a state of mind as the bomber and missile "gaps." The conventional buildup has added enormously to the cost of national defense; there can be no considerable reductions in this cost while it continues. Alongside such expenditures, the savings from closing down airfields and depots will produce little more than minor passing jiggles in the spending curve.

A more serious consequence of the preoccupation with conventional options has been the increasingly cautious investment in the more speculative military technologies. The capital investment on the side of the technological advantage, which is to say in advanced systems—a form of indirect economic pressure the adversary finds most difficult to meet over the long pull—has begun to decline, while the investment in people has been rising both relatively and absolutely. If there is to be a substantial drop in defense costs it can come only through a shift in the investment allocations, and this would mean, for Johnson, a thoroughgoing reappraisal of the economic and military validity of the Kennedy-McNamara strategy assumptions.

The Defense Industry Is Facing Trouble* —

CHARLES J. V. MURPHY

There is no longer any mistaking the warning signals that the Pentagon has gingerly raised in recent months. The country's great defense industry is once again facing trouble. A mood of suspicion, apprehension, and even anxiety has begun to pervade the front offices of the major producers. There is suspicion because the Department of Defense continues to insist that no drastic changes are under consideration, whereas all the signs prove that a sharp downturn in military procurement already is in process. There is apprehension because no new massive programs looking to further experiment, invention, and production are taking tangible shape beyond the contracts being disposed of at present. And there is deepening anxiety over what is to become of the unique bodies of engineering and scientific talents that the military prime contractors began to assemble a decade or so ago when the tide of technological innovation was on the rise.

The entire defense program, of course, currently engages only about 10 percent of the total U.S. production of goods and services and about the same percentage of the labor force. At the same time, the defense community is an intensely concentrated and therefore highly vulnerable one. In certain industries —airplane and missile manufacturing, electronics, shipbuilding— military or defense-related federal business supports from one-half to as much as nine-tenths of the work being done. Furthermore, more than one-half of all industrial research in the nation is generated by the military programs; the military also pay for about one-quarter of all pure research. However diffused might be the impact of a sharp cutback in military procurement upon most American communities, the same impulse would strike such places as Los Angeles, San Diego, Seattle and the entire state of Washington, Hartford and the Connecticut Valley, not to men-

---

* *August 1964*

tion the electronic communities strung along Route 128 outside Boston, and the west shore of San Francisco Bay, with devastating force.

These communities are worried. In California, which at present holds about 23 percent of all prime military and about 50 percent of all NASA contracts, Governor Pat Brown some months ago created an Advisory Panel on Aerospace and Electronics Industries. The panel is made up of the top executives of the major defense companies and of economists, who consult directly with the Governor. In June 1964 he summoned a number of these advisers or their deputies to the San Francisco airport to chew over the growing problems—a still relatively small but quickening increase in unemployment and a growing uncertainty about future orders and prospects.

In an effort to reassure the defense industry, the Defense Department will send a curious road show into all the major defense-producing centers in the fall and winter of 1964. Under the scheme a select team of Pentagon briefers and planners will be provided, to the degree that security permits, with what might be called a shopping list of the goods and services—the hardware and the research and development programs—that are tentatively included in Defense Secretary McNamara's five-year defense plan, covering the 1965–69 fiscal-year span. Executives in the major industrial centers will also be lectured on the prospects, such as they are, of arms control and the economic consequences of progressive disarmament, should disarmament in one form or another prove to be in the cards. Finally, an important part of the government's agenda will be devoted to outlining for the defense producers how their extraordinary flair for systems management and their capital and intellectual resources in the higher technologies might best be regrouped for opening up whole new kinds of markets—urban transit, oceanography, the invention of spectacular new materials and processes.

While all this should make the defense industry much better informed, it is scarcely calculated to allay its anxiety. What is going on under the bland surface that the Administration understandably is anxious to maintain through an election summer and fall is obvious enough. Another deceleration in defense spending for hardware and technical services is already quietly under way. The phenomenon has been blurred, by and large, by the fact that the defense budget as a whole has not changed very much in size between John F. Kennedy and Lyndon B. Johnson. In the military budget for fiscal year 1965, McNamara's request for nearly $51 billion in new obligational authority to finance the forces and buying programs was only about $120 million less than he asked for in fiscal 1964. His planned expenditures of $51.2 billion, moreover, were less than 2 percent off his peak spending figure of $52.3 billion (estimated) in the fiscal year that ended in June 1964.

The catch in these figures, so far as the defense industry is directly concerned, is that by far the biggest function of the military budget, about three-fifths of the total, is spent in the main on general support elements—pay, construction and housing, civil defense, and other items of upkeep—that provide relatively little business for the defense industry. This community makes its living from the two categories that together constitute the remaining two-fifths of the budget—the procurement of hardware and weapon systems on the one side, and research and development in their intricate and diverse forms on the other. It is here that the Kennedy-generated defense-spending wave has unmistakably crested, and the troupe of briefers that the Defense Department is about to send into the hinterland will have the difficult chore of explaining why this has happened.

A survey completed by the Aerospace Industries Association in the spring of 1964 disclosed that its member companies had laid off about 3.2 percent of their work force between September and March, and the consensus then was that 3.4 percent more of the workers would be dropped by the end of the summer. The survey sample took in fifty-five companies operating 143 plants and covered about 70 percent of the work force that a year ago totaled about 1,250,000. On this showing, it appears that the industry as a whole will have dropped about 81,250 workers, or slightly less than 7 percent of the total, during the twelve-month period ending in September, and the decline is certain to continue.

As a warning signal, these particular statistics taken by themselves could be likened to the cloud of prophecy that at the first speculative glance was no bigger than a man's hand. McNamara is not saying at this stage just how far he is prepared to extend the reduction in spending, or the ratio of investment he proposes eventually to establish between the procurement of hardware and research and development, and between these two categories and the rest of the military budget. The only fact that is clearly in view is that while the budget as a whole remains for the time being close to its peak peacetime levels, the great buy in the strategic nuclear systems—the investment that profoundly changed the character of the defense business—seems to have come to an end.

No one who has been following McNamara's recent moves, not to mention his frequent disquisitions on strategy, should be surprised by what is happening. Ever since he established to his satisfaction early in his regime the superiority of the U.S. strategic retaliatory forces over the Soviet offensive, or first-strike, forces, he has been gripped by a fairly uncomplicated conviction. It is that the U.S. lead in rocket and nuclear technologies, combined with the preponderant power of the strategic forces deployed and being formed, is far too much for the Soviet Union to overcome in the foreseeable future. Believing this, McNamara holds that the U.S. can therefore greatly slow down its vast capital expenditures on experiment, and safely stand for some years to come pretty much on the weapons already in hand or about to emerge from advanced development.

In any case, a great wave of development seems spent. The last B-52 came off the Boeing line in Wichita in the summer of 1962 and the B-70 concept is finished as a weapon system. No new strategic bomber systems of any kind are coming along and nothing strikingly new is being brought forward among the ICBM's either. The last Polaris submarine, completing the Navy's fleet of forty-one, is scheduled to slide down the ways about two years from now. The funding of the last submarines was covered, in fact, by last year's appropriations. The only large additional capital investment contemplated for the seagoing part of the strategic deterrent is for the purpose of replacing the production missile with an improved one. The main buy of the Atlas and Titan liquid-fuel systems is finished and several of the earliest squadrons, representing in numbers a rather sizable fraction of the aggregate, are to be retired over the next several years as obsolescent. The big capital funding for the solid-fuel Minuteman system has been completed; outlays being made now are essentially for an improved guidance system and a more powerful warhead, which are to be incorporated in about half of the rockets already in silos.

While fairly large sums are being released for the Army's anti-ICBM research program, the Nike-X experiment, McNamara has resolutely refused to authorize any move into the engineering-development stage that would necessarily precede the production of hardware in volume. On the contrary, the leisurely pace and narrow scope of the program suggest that he is unwilling to commit more money than is absolutely necessary to reinforce his judgment, and that of his principal technical advisers, that such a defense system is, at the existing level of technical experience, much too costly for either the U.S. or the U.S.S.R. sensibly to attempt. Finally, he has no intention of releasing to the Air Force the considerable sums it desires for testing such potential military options as may lie latent in space.

THE TELLTALE FIGURES

Once the capital funds for the Minuteman and Polaris systems are used up, the former aircraft "primes," which now call themselves aerospace companies, will be left, unless some great crisis materializes over the next several years, with only two major military systems actually in line production. One is the TFX (now formally renamed the F-111) tactical fighter-bomber, jointly under development by General Dynamics and Grumman Aircraft. The other is a big jet transport, the C-141, for which Lockheed Aircraft has received a large start-up order. This machine is to enter the airlift that McNamara has been rapidly expanding for the swifter deployment in an emergency of the general-purpose forces.

No one in government, let alone in industry, is prepared to predict what the effects would be on the defense industry of a prolonged standstill in the evolution of strategic weapon systems. In a very real sense, the onrush of invention in this field provided, so to speak, the leading edge for the technological buoyancy that lifted the entire aerospace industry to affluence. The industry got a big initial stimulus when Kennedy entered the White House. In the budget for fiscal 1962, the last prepared by the Eisenhower Administration, the aggregate funding set up for the strategic retaliatory forces came to $7.6 billion, about one-third of the entire Defense Department procurement and R.D.T. and E. (research, development, test, and evaluation) programs. This sum was to pay for the operating costs of such forces, as well as for the continuing purchase of missiles and related gear and for the improvement in R. and D. of going and new systems. One of the earliest Kennedy-McNamara decisions with regard to these forces was to raise the fiscal 1962 funding by $1.5 billion to $9.1 billion. The reason for the sharp jump was the desire on the part of the Kennedy Administration to move the major U.S. retaliatory forces into a theoretically invulnerable second-strike posture. This it proposed to do by fitting out the entire Polaris fleet and deploying the Minuteman force a full two years sooner than the Eisenhower schedules contemplated.

Since fiscal 1962 the annual funding has gone down steadily— $8.4 billion in fiscal 1963, $7.3 billion last year, and $5.3 billion proposed for the current year. Now the expectation is that two years hence, as the improvements in the Polaris and Minuteman systems are disposed of, the annual cost of the entire strategic apparatus will settle at $4.5 billion and may well drop as low as $4 billion. All but a fraction of this drop has been at the expense of procurement and R. and D., which stood somewhat in excess of $7 billion three years ago. It will dwindle in the coming year to $3 billion, or only about 45 percent of the sum that the Kennedy Administration was committing to industry in its first year. Should McNamara achieve his tentative goal, outlays for procurement and development for the strategic forces would drop in 1966–67 to between $1.7 billion and $2.2 billion.

Here, manifestly, is the principal source of the anxiety that permeates the aerospace industry. It has been in the technologies associated with or flowing from the great strategic systems, offensive and defensive, that the electronic and aerospace companies have experienced the sharpest rates of growth. The big question is: What's going to happen as the full impact of the cutback in procurement and R. and D. spreads out from the prime contractors, such as Boeing and North American and Lockheed, to their second and third tiers of subcontractors and suppliers scattered across the nation? . . .

A DEEPENING DILEMMA

And so it is, as one travels from one old-line defense producer to another, from the West Coast back through the Midwest into the Connecticut Valley, that one has the sense of entering a world for the most part still affluent, still virile and aggressive, yet edged with foreboding, and in some instances close to crackup. The emerging situation is marked by at least two distinct features. Anywhere from a dozen to twenty and even thirty companies are maneuvering hungrily against one another for the handful of possible systems contracts that dimly persist on the federal horizon —the Air Force's Manned Orbital Laboratory and NASA's much larger but demilitarized counterpart, the super-super CX-HLS military transport, and the potentially immense but still groping experiments concerned with establishing the validity of a rocket defense against strategic rockets. A company fortunate enough to land one of these big jobs could count on remaining an elite research and production establishment for quite a few years to come. The companies that lose out are the ones that will be early candidates for merger, consolidation, even extinction.

The second feature of the rising situation reflects the first. An essential attribute of any company in the aerospace business, if it wished to qualify as a manager of prime systems, has been a truly great versatility in many scientific disciplines and engineering skills. Without these skills, a company could not bid, let alone attempt the work. In the present situation, with only one new major system (the F-111) moving to the hardware or production phase, the competition for analytical work has become intense. Exploratory-study contracts are being scattered about by the Defense Department, but these do not begin to soak up the supply of scientific talent that represents a considerable fraction of the continuing overhead of the major companies. No doubt there has been a good deal of water in these supposed technical assets. A general sloughing off here, it is widely agreed, will be a good thing for industry and government both. All the same, after the deadwood has been disposed of, many companies will be left with an unresolvable dilemma—how to hold a fine engineering staff together.

CHOICE FOR THE U.S.

It is the nation's dilemma, too. Above and beyond the economic consequences to the aerospace industry, changes in the structure of the defense industry will affect the nation's capacity for action. McNamara's main proposition is that the wave of technological invention that started with the splitting of the atom has run its course for the time being. No earth-shaking technical surprises on the order, say, of an ICBM with a thermonuclear warhead or even an effective defense against an ICBM are to be expected in the near future. As early as February 1963, the Secretary explained to the House subcommittee on military appropriations his seeming indifference to the case for a possible military exploitation of space with the statement, "If anything, I think we have gone too far in our R. and D. projects, because we are grasping [at] straws to find new weapon systems."

To be sure, McNamara is not writing off the importance of research and development. Total military spending for R.D.T. and E. (apart from NASA's) for all services may run in the future to some $6.5 billion a year. But only a part of this will go to systems for the strategic retaliatory forces, which have been of such importance to the great prime contractors. Moreover, McNamara is wedded to his so-called "technological building blocks" theory, which, while appearing to stimulate the development of new weaponry on the broadest scale, actually has operated to inhibit its development. Ideally, the theory would carry new projects along up to the major engineering phase, always the most expensive, and then, so to speak, hold them on the shelf. But the services complain with accuracy that under McNamara fewer and fewer inventions are reaching the hardware stage, and that this policy involves real sacrifices. For engineering and production often lead into improvements in the weapons. The building-block theory seems to dismiss the advantages that accrue to the side that persistently carries its technological building blocks into full-dress engineering test.

Underlying the whole present approach is the political assumption that the U.S. should not push its new weapons development to the point where the Russians might deem it "obtrusive" or "provocative," and that, with or without a clear *détente* with the U.S.S.R., the U.S. military budget can be greatly reduced. On this point, however, the recent counsel of two eminent men needs heeding. There is, on the one hand, the judgment of James Killian, who was Eisenhower's senior scientific adviser, that it is a dangerous delusion to believe that "we have reached some kind of plateau in our invention and development of weapons." And there is the comment of Lee Atwood of North American. "My company," he says, "has not been favored with a sanction requiring the federal government to keep its 100,000 people employed. All the same, if it is in the cards that federal procurement of new systems is to start down fast, then it will be a signal to the rest of the world that the U.S. is relinquishing its lead in the space and military technologies. That will be hard to win back."

*Hitching the Economy to the Infinite** _____

GILBERT BURCK

There is no end to space, and so far as the U.S. economy is concerned, there will probably be no end to the space program. Man has hitched his wagon to the infinite, and he is unlikely ever to unhitch it again. A failure or two in the sky can be only temporary, a spur to the next success. And the next success will be merely the prelude to even greater triumph—a project to build Fort Kennedy on the moon, bigger and better voyages to Mars and Venus, immensely costly expeditions to Jupiter, Saturn, Pluto, and so on ad infinitum. As D. Brainerd Holmes of the National Aeronautics and Space Administration remarks, "The lunar program makes sense only if we go on from there." The space venture, in short, is likely to be more durably stupendous than even its most passionate advocates think it will be. It is bound to affect the nation's economy powerfully and in many ways.

During the next decade alone the U.S. will loft several hundred scientific satellites and dozens of lunar and planetary probes, and undertake upwards of forty manned space flights. By 1970, according to the most conservative initial estimates, NASA and the military will be spending around $15 billion a year on space, including $5 billion on missiles. But almost every space project so far has cost two to three times its conservative initial estimates. Mistakes are bound to be made, failures are bound to occur, and

_____

* *June 1962*

costs and ambitions bound to soar. The space effort (as it is coming to be known in official jargon) will very likely cost more than $20 billion a year by 1970.

Nothing is more fecund, industrially and socially, than large mobilizations of scientific knowledge and effort; and this is the greatest mobilization of them all. Precisely because the benefits it will bestow on the world will be incidental to the main effort, they may eventually come faster than man's capacity to use them economically. The space effort has already given man an immense psychological boost. Just as the Russian space successes have bolstered Soviet power internally by winning world power and prestige, so U.S. space projects are fortifying the old American optimism, confidence, and audacity. In thousands of offices and plants as well as in the endless anonymous corridors of Washington, prudent men who customarily discuss mundane prospects warily now talk with easy assurance of landing on the moon and exploring Mars. And they are even more sure of the benefits flowing from space techniques. Hundreds of American-made satellites will soon be buzzing the globe, guiding its navigation, mapping its impenetrable jungles, solving the cosmic riddles of its erratic weather, searching its hostile terrain, and relaying libraries of information and millions of photographs to receivers below. In the long run the space effort promises immense consumption dividends, a "fall-out" of better products and ways of doing things from generating power to calculating probabilities, from packing eggs to treating ailments, real and imaginary.

A MILITARY THRUST, AN INFLATIONARY BOOST

Too often forgotten, however, is the fact that such pleasant rewards will be bought at a heavy price—a price that, all other things being equal, the U.S. might be reluctant to pay. This decade's program alone, which may be only preliminary, could impose unpalatable if not severe burdens on the nation. It will very likely kill all chances of reducing in our time the government's share of the economy. It will change, strain, and probably distort the distribution of the nation's resources. With all its emphasis on planning, both national and international, it could ultimately do violence to private enterprise itself.

Nor will the fabled practical benefits offset the cost of the program for a long time. Washington is teeming with lobbyists and other space partisans assiduously promoting the notion that space is the greatest surefire blue-sky investment ever, sure to pay off at 1,000 percent almost immediately—as if the benefits were the primary aim of the program. Actually, the chief reason for allocating so prodigious a part of the national resources to an accelerated space program is the paramilitary necessity of being in space with the most and the best; and the fact that the U.S. has divided the effort into military applications run by the Department of Defense and general applications run by NASA does not alter the situation. (The Russians themselves regard NASA as a device for continuing space activities if an arms agreement is signed, which in a way it would be.) Although the space effort may realize a bonanza of practical benefits, it is hardly an efficient way of getting them.

By the time the satellites begin to pay off measurably, say 1970 at the earliest, the U.S. may have spent $75 billion to $100 billion on space activities, and another $50 billion on missiles. Annual interest on such sums, if reckoned at the prevailing government securities rate, will be around $4 billion, enough to pay the nation's yearly shoe bill; and what might be called the accumulated interest will come to another $20 billion by 1970, enough to run the whole U.S. railroad system for two years or to pay for most of the country's education for a year. . . .

The implications for 1970 and beyond are portentous. Barring a genuine arms agreement—i.e., barring a revolution in the Soviet state religion—military costs other than missiles may well rise from their present $43 billion to more than $70 billion by 1970. So military and space outlays together could come to $90 billion or more a year. What could this mean? In its projections of the U.S. economy of the 1960's, *Fortune* estimated that GNP (in 1959 prices) would rise from about $500 billion in 1960 to $750 billion a decade later, or at a compound annual rate of 4.2 percent. So far, this appears a sound projection. *Fortune* also estimated that by 1970 defense outlays, including several billion a year spent overseas for military aid, etc., would not exceed 10 percent of GNP, or $75 billion. But if defense plus space outlays rise to more than $90 billion, the growth of the rest of the economy will be correspondingly retarded unless people work longer or raise their output per hour. Only an industrially opulent country can mount a space effort worthy of the name. But even the most industrially opulent of all nations cannot take the imponderable demands of a huge space program in stride unless it uses its resources with sharply increasing efficiency.

FEWER AND BIGGER CONTRACTS

The immediate effect of the space venture on the U.S. economy, besides pumping a lot of money into it, has been to change the pattern of much business profoundly. Space vehicles are the most complex structures ever built, running to thousands of components, subassemblies, and specialized devices; no single company yet has the immediate resources to manufacture whole vehicles. A given project is ruled by the prime contractor, which practices what is known as systems management: the integration of production and research and development, including its own and that of government and university laboratories, into a final working vehicle. Many companies handle more than one prime contract, but in addition they usually are subcontractors on several others, and thus no one company covers the biggest programs exclusively. The giant North American Aviation Corp., for example, is the prime contractor for the Apollo lunar spacecraft, but it is also a large subcontractor. McDonnell Aircraft estimates it has called in more than 4,000 subcontractors and suppliers on the $145-million Mercury capsule contract alone.

But even this pattern is changing rapidly as the central effort of the aerospace program shifts from missiles to propulsion and electronics. Missile production, after rising a little, may peak off at something above $5 billion. Other outlays by NASA (for such things as the moon program) and by the military (for such things as propulsion systems) are climbing toward the $10-billion mark, which they may reach as early as 1965. "Already," says Harry H. Wetzel, vice president of the Garrett Corp. of Los Angeles, which makes environmental control systems, "the aerospace business is a new game." As Wetzel and others see it:

1) There will be fewer and bigger contracts.

2) Production runs will decline steadily, and completely reverse the traditional four-to-one ratio of shop to engineering personnel. That is, companies will spend more on engineering and less on actual production; in fact, straight production capacity is already

excessive. In 1960, Lockheed says, the company's R. and D. awards came to more than the whole nation spent on defense R. and D. in 1950.

3) The aerospace companies will need not only engineers, but physiologists, psychologists, space-medicine men, chemists, and systems engineers.

4) As the space program proceeds to moon shots and planet exploration, reliability will become increasingly more important, and will demand more research facilities that can simulate space environments, more control engineering, more surveillance of sub-contractors' and suppliers' quality controls.

This trend may be hard on small business, and doubtless will result in many mergers—of small companies with big, and small with small. For the important contracts from 1965 on will be based on ground support and airborne guidance and control systems, which require large engineering organizations. "We can't exist without small business," cautiously explains Jack Parker, General Electric's vice president in charge of electronic and flight systems. "Yet as the emphasis on quality and complexity becomes greater, it is apt to reduce the amount of work small business may want." Says a blunter spokesman for another large company, in authentic space jargon, "Captive production will increase not only because companies will want to maximize dollar volume in-house, but because schedules must be met reliably. The need for specialized equipment and technical sophistication will inevitably reduce off-site work."

NASA is going out of its way to encourage little business; and the very nature of the space and missile program, with its demand for all manner of custom-made specialties, may continue to favor small firms devoted to electronic devices, engineering techniques, special research, and other relatively esoteric services and products. Small companies, as a matter of fact, can offer scientists unique advantages such as participation in top-level decisions; some offer higher salaries and more fringe benefits than big companies, a few offer more money than their own top executives get. T. F. Walkowicz, aeronautical engineer and associate of Laurance Rockefeller, who helped establish such Rockefeller-financed companies as Itek (information technology) and Geophysics Corp. of America (instruments for space research), concedes there will be a shake-out, just as there was in electronics, but argues that the brightest companies will survive and grow. "Brains are what count today, and nobody has a monopoly on brains."

WANTED: A MILLION MORE SCIENTISTS AND ENGINEERS

The space effort is the first paramilitary effort in history not accompanied by a demand for heavy hardware and mass-produced materials. Its great demand, instead, is for professional people, and it may relatively soon employ up to a million. Since more and more money will go into manpower, particularly engineers and other technical specialists, the well-worn question of whether the U.S. is producing enough professionals is no longer academic. By 1970, thanks in large part to the space venture, the U.S. will need more than two million scientists and engineers, or about double the number employed in 1959. A million more will be hard to find. NASA itself will have hired 4,500 specialists by the end of fiscal 1963; since, however, it has gone to a great deal of pains to get talent and also because many professional people would rather work where the big decisions are made at relatively low salaries ($8,000 to $20,000), it has managed to hire about 2,000 and expects no great trouble in corralling the other 2,500. Some experts argue that if engineers and high technical talent were used efficiently—i.e., not assigned to sales work and routine technical jobs—the shortage would not be so bad as it seems. But the majority agree that the shortage is already severe, and is bound to get worse as the space industry expands and R. and D. becomes more intensive.

The adventures of a job broker named David O'Brien, who calls himself a headhunter and patrols the country for talent, are to the point. Every week O'Brien gets 200 to 300 job "descriptions" or requests for men, and has to scratch hard to fill a tiny fraction of them. Recently, he says, it took $9,000 worth of newspaper advertisements to recruit two engineers, and $35,000 worth of his time produced only thirty-eight people. To get a couple of plasma physicists, one firm offered to form a small subsidiary for them. Companies everywhere are hoarding talent, just as industry hoarded lower skills during World War II; and outfits that don't need scientific personnel interview continuously simply to find out what other companies are doing. A class of mobile technicians somewhat like the old-time railroad boomer has sprung up; they work a while for one company, and then pick up and leave for another one. Many firms welcome them because the itinerants can often give them a good line on what the competition is doing.

To complicate the manpower problem, observes Herbert E. Striner, director of Stanford Research Institute's urban-studies program, many colleges and universities are not training scientists and engineers as well as they should. Most universities and colleges are avid for government research contracts, which frees money for other research facilities, fellowship funds, and salaries. But some, Striner argues, put graduate students to work on applied research instead of giving them a sound training in basic research.

The President's Science Advisory Committee hopes to make specific recommendations for stimulating the production of scientists, and many other authorities are discharging wisdom on the subject. So as the demand for professional and scientific personnel rises and is reinforced by incentives, the supply is certain to rise eventually too. For a while it probably will not rise fast enough to meet the demand, and important civilian research and development may be temporarily deprived of talent.

In the longer run, however, the space effort will be the prime force in increasing the U.S. scientific and professional population. And in the process it will accelerate greatly the secular tendency for U.S. business to depend more and more on R. and D. This trend, in turn, according to a preliminary study made by Dr. Howard Vollmer of the Stanford Research Institute (sponsored by the Air Force), may eventually change the "organizational structure" of all U.S. industry. That is, it may make U.S. industry less bureaucratic and more intellectually challenging, "with greater opportunity for professionals to participate in work-related decisions."

MASS PRODUCTION IN SPACE

The first large-scale matching of corporate enterprise with the commercial possibilities of space is taking place in the communication-satellite program. Possibly no invention will have ever jumped the rugged gap between concept and commercial application so quickly and dramatically as the communication satellite. Like much in the space effort, it has been overtouted. No less an authority than Lloyd V. Berkner, chairman of the space-science board of the National Academy of Sciences, has predicted that it could eventually earn $100 *billion* a year. Although such talk has already run aground on cruel reality, the principle of the communication satellite does make economic sense. What it amounts to is a device for the mass production of long-distance wireless communication; once it achieves volume and overcomes a host of problems, it could be nicely in the money.

The economic validity of the communication satellite rests on a genuine technical advantage. Because lower frequencies are overloaded, progressively higher frequencies are necessary to handle the growing volume of radio communication. But when frequencies attain thousands of megacycles per second, the waves travel in a straight line from the transmission tower, are blocked by hills or buildings, and cannot reach beyond the earth's surface or the horizon. Even in flat country, therefore, their optimum range is about thirty miles. There is no technical problem on land, where relay stations can be built at appropriate intervals; but it makes microwave radio impracticable over the ocean. Transoceanic communication is limited to submarine cables or relatively small capacity or lower-frequency radios. Hung high in the sky, satellites could relay a huge volume of traffic, including TV and data-processing signals, across the seven seas. . . .

NO MORE NATIONAL PRIVACY

Probably the quickest space payoff will come from satellites like NASA's upcoming "orbiting observatories," which will carry telescopes and other astronomical and geophysical instruments. Such satellites could map the world as it has never been mapped before. "When it comes to mapping, the satellite is to the airplane as the airplane is to the ground surveyor," says Richard S. Leghorn, president of Itek Corp. and chairman of the National Planning Associations' Committee on Security through Arms Control. "The present proposal to map Antartica with planes could be done with satellites for half the money and in a fifth of the time." All that needs to be decided, says Leghorn, is whether the government or private industry is to run them.

Once the decision is made, observational satellites could begin to earn money immediately, on jobs now scheduled. Itek itself stands to gain by an early decision, for as a specialist in information storage and retrieval it has developed a machine that can read diagrams and pictures and otherwise relay information graphically without programming—i.e., without reducing information to a machine code. "There's no such thing as backyard privacy if we orbit the world constantly," Leghorn likes to point out. "We're ahead on information satellites; we should take advantage of them to open up the Soviet Union to view. Great areas there are barred off, but what would be the use of barring them off if we know what's there?"

Probably the most broadly remunerative of the space vehicles will be the government-operated weather satellites, designed not only to predict short-term weather movements but to gather enough data to enable men to understand just how these movements are generated. Four RCA-made and NASA-supervised Tiros (television and infrared observation satellites) were launched between April 1960, and early 1962. Orbiting the world every hundred minutes or so, and equipped with two TV cameras apiece, they recorded significant new cloud formations over enormous ocean areas. All except Tiros I gauged solar energy reflected and scattered by the earth's surface and atmosphere as well as infrared radiation leaving the earth and its atmosphere. Relevant findings were analyzed promptly and passed on to weather forecasters here and abroad. Although Tiros IV missed the epochal east-coast "Ash Wednesday storm" in March 1962— it was orbiting the Northern Hemisphere by night at the time— Tiros III tracked seventeen tropical storms, and gave advanced warning of Hurricane Esther.

Within a year NASA plans to launch at least three more Tiros and an advanced Nimbus satellite, which will orbit the earth from pole to pole. It is possible that the Russians will cooperate in such a venture, perhaps by lofting a second Nimbus-type satellite. At all events, such satellites will enable the U.S. Weather Bureau to trace the progress of any disturbance anywhere. To view a large part of the world from a steady vantage point, moreover, NASA and the Weather Bureau are planning an Aeros high-altitude orb.

How much all this will save the world it is hard to say. A dozen or so years ago, when the Weather Bureau tried to determine the value of storm warnings and correct forecasts, "business and agricultural interests" suggested that such forecasts could save $3 billion a year in water resources and up to $2.5 billion a year in farm products, to say nothing of a hundred million in transportation (exclusive of air transport). But F. W. Reichelderfer, bureau chief, now feels such figures are meaningless. "Everybody benefits from better weather forecasting," he says, "so we're trying to value something we really can't measure. We know, however, the benefits are there. Just think how much could have been saved if Tiros IV had been around to forecast that east-coast storm last March." Accurate weather forecasting could make farm supports an even greater absurdity than they are. Underlying the whole support program is the assumption that farming, owing to the weather, is egregiously risky. With the risk eliminated, there would be less reason for subsidizing farmers than for subsidizing small manufacturers or storekeepers.

Despite the predictions of the space enthusiasts, it will be a long time before man can even attempt to begin to control the weather. First he must thoroughly understand it, and he still has a long way to go. But he will find out more about it in the next few years than he has in all history.

THE BENEFICENT PROMISE

"In whatever direction our technology is moving," an IBM engineer puts it succinctly, "the space program is advancing us faster." Thus the "fallout" of other kinds of benefits from the nation's investment in space research and development, though some will be long in coming, may be incalculable. To get space discoveries and inventions where they will help the civilian economy, NASA has set up an Office of Applications that will identify "inventive elements and apply them to industry while they are new." One of its first moves has been to hire the Midwest Research Institute of Kansas City to pick up potential applications, document them, and circulate news of the possibilities among industry people.[1] It has also retained the Denver Research Institute for a different kind of investigation: to find out whether industry is already making products and using processes originating in the space effort. After careful screening, Denver Research found 145 such examples, and thinks it will find more. But the big advances lie at some point in the future when the new techniques have had time to blend with the old and join the economy. When they do, space will be largely responsible for many new looks here below. Among the promising areas of development:

• *Materials.* Structural demands of rocket and spacecraft vehicles, the intense power requirements at takeoff, the sustained power required in flight, and the intense heat encountered on re-entry are making for a sharp advance in the strength and property of materials. In the area of metals and alloys this will lead to successful hypersonic planes, the development of simpler, more efficient aircraft and automobile engines, and, perhaps twenty years hence, to lighter and stronger building structures. The development of powerful new fuels is leading the chemical industry to use extreme-temperature, high-pressure techniques, one of which, indeed, is already being used to produce liquid hydrogen. A large array of entirely new metals and materials will be available for untold uses.

• *Reliability and miniaturization.* Because space-vehicle machinery must be both small and absolutely reliable, industry's trend toward miniaturization and reliability, already illustrated by the development of transistors, diodes, etc., will accelerate. Computers will be among the first to profit by the new techniques; computers that used to fill large rooms will soon be housed in

---

[1] Business, however, has been complaining that it has been discouraged from adapting new products and processes developed while working on NASA contracts, because patent rights on those products and processes automatically become government property unless the administrator waives the government's rights. The Department of Justice has entered a strong plea to keep things that way. The issue, whose importance is obvious, seemed to be building up to major proportions when the patent subcommittee of the House Science and Astronautics Committee voted to revise NASA practices. If its recommendations are adopted, NASA could be brought more in line with the Defense Department practice of retaining license rights—but not title—to patents taken out on inventions and improvements made by companies while working on military contracts.

packages the size of a small TV set. The Burroughs D210 computer, designed to guide missiles, occupies less than ¼ cubic foot, uses less power than a 60-watt bulb, operates 50,000 hours without failure, and costs only $25,000 to $50,000 against more than $1 million for the present Atlas computer. Various forms of microcircuitry, developed for space vehicles, some already used widely, will probably result in miniature consumer goods, like radios, at reasonable prices.

• *Automation.* Advances in guidance systems for space vehicles will improve and speed up automation techniques. "Everything we have learned about guiding the Titan," says one IBM man, "will be useful in guiding machine tools." By way of humble example, Allied Research Associates of Boston has used space innovations to develop a machine that automatically sorts cigars for uniformity of color.

• *Bonding techniques.* Because high vacuums are essential for space environmental test chambers, and because many of the specialty metals for space vehicles are being made in vacuum, high-vacuum techniques are being accelerated. Scientists of the National Research Corp., for example, have recently shown that certain metals, if cleaned and put into an almost perfect vacuum, bond together tightly and permanently as if welded. This demonstration will help industry make bearings that will not congeal and clog in the vacuum of space; on the other hand, it will probably result in new nonwelding techniques for bonding many metals here on earth.

• *Aerial observation.* Interpretation of aerial pictures, now being used by Itek Corp. to advise grape growers of California on the quantity and quality of the crop and so to forecast market price, will be extended to hundreds of uses. The problem of storing and retrieving vast amounts of technical information, brought into being by the space age, will be solved by digital graphic systems such as Itek's EDM machine.

• *Klimps and Kudl-Pacs.* Space components are easily damaged, and must be handled a lot, so new packaging techniques have been developed for them. North American Aviation's subsidiary, NAVAN Products Inc., has invented an L-shaped wire fastener it calls a "Klimp," which is replacing nails in packing boxes, and "Kudl-Pac," a thermal-plastic, polyurethane-lined case that adapts itself to a variety of shapes and can be used over and over again. NAVAN has promoted this product by sending prospects a real live egg enclosed in a Kudl-Pac.

• *Packaged power.* Probably the broadest area of practical development will grow out of the new, compact, self-contained sources of power needed by satellites and spacecraft to operate their equipment and to maintain men and their environment independently in space. Already being developed by private and government research for eventual commercial use, they include: (1) Silicon solar cells, converting sunlight directly into electricity, which are being used to power such disparate things as portable radios, railway crossing lights, and community radio receivers in Indian towns. (2) Thermoelectric materials, which can convert low heat directly into electricity, or electricity into heat or cold by reversing the direction of the current. (3) Thermionic tubes, which convert high heat directly into electricity. (4) Fuel cells, converting chemical reactions directly into electricity. (5) Highly compact atomic-power packs, tapping electricity directly from the atom through a converter. (6) Magnetohydrodynamic generators, which convert the movement of a very hot and ionized gas stream ("plasma") into electricity by passing it through a magnetic field. Such a device will make possible high-efficiency power stations: Avco Corp. and a group of seven electric utilities led by American Electric Power Service Corp. is supporting a research program on MHD generators, which may turn out to be 40 percent more efficient than the most modern power generator. As a result of its work in plasma, incidentally, Avco is marketing a "PlasmaGun" or high-heat gun using a tungsten electrode and water-cooled copper nozzle for applying such coatings as tungsten, molybdenum, titanium carbide, and tantalum carbide to metallic and ceramic surfaces. Achieving temperatures up to 30,000° F., the gun can also be used for flame cutting and materials studies.

Compact power packages will probably be developed to the point where they can generate electricity on the spot for home lighting, appliances, and industrial processes. The natural-gas industry is financing a research program on fuel cells, reacting natural gas with an oxidizer to make gas the sole source of domestic energy—heat as well as electricity. Thus walls for homes and buildings may be designed with their own built-in, self-contained heating, cooling, lighting, and electrical systems, feeding on fuel cells, or free energy from the sun. These and other devices, already being carried over from the space industry by such giants as General Electric and Westinghouse, may revolutionize the generation and distribution of power on earth.

• *Solution to overpopulation.* Gazing far into the future, some scientists believe that the greatest benefit the space effort will confer on the human race is to enable man to migrate to other worlds. Theoretically, atmosphere can be created on planets where it is nonexistent or very thin, perhaps by seeding the planets with a catalytic substance to release oxygen now locked up there in compounds like carbon dioxide. "If you want to look ahead a hundred years or more," says Murray Zelikoff of Geophysics Corp., "I think the real purpose of the space effort is to colonize the planets. How else can we solve the population problem? It's not only politics that moves men, but social and biological factors. Subconsciously these are moving men to outer space."

FEET ON THE GROUND

Such a prospect is still far out, but it no longer belongs in the comic strips. The space project is surely enlarging man's notions of the potentialities of the universe, and is accustoming him to think in terms of longer periods of time. Engineers look ahead at least twenty years in planning a space program, and to the extent that business is involved, its scale of thinking is correspondingly enlarged. As General Electric's Ralph Cordiner has remarked, when business deals with space it deals with a technology that needs a planetary scale to stage it, decades to develop it, and a much bigger investment to cross the threshold of return than is customary today.

Private enterprise is not disdaining the challenge. As we have seen, it is stepping into the communication-satellite business; and if other jobs, such as launching operations, can be put on a paying basis, it may gradually take them over. With its own money, industry is already constructing space-simulating facilities, such as GE's laboratory at Valley Forge, Pennsylvania, and RCA's space center at Princeton, New Jersey.

Nevertheless, the great space effort is primarily dependent on government planning, national and international. Consequently, it is boosting the ardor and ambition of those who believe the world is headed for more state planning, and that the scope of private decision is inevitably narrowing. They "observe" that planning for space will train men to plan ahead in other fields, that the idea of government and free enterprise as distinct entities is no longer adequate. For them the great implication of space is that it will somehow free man from his preoccupation with profits and losses and other sordid things that tyrannize him here on earth.

But alas for the idealists, it is precisely this tropism of world-lings for minding their business that has enabled the space program to be created. Only this mundane preoccupation can carry the great program along, world without end. Contemplating the starry heavens above, as Immanuel Kant once did, even a normally reflective person finds it easy to muse on the shortcomings of mankind. But it should also be obvious that the space program, no matter how abundantly it pays off, will be a big and growing investment, and that, like all investments, it cannot be made until people first produce something to invest. To rise in the sky, the U.S. will have to keep its feet on the ground.

part 5

BUSINESS AND LOCAL GOVERNMENTS

MOST OF the governmental bodies with which businessmen deal in their day-to-day operations, and in which they participate as citizens, are not federal or national units, but thousands of smaller governmental units—state, city, and district. The actions of these units vitally affect many businesses, which are controlled or regulated by all sorts of local decisions about schools, zoning, sewerage, and the financing of these services. Local governments may also promote or encourage business by the ways in which they assess charges for the services provided to businesses and to all citizens. In recent years there has been much talk about the "business climate," the political atmosphere created by local units of government, and about the impact of local government decisions on the costs of doing business and even on the ability to operate at all.

Most states and cities today are eager to increase the volume of manufacturing going on within their boundaries, and there is vigorous competition between states and communities to attract new plants. "Higher and Higher Go the Bids for Industry" as more and more inducements are offered to attractive prospects. However, inducements that seriously erode the tax base and restrict development of necessary local services may create more harm than benefit. While many communities have concluded that new jobs and increased prosperity are worth any price, some instances of overzealous municipal financing of industry have stirred up national criticism. A number of corporations are beginning to take a second look at inducements to see whether their responsibility requires "paying our own way."

A consideration of services and charges or taxes suggests why businessmen are interested in local government. Many services traditionally have been the responsibility of local units of government, even though these units are helped by state or federal financial aid. Industry in its search for locations will pay for some services it needs, and can expect to help pay for others it does not need. Often, however, local government does not fulfill its responsibilities to business or the community in general. "The Worst Public-Works Problem" discusses water and sewerage, services which are often woefully deficient even though they are powerful tools for shaping communities.

"The Taxes Closest to Home" are closely related to the level and quality of services provided. The existing financial mess for many cities and states can be largely alleviated by the growth of the economy, for state and local tax systems have shown a remarkable capacity for siphoning off their share of growth. Nevertheless, the whole tax apparatus needs overhauling and some enlargement, keeping in mind broad standards of equity and economic soundness. Much could also be accomplished by a better quality of administration and by economy in government operation.

Part of the difficulty in reforming tax systems has lain in rural domination of state legislatures, and in the legislative "bias against adequate taxation." People have gradually gerrymandered themselves by moving to metropolitan areas, and the practical consequence has been for disfranchised city voters and their mayors to turn increasingly to the federal government. The 1962 Supreme Court decision in the Tennessee apportionment case, followed by many other decisions, required a start on state legislative redistricting as an act of fairness. Businessmen should be gratified by this change, for business is often a victim of the lag between political ideas and the realities of a fast changing society.

Higher and Higher Go the Bids for Industry*

EUGENE LICHTENSTEIN

Nearly every local and state government in the Union appears to be convinced today that prosperity (in some cases, survival) depends on the rise of manufacturing within its borders. Not only states, but towns and counties, power companies and railroads, find themselves in fierce competition for migrating or expanding corporations. More than 11,000 public and private organizations are in the game. Each holds out its special promise, its unique offer. Specifics begin with come-on offers of all-expense-paid Baedeker tours of a state's natural and man-made resources and run all the way to a community guarantee of a ten-year tax honeymoon, plus assurances that the plant will be financed down to its last blueprinted detail.

The campaigns have certainly contributed to the improvement of the face of the land. Bridges are being thrown up and vast superhighways rolled down to smooth the path of corporate progress. Industrial parks have sprouted on gray and desolate sandlots. Universities and colleges have been upgraded, and teachers lured away from rival states, in order to attract research and development corporations. And, most important, state programs designed to train the illiterate and the unskilled have finally got under way as officials have discovered that, for most industrial firms, a community's greatest asset lies in the character and skill and attitudes of its people.

So by and large the scramble for new industry is a fine thing, but there is growing evidence that at least one warning is in order. As the competition grows hotter, more and more states and communities are offering financial inducements, sometimes with a disregard of future punitive costs to themselves and their

---

* *April 1964*

new corporate citizens. The Federal Reserve Bank of Boston, noting in a current study the rapid rise of new state industrial financing programs, has expressed grave concern. For the proliferation of financing programs, whether good or bad, can be seen almost anywhere one looks. Twenty-six states have passed legislation permitting the sale of municipal bonds for industrial purposes (in 1950 only three states had such a law on the books), while in nine others some form of direct state aid is available.

Arkansas, for example, called a special session to push through its bill authorizing municipalities to issue tax-exempt revenue bonds in order to finance new industrial plants. One reason for the urgency was that the Seiberling Rubber Co., short on capital and long on expansion plans, had promised to locate in Batesville. Five New England states, hoping to stimulate new industrial construction, passed legislation permitting guarantees of mortgages on plant expansions as well as new buildings. North Carolina, which prides itself on the fact that it does not use state funds for industrial financing, nevertheless boasts more than 200 private community development corporations, each one of which is ready, willing, and able to come up with part of the capital for a new plant. In this competitive climate even heavily industrialized regions such as Ohio have been forced to adopt loan programs as a form of self-defense.

Indeed, what once was rationalized as a financial boost for areas of serious unemployment is now frankly recognized as a competitive device. Take the case of Georgia. Prior to 1962 twenty-five Georgia counties and cities with underemployment problems voted to authorize the use of tax-exempt bonds for industrial facilities. Then, in 1962, fifty-six additional Georgia counties authorized the same financial inducement, claiming that the original group (as well as other states) had an undeniable competitive advantage in the battle for industry.

COMPETITION IN THE NEIGHBORHOOD

It is true that corporations still concentrate on such economic necessities as labor supply, production costs, markets, raw materials, and transportation—and such noneconomic intangible factors as community attitudes, climate, educational opportunities, and the preferences of the boss's wife—before determining where to locate a new plant. But once a region has been selected for basic economic reasons other factors come into play. This makes neighboring communities and states even more bitter competitors than rival regional areas. Kentuckians know that any corporate executive considering their state must take a look at Tennessee and probably Ohio. Rhode Island finds itself competing against Connecticut and Massachusetts for plants and warehouses seeking a New England market. Thriving North Carolina is competitively wary of Atlanta, a strong distribution center for the southern market, and of Virginia, somewhat closer to the source of government contracts in Washington. It is in such situations that state and local governments feel they must wheel up some financial device.

Thus what began as a bootstrap operation in most of the states appears now to be getting somewhat out of hand. To date, the dollars involved are not a true indicator of the size of the problem. For while some $500 million of municipal industrial bonds have been sold in the last twenty years, the bulk of the total has been marketed in the last four years. Expectations are that the figures will continue to accelerate.

At their best, state and municipal financial aids to industry provide a leg up for small, expanding firms with little capital, while stimulating active community programs of self-help. At their worst, they give corporations an unfair financial advantage over competitors at governmental expense; and while the benefits of added jobs and income may be desirable, municipal industrial financing can squeeze a community rather tightly and cause severe financial strain. In short, it is a dangerous and dubious practice if applied incautiously.

Economist Edwin Gooding of the Federal Reserve Bank of Boston has speculated that the trend may eventually put the states into the banking business, offering widespread interest-free loans (interest on some state loans is now as low as 2 percent) in one grand sweeping industrial-development program. Officials in the Investment Bankers Association, who have been raising Cassandra-like cries for more than ten years, proclaim there is a fundamental wrong in the use of tax-exempt-bond privileges for industrial purposes; if nothing else, it jeopardizes the tax-free status of municipal bonds. Not surprisingly, emotional shouts of socialism have been leveled by opponents of municipal financing who are apprehensive over the prospect of local or state governments being even tangentially engaged in private enterprise.

What is clear is that, protests aside, state and municipal financing is increasing under the press of militant competition. Already some states would like to shuck some of the financial inducements, particularly the use of municipal industrial bonds, but feel they dare not lest they lose out to a competitor. Thus it seems to fall to industry to exercise a proper responsibility. Otherwise, the issue will only too quickly explode beyond the range and control of states or corporations. At which point there will surely be cries for federal legislation to regulate the tax-free packages that have been so neatly put together.

THE HIGH STAKES

The drives for industry-at-any-price have increased since "unemployment" became such an explosive political word at state and local levels. A recent U.S. Chamber of Commerce study shows that a plant with 100 new jobs brings to a community an annual dowry of $710,000 in added personal income and $229,000 in fresh bank deposits. The mayor can anticipate 359 new citizens, and housewives three new stores; established merchants can begin mulling over expansion plans with the expectation of more than $300,000 of additional local retail sales. And while it is granted that these "humanized" statistics are more promotionally than methodologically sound, they have nevertheless conveyed to the political leaders the sense of what an increase in jobs might mean to a community. It is little wonder then that the states and local townships have spruced up and taken off after industry, ring in hand and all the "I do's" eagerly promised in advance.

The industry-wooing business is only some twenty-five years old, but it has flowered in a period of great transition. Mississippi started things with its Balance Agriculture With Industry Act in 1936, which authorized the use of municipal bonds for financing new plants. But Mississippi's aims were local and noncompetitive: it merely hoped to switch from its complete dependence upon agriculture. That the initial response to the program was small had more to do with the economic facts of life in the mid-Thirties than the appeal of the idea.

It was only at the end of World War II that the South found itself in a position to make a bid for northern industry. Manufacturing had diversified as well as expanded in the South during the war years. In the late Forties not only were there existing plants to attract northern manufacturers, but there were also more skilled workers, and more people with higher per capita incomes, suggesting that a significant market existed in the region.

Essentially it was the prospect of three factors, markets, materials, and labor, all interrelated, that gave the South its postwar opportunity to attract industry. Companies producing automobiles, farm equipment and building materials liked the new consumer market; those in lumber, leather, and paper were in turn attracted to the developing southern industrial market. Creameries and milk plants, petroleum refineries, and phosphorus plants were drawn to the raw materials. Northern textile and shoe companies liked the labor market: women could work after 6:00 P.M., unions were virtually nonexistent, and workers tended to view the employer as a member of the community instead of merely as the enemy. The entire trend seemed a vast deterministic conspiracy when a series of freight-rate increases made it cheaper for many industries to assemble the finished product near the source of supply.

As if these somewhat mechanistic forces were not enough, a number of northern plants were rapidly becoming obsolete; confronted with a decision to expand their present facilities or relocate, many chose to move. For not only were land costs lower in the South and markets appealing, but also several southern states began to push offers of long-term tax exemptions and 100 percent financing of new plants.

The New England states saw no alternative but to adopt weapons of their own. As they lost the old-line major manufacturers they began to seek out traditional firms that wanted to expand, or new ones that wanted to locate in New England. Maine and New Hampshire, in efforts to spur a sagging economy, each authorized the use of a state-wide private building development corporation. New Hampshire, in addition, later established a state agency that was empowered to borrow treasury funds on a three-year loan basis, the money to be spent for developing industrial parks. In a somewhat un-Yankee fashion, the state agency was also given authority to engage in speculative building projects—i.e., constructing plants without having specific tenants signed up in advance. In Rhode Island, state officials put together a package that produced 100 percent financing of plants.

In sum, the New England development corporations became so effective at sparking conventional lending institutions, and assisting small growth firms in their move ahead, that Southerners and Midwesterners quickly began to adopt the device themselves, adding it to whatever public-financing lures were already on the books.

A NEW INDUSTRIAL EQUATION

Meanwhile, carried along by the force of its own volition, industry was changing its ways. One of the industrial lessons mastered in the war was that assembly-line operations could be broken down into units, each unit becoming a plant operation unto itself. A finished product no longer had to be manufactured in one central plant, but could be produced in parts, all over the country, each plant unit locating near a source of supplies or raw materials. Consequently each region soon collected its own diversified set of industries, and its own expanding market. Manufacturers began to set up regional headquarters and production units as well as supply lines and warehouses within many of the large geographic areas of the U.S.

Not only was this a way to cut soaring transportation costs, but it was also becoming a competitive necessity as customers insisted upon prompt and special service. Armstrong Cork located a bottle-cap factory in Dallas as much to meet the area's rising demand as to offset the advantage that a southern base afforded a competitor. More recently Olin Mathieson settled on a new $14-million plant in Charleston, Tennessee, so that its largest customer in the area, Bowaters Southern Paper, could be supplied directly by pipelines running from the Olin plant.

The postwar portable-typewriter boom made it clear to Royal McBee that it must adjust methods of distribution and expand production of its portable machines. Keeping the plant in or near Hartford offered undeniable advantages: proximity to corporate headquarters; familiarity with the community; and retention of an important tradition, namely, the New England character of the Royal typewriter half of the firm. However, balanced against these affirmative propositions were the prospects of higher labor costs in the Hartford area, and the need for a distribution center strategically placed so that it could afford maximum access, at minimum cost, to Royal's future market. In the end, the company decided on a new portable center for Royal in Springfield, Missouri. For there was a supply of available labor at a lower wage rate and Springfield was just about the ideal distribution center for the company's predicted future national market. And despite the modest immediate assistance that the city offered (supplying facilities for the company to train its future employees), it was finally the community leaders' strong positive attitude toward new industry in general and Royal McBee in particular that sold the company's executives on Springfield.

Just as the states began to adjust to the new industrial equations, they discovered R. and D. It is not much of an exaggeration to say that nearly every plant hunter in the country has checked off R. and D. firms under the heading of "top priority." "What R. and D. requires, we desire," may well be the motto of all fifty states. Primarily it is the desire for R. and D., with its clean plants and clean-living Ph.D.'s that has given major impetus to such needed face-lifting as improved university and recreational facilities, and even prompted drives to ameliorate slum conditions. Thus the modest thought behind Mississippi's BAWI plan has resulted in a fiercely competitive war between the states with beneficial side effects ranging through transportation, education, new multimillion-dollar appropriations for science and research, and even vast vocational-rehabilitation training programs. But as neighbor measures neighbor, as each state balances a real or imaginary advantage that its opponent has, financial inducements are coming to play a larger and, in the community's view, more necessary role, frequently tipping the balance of decision.

INDUSTRY'S BIDDING POWER

Hard-bargaining industry now finds itself in a buyers' market, and perhaps cannot be blamed for taking advantage of it so long as tax advantages and financing are important to corporate profits.

When U.S. Rubber decided to build a new plant several years ago, the company officials knew they were limited to a site near

Atlanta, U.S. Rubber's major distribution center for the Southeast. Many sites had been checked and re-checked, and several dozen items on a master checklist investigated and analyzed. In the end, a number of communities qualified, but it was the city of Opelika, Alabama (population 16,000), in Lee County, that was finally selected. Opelika had offered to finance the construction of the plant through the sale of municipal industrial bonds. For U.S. Rubber the fact that the plant would be rented rather than owned meant the company would pay no property taxes, since the Opelika Industrial Development Board, a non-profit corporation established by the town, would be the legal owner of the plant. The lease payments, of course, are an operating expense, and U.S. Rubber saved an initial outlay of capital while gaining a spanking new $20-million plant. The moral of the story has not been lost on Opelika's neighbors, many of whom will feel compelled to outbid Lee County next time around. Just as other corporations are likely to demand equal financial consideration the next time they expand or locate a new plant.

Harvey Aluminum, with a new plant under construction in Lewisport, Kentucky, which is being financed by a $50-million municipal bond issue, has come in for some strong criticism. Since Harvey's completed plant will employ more than 1,000 people and Lewisport has only 700 residents, critics have suggested there is some disproportion in the arrangement concluded between company and town. Certainly, without the offer of municipal financing it is doubtful that Harvey would ever have located in Lewisport—which now has the task of providing additional facilities from a limited tax base.

However, tempting financial offers may well pose a tangible danger for a corporation—namely, that it might underestimate some of the hard, essential economic facts of life. One company, C. M. Hall Lamp, maker of automobile parts, moved most of its production from Detroit largely as a result of union difficulties and mounting labor costs. Clinton, North Carolina, in 1958 undertook to enlarge a one-story plant for the accommodation of Hall, leasing it to the company on reasonable terms. In only two and a half years Hall's president decided that Clinton's disadvantages far outweighed the gains.

To begin with, most of Hall's customers were located in Detroit, which meant a sudden increase in the company's freight costs.

Then, too, it soon became clear that business losses were accumulating as a result of Hall's inability to supply quick, personal service—particularly on the engineering level—to the auto manufacturers in Detroit. Finally, in 1961, Hall flicked out its southern light and retraced its footsteps to Detroit. The company's candid appraisal was that the sojourn was "a costly one."

HIGH HOPES

From a local standpoint, the concern is whether the form competition has been recently taking does not create more harm than benefit. Adopting excessive financial inducements, a community can seriously erode its tax base and restrict the development of such necessary local services as schools, roads, and hospitals. What must be determined is whether the promise of jobs and increased prosperity to the community is worth the price.

Elmira, New York, is an example of a city that decided it *was* worth the price even if this meant raising itself by its own bootstraps. Near Elmira, ground has been cleared for the Great Atlantic & Pacific's new $15-million food-processing plant. Elmira had been a fairly prosperous industrial community through the 1940's and early 1950's, but by the time the Korean war boom had ended the town had come to a dead halt. The first major positive step was taken in 1959 when several of the local merchants banded together to refurbish the downtown area, building a new Elmira shopping center. Spurred on by this, a number of businessmen decided to revitalize Elmira's traditional industrial-development association, organizing the Chemung County Development Corp. and soliciting members and funds from men in the community. They began by developing a twenty-six-acre industrial plot just outside of Elmira, attracting two new companies there by 1962.

It was just about this time that the Great Atlantic & Pacific Tea Co. discovered Elmira. A&P was looking for a new site for a food-processing plant that, when completed, would employ close to 2,000 people. Chemung pieced together a 104-acre land parcel, but discovered that financing would be an important factor. To compete with other communities, the development corporation offered the site to A&P for $208,000. An additional $300,000 was necessary to cover land and site-preparation costs. Chemung employed a professional fund raiser and within twelve days more than $700,000 was pledged by the area's business, industrial, and professional community.

A&P is still more than a year away from the date its new plant begins operating. Nevertheless, Elmira feels with some justification that although there are financial burdens ahead and the town may undergo marked change, the choice was a wise one and the risk and the strain are supportable.

A COMPANY TOWN

For speculators, realtors, and community leaders, municipal financing opens up all sorts of imaginative—and perhaps explosive—possibilities. In the heart of St. Louis County, 3,800 acres of farmland were incorporated in 1959 into the village of Champ. Champ has fifteen voters today, and its sole reason for being, according to owner Bill Bangert, is for the purpose of constructing an industrial village. Bangert is the head of the village governing council—the four other council members are his tenants—and he envisages a village containing more than a billion dollars worth of industrial plants but only between ten and twenty voters—i.e., the only residents in the 3,800 acres of Champ, he explains, should be key management personnel, whose interests coincide with those of the resident industries. Workers in the plants will live outside of Champ. The companies to whose welfare Champ is dedicated will exercise their voice by establishing an industrial commission that will advise the village's council; each company's votes on the commission will be determined by the number of acres it occupies.

Champ's come-on reads like a model written expressly for corporations. It is located three minutes from the airport, at the juncture of two major highways, with excellent gas and water facilities, and the St. Louis labor pool within twenty-five minutes' commuting distance. Local building codes will be tailored to industry, since the city fathers have stated they have no intention of harassing companies that move to Champ. Additional water lines, sewerage facilities, and roads will be paid for by the village, which anticipates more than $1,500,000 in revenue from Missouri's utility companies (under state law, communities can charge a 5 percent tax on gross receipts accruing to the utilities from the municipality). Police and fire protection will also be linked with industry, for Champ expects to deputize plant guards, authorizing them to function as law-enforcement officers as well as company employees. Indeed, if this experiment succeeds, imaginative realtors throughout the country may become municipal midwives, delivering new villages across America, and the phrase "company town" may eventually assume an entirely new meaning.

At present only one manufacturer, R.C. Can Co. of St. Louis, basically a fiber-container company, has agreed to locate in Champ. The village unanimously approved a $3,250,000 municipal revenue bond issue to finance the plant for R.C. Can, but before the bonds could be marketed Missouri's attorney general brought suit, contending that it is illegal for a group of citizens to incorporate themselves into a municipal village solely for the purpose of gaining a tax-free bond umbrella. The case was argued before a special commissioner last December and his recommendations are expected shortly. The case will then have to be argued before the State Supreme Court. Undeterred by the state's action, Bangert borrowed funds to finance the plant himself, arranging, with R.C. Can's approval, to market the bonds if the case is decided in his favor. Hanging fire are decisions by several other companies, all tempted by Champ's inducements— not only municipal financing for industry, but a village designed precisely to serve the interests of industry.

A NATIONAL CONCERN

Overzealous municipal financing of industry is beginning to stir up criticism on a national, as well as a local, level. The cause has brought together a strange assortment of allies. Unions have charged that state inducements have become a form of corporate blackmail, with companies threatening to pull out of union plants and flee to areas where right-to-work laws prevail—unless of course the union knuckles under.

Pointedly, the Investment Bankers Association has suggested that the misuse of tax-free bonds brings into question the status of all municipal bonds. However, the greater threat is that corporations themselves may step up their pressure for municipal financing, as they find new ways to take advantage of municipal largess. Example: If a corporation buys the entire municipal bond issue itself—a practice neither investment bankers nor corporations like to discuss—then it reaps the double benefit of collecting interest on bonds that enjoy a federal-tax exemption while avoiding the payment of local property taxes.

The IBA's solution is to deny deductions for rental payments on plants financed by municipal bonds. A bill to this effect was introduced in 1961 by Congressman Robert Griffin of Michigan, but it never got out of committee; last year he introduced a similar bill, which is still pending in committee.

The Supreme Court of Idaho, interpreting its state constitution, ruled against the use of municipal bonds for industrial financing. The court charged that plants *not* financed with public funds are discriminated against and have grounds for complaint, for they have been placed at a competitive disadvantage by use of public funds. Indeed, the court saw the shadow of socialism hovering in the background. "If the state-favored industries were successfully managed, private enterprise would of necessity be forced out, and the state, through its municipalities, would increasingly become involved in promoting, sponsoring, regulating and controlling private business, and our free private enterprise economy would be replaced by socialism."

The example of Deming, New Mexico, is very much a case in point. In Deming the local officials took the logical next step. How do you secure manufacturing when growth is necessary and companies refuse to be lured into your back yard? The answer is deceptively simple: you buy a company. Deming purchased the Auburn Rubber Co., a plastic-toy company located in Indiana, and brought the plant's assets along with twenty-three key managerial personnel down to New Mexico, financing the transaction by the marketing of $4,480,000 in municipal bonds. Since Deming is not permitted by state law to operate a corporation, it leased the plant to a new company known as the Auburn Rubber Co. of New Mexico, 50 percent owned by *one* of its executives and the other 50 percent by the local go-getting development corporation. So far, despite major union and relocation difficulties, Auburn has managed to sustain itself in its new setting but not by much of a margin.

A CORPORATE RESPONSIBILITY

As their experience with financing techniques accumulates, a number of corporations are beginning to take a long second look at inducements. In one sense this reflects an awareness that the federal government will come into the picture if abuses become excessive and corporations take to expanding at public expense. The exercise of corporate discretion also suggests that enlightened industry knows that it has a responsibility to the community in which it lives. Westinghouse Electric turned down an informal offer of free land from Montevallo, Alabama, explaining rather bluntly that it preferred to pay its own way. Another corporation executive, detailing his reasons for selecting a Maryland site, revealed that he liked the fact that state officials, although willing to grant many concessions, were also firm in drawing the line about what they would not do. That they refused to be pushed around seemed a definite asset; after all, what would happen if the next company that came around was even bigger and demanded even more concessions? Some companies actually oppose the use of financing on principle; still others are concerned about future relations with a community that has financed a plant and is in effect the landlord. What happens if there's a labor dispute, or if a new mayor decides he wants to tell the company how to run its business?

"We pay our own way," explained one vice president, "and we prefer it that way. It's sound business. And it leads to respect." In the end someone has to pay for the benefits an American community offers, and that someone is the corporation as well as the citizen.

The Worst Public-Works Problem*　———

EDWARD T. THOMPSON

Fourteen miles southwest of downtown St. Louis is a subdivision of $30,000-to-$50,000 homes called Ronnie Country Club Acres. Its twenty-five families are happy in homes in such a desirable neighborhood—until it rains. "Then," says one despondent resident, "the septic tanks overflow and sewage lies in the yards or runs down the street." The people of Ronnie Country Club Acres

---

* December 1958

have spent a lot of money trying to rectify the condition by improving drainage fields or putting in storm drains. The owner of one of the houses secretly installed a pipe that takes any overflow from his septic tank and discharges it alongside the state highway. But none of these expedients has solved the problem; it's still unpleasant when it rains on Ronnie Country Club Acres.

The situation that has overtaken these St. Louis suburbanites, with their large investments, is one that is familiar across the U.S.; it is one small item in the most neglected of all the public-works problems arising out of postwar prosperity, mobility, and population growth. *Fortune* has analyzed the highway situation, into which the government may be charging blindly, but at any rate is charging, and the vast school-building program that is actually catching up on the famous "classroom-shortage" of a few years ago. But water supply and sewerage remain a signal failure in public works. These vital deficiencies are being attacked haphazardly, reluctantly, and locally, instead of on an area-wide basis, which is the only effective approach. And not only are water and sewerage facilities woefully deficient, their potential as a powerful tool for shaping communities is being almost totally overlooked.

Not surprisingly, the deficiencies in both sewerage and water facilities, which have been growing steadily more serious for nearly twenty years, are most serious in the sprawling suburbs. The nation's exploding metropolises have filled the country with a hodgepodge of water and sewer systems bounded by political lines instead of natural drainage basins, systems that were often inadequate even before they were completed, much less paid for. The U.S. Public Health Service, in a community-by-community survey, found that nearly half of the 100 million Americans who have community sewers do not have adequate sewage treatment facilities. The Business and Defense Services Administration estimates that some 40 million people need new or improved sewage-collection systems. BDSA also says that almost half of the 117 million people who use public water supplies can't be sure of having enough water available on a hot summer day to put out a major fire.

It is relatively easy to stir up indignation over industrial pollution, a well-publicized problem that will be solved, if at all, by private not public works. Similarly, it is not hard to gain support for such water projects as the Missouri River Basin program, which through flood control, irrigation, and new power sources will change the fortunes of huge areas of the country. But sewer and water needs are less visible. The ordinary householder is satisfied as long as clean-looking water flows from his faucets, and as long as the sewage goes someplace where he can't smell it.

In all, says BDSA, the U.S. investment in municipal sewerage systems is at least $6.9 billion short of what it should be, and in waterworks is short by $4.6 billion of the needs. In the next seventeen years, to correct today's deficiencies, and to provide for the expected surge in population and for depreciation of existing facilities, BDSA estimates, the nation should spend at least $44 billion on waterworks, sewers, and sewage treatment plants. This would mean spending $2.6 billion a year—which is about twice the average rate of outlays for this purpose since 1946. Of the two problems—water and sewage—the latter is by far the more critical. Says one BDSA official: "I don't think the municipalities will catch up on sewers for forty years."

MORE PEOPLE, MORE WASHERS

The U.S. has no absolute shortage of water. The shortage is one of reservoirs, transmission lines, and pumps; these have not been adequate since 1940. During World War II new waterworks construction was virtually nonexistent, and from the end of the war through the Korean emergency, rising costs and material shortages kept the pace of construction well below what was needed to keep up with the population. Since 1940 practically all of the increase in population (from 132 million to 175 million) has been in urban areas; the population dependent on public water supply, says BDSA, has risen from 82 million to 117 million. At the same time, the advent of such appliances as automatic washers has raised the per capita consumption of public water from 122 gallons to 160 gallons per day. By 1975 some 149 million people (of a total population of 209 million) will be in communities with public water, and their per capita needs will be at least 200 gallons daily. The total cost of new waterworks construction needed between now and 1975 is put at around $20 billion.

By 1975 at least 134 million people will be in areas with public sewerage, compared to 100 million today. To provide them with adequate sewage disposal, $24 billion should be spent. A great part of this spending is needed for sewage-treatment facilities. Until recently, most sewer systems were considered adequate if they simply provided collection lines. The raw sewage could be dumped, as it still is in St. Louis, New Orleans, and many other areas, into a convenient stream or river, which through dilution and natural bacteria action would often purify itself within a few miles. But as population became more dense, the amount of raw sewage discharged began to exceed the purifying capacity of the streams. Federal and state authorities agree that the Mississippi just below St. Louis is "highly polluted." Most large cities and many smaller communities recognized the dangers of pollution and built so-called primary treatment plants—in effect, settling tanks that reduce organic pollution by about one-third. Now, however, the quantities of sewage have risen to such a level in areas like Denver and Washington, D.C., that more intensive treatment is needed—secondary treatment, which, by aeration and settling, leaves the effluent 70 to 90 percent "clean." Primary-treated sewage from Denver now enters the South Platte River, which is a source of irrigation water for downstream farmers; even though the state warned of a health hazard in 1956 and recommended secondary treatment, Denver is still not spending the necessary money.

NO SALES APPEAL TO SEWERS

Besides the sheer population growth, a complicating factor in the problems of water and sewerage is the pattern of that growth. When new houses are erected on sites contiguous to built-up areas, it is a relatively simple matter to extend community water and sewer lines to them. But the subdivider, in his search for cheap land, generally jumps out into the countryside, then tries to persuade the city to bring water to him. Usually he is willing to pay for the installation of water lines, within his development, plus at least his proportionate share of the water main from town. In most cases, the town is willing to pay the incremental costs because it can be fairly sure it will recover them in increased water revenues as the area builds up. Sometimes, however, as in many parts of Florida that have a high water table, the cost of bringing water from town is greater than drilling a central well or wells at the development, so the developer builds the facilities and then either goes into the water business himself, or deeds or sells the equipment to a private utility. In either case, the home buyer pays the cost in the price of his house.

Sewerage is another matter. A developer may install sewer lines, pay for the trunk line from town, add the cost to the price of his houses, and leave the owner with a permanent system. But most developers don't operate that way. Unlike a good water supply, which practically all buyers insist on, sewers have little sales appeal. Buyers seem to ignore the rather obvious fact that up to 95 percent of the water that enters a house must be carried away by some sort of mechanical means. So the developer puts in septic tanks at perhaps two-thirds the cost of sewers, without, of course, informing the buyer that these devices may be adequate for only five or ten years, and that in the meantime there will be maintenance costs. When the septic tanks start giving trouble, the house owners often find that the only solution is a sewer system. Then they not only have to write off their investment in the septic tanks, they have to pay considerably more for their sewers than they would have when the houses were built because properties and streets have to be torn up.

Septic tanks are all right if certain conditions are met: if the drainage field is big enough and the soil drains easily. Authorities agree, however, that the average development lot of less than a quarter acre is seldom sufficient even with the best possible conditions.

"BREAK UP THE COMPETITION"

Planners and engineers, in a rare display of unanimity, believe strongly that metropolitan action is vital if the country is to get the kind of sewerage it needs. They cite several reasons for their belief. Individual municipalities within a metropolitan area do not pass the laws necessary to curb the installation of septic tanks; each town is afraid that if it is too strict with a developer he will simply build his houses elsewhere. The separate towns can't or won't do anything to bring uniformly high standards to the multiplicity and variety of sewerage systems that already exist in every metropolitan area. On the Virginia side of the Potomac River across from Washington, for example, there are fourteen sewage-collection agencies operating nineteen treatment plants; in addition, there are 70,000 people without sewers at all.

The lack of concerted action is due partly to the fact that the man at the top of the hill just doesn't care about the problems of the man at the bottom. Sioux City, Iowa, for instance, despite long-standing complaints from people downstream on the Missouri River about pollution, has refused to build a sewage-treatment plant. Moreover, "clusters of governments can't make over-all policy," as Robert Wood, political scientist at the Massachusetts Institute of Technology, points out. "One city can make its own residents happy, but not much else. Even if governments want to solve problems on a broad scale, officials are hamstrung by outdated laws and the nationwide scramble for resources. We need to break up the competition among communities." Sewage treatment makes sense, of course, only if an entire area participates. There is little incentive for one town to clean up its sewage if thirty others around it aren't equally conscientious.

Finally, argue the planners, there is the economic advantage of metropolitan sewerage. The capital investment required for a treatment plant to serve 500,000 people is only about three-quarters as much per capita as for one that serves 50,000 people in the same area; per capita operating costs are usually less in a big plant.

These are not necessarily arguments for establishing over-all metropolitan governments; but they are potent arguments for setting up public-works authorities able to operate on a metropolitan scale.

"MOSCOW OR SEATTLE?"

Seattle and its environs are typical of what planners call the "conglomerate mess" of suburban sewer facilities, and of what can happen when communities fail to take an area-wide approach to the problem. The Seattle area now has a population of about 850,000, over 65 percent of it within the city limits, the rest in surrounding fringe communities. The area is expected to have a total population of a million and a quarter by 1980 (only half of it inside the city limits). Until this summer, sewerage service was controlled by forty-nine agencies.

Though there are twenty-five sewage-treatment plants in the area, raw sewage from about 425,000 people is regularly discharged at sixty different points into Puget Sound, the Duwamish River, and Elliott Bay. Treated sewage from 80,000 people enters Lake Washington directly from ten treatment plants and indirectly from at least 4,000 septic tanks. In addition, when it rains heavily, overflows of raw sewage enter Lake Washington and Green Lake more than forty times per summer. As a result, the concentration of certain plant nutrients, mostly phosphorus and nitrogen, has increased to the point where plant life is choking the lake.

Almost one-third of the total population is without public sewers, and to keep up with residential development some 6,000 private septic tanks are being built annually at a cost of $2 million. Engineers consider many of these no better than a temporary solution. Much of Seattle itself uses combined sewers that carry both sanitary sewage and storm runoff (a situation common to most big cities). Because of inadequate provisions for storm flows, many of these sewers overflow when it rains, flood basements, and discharge sewage into streets.

The logical area for future growth is around Lake Washington, but its greatest attribute—the lake—is being ruined. The communities on the eastern shore of the lake recognized the problem, and also recognized that they could solve it only in concert. So three years ago the towns tried to get together on a joint trunk sewer line that would take the sewage out of the lake and put it in Puget Sound. But the well-intentioned attempt quickly turned into a battle. Two of the communities, Bellevue and Lake Hills, couldn't agree on what plan to adopt; nothing got built.

Meanwhile, a group of private citizens led by James Ellis, an earnest young attorney, and strongly encouraged by Seattle's able mayor, Gordon S. Clinton, had been pushing the cause of metropolitan government for the area. Ellis, in fact, had helped draft a new charter for King County, in 1952, which would have created a county-manager form of government. Opposition slogans such as "Is This Moscow or Seattle?" plus the lack of a compelling reason for administrative change killed it at the polls.

In 1956 the city and county finally did get together to finance a $130,000 sewerage study by Brown & Caldwell, San Francisco consulting engineers; the state pollution-control commission contributed $10,000 toward the study. Concurrently, Ellis' group drafted and pushed through the state legislature in 1957—by one vote—a law that allowed the formation of a Metropolitan Municipal Corporation empowered to plan, finance, and administer six services for the area: sewage disposal, water supply, public transportation, garbage disposal, parks and parkways, and comprehensive planning. In March of this year, metropolitan Seattle residents were presented with an abbreviated proposal to create such a corporation with authority over sewerage, public transportation, and comprehensive planning.

"SAVE LAKE WASHINGTON"

But even this was too much for the voters. The proposal passed in the city of Seattle, but was defeated in the areas outside. "The county areas were afraid of a supergovernment dominated by the city," says Mayor Clinton. Plans were made immediately to have a new vote in September, but this time on an even more abbreviated version of the first plan. The corporation would have authority only over sewerage; local autonomy would be strictly observed; the area to be covered by the authority, originally 575 square miles, was cut about in half. Perhaps the most important, a single issue was dramatized: "We must save Lake Washington." The people at last voted yes.

Brown & Caldwell had recommended that two large treatment plants be built (one south of Seattle, one north); these will be fed by two huge interceptor lines that will pick up the sewage from present and proposed collection lines. Because of ridge topography in some areas, seven small additional treating plants will be built. Total treating capacity is to be nearly 300 million gallons per day, enough to last the area for seventy-five years. The proposal called for a three-stage program to cost $83,200,000 in the first ten years, $35,400,000 in the second ten, and $45,-400,000 in the final stage. All of the first-stage projects and the most pressing parts of the second are in the geographical area covered by the new authority, and are now being studied in detail. (The report also recommended that the city of Seattle spend $69 million of its own money to separate storm and sanitary sewers.)

SO NOTHING GETS DONE

Ardent planners may not be too happy about Seattle's plan. They argue that first things should come first, and in their book the first thing is a metropolitan government that can handle *all* the problems of area-wide significance. Once the organization is established, it can attack the specific problems.

This argument has an orderly sound and, in fact, it is precisely what James Ellis and other Seattle Metro backers wanted in the beginning. But when, as happened in Seattle, the people of the area decide they just don't want a super-government, the argument breaks down: urgent and specific problems don't get solved. In the region around Nashville, Tennessee, for example, better sewerage is badly needed, and the planners tried to use the situation as a lever to set up metropolitan government. Metro was so soundly defeated in Nashville last June that the chances are it will not be proposed again, or at least not very soon. Meanwhile, no steps are being taken to get an area-wide sewerage authority, and the potential hazard to health increases.

Partly because of sewerage problems, the people of Dade County, Florida, voted in 1957 to adopt metropolitan government. (It is the first, and so far only, large area in the U.S. to try this system.) But Dade's Metro government has been so harried by political problems that only the barest start has been made to meet sewerage needs. A sewer authority elected in 1957 would almost certainly have been much further ahead.

Independent authorities pose some difficulties, of course. As *Fortune* has pointed out, they can easily become a power unto themselves. Being "non-political" appointees, the commissioners may hold themselves aloof from normal democratic pressures; this is fine if upstream and downstream views don't compete, but, particularly in water and sewerage problems, they almost always do. Moreover, there are many organizational and public-relations problems in setting up a metropolitan water or sewer authority. For example, should communities that have already solved their problems be required to surrender their expensive facilities to the agency, and in addition help pay for facilities for their less foresighted neighbors?

But the fact is that metropolitan water-and-sewer authorities *are* operating successfully, and have been for some time. Both

Boston and Chicago have had metropolitan sewerage agencies since 1889, the Metropolitan Water District of Southern California was created in 1928 to provide water for the Los Angeles area. In every case, despite the problems and drawbacks, these authorities are doing a far better job than the individual communities in the areas ever did, not only of correcting water and sewer deficiencies, but of planning ahead for an expanding population.

GOOD GAMBLE

Once water and sewer lines are installed, population builds up around them. It is possible for a metropolitan authority to put lines in sections where it wants population to expand and withhold them from sections it wants to keep for open space. Water and sewer facilities can be an even more useful weapon against urban sprawl than zoning laws. But they are seldom used this way.

Similarly, water and sewerage can be used to attract industry. Many cities and towns will agree happily to provide such services to a company if it will formally decide to locate within the town's boundaries. But almost no communities in this country have been willing to take the next important step, that is, to build water and sewer lines into an area not currently industrialized so that the chamber of commerce can then say to industry: "We're ready for you right now, no waiting."

The arguments of the politicians against both of these policies go something like this: "We have so many existing needs that we can't even think about building out ahead of population growth or in anticipation of new industry; we can't afford to put in lines that maybe nobody will be using for several years; we can't afford to gamble with the public's money." But with the flight to suburbia almost certain to increase rather than diminish, and with practically every community in the nation scrambling to get choice industry—research labs, electronics firms, etc.—it may well be a bigger gamble not to be ready ahead of time.

"WE CAN'T AFFORD ANY MORE"

The most common response of local officials when asked why they aren't tackling their water and sanitation problems more vigorously is, "We know we're way behind, we know we're polluting our river, but we just can't afford to spend any more than we are." What they mean is that they *won't* spend any more.

It is true, that water and sewer projects are expensive. New York City, which may face the threat of having to close its beaches because of pollution, recently estimated that it would have to spend some $170 million just to separate sanitary and storm sewers, and another $110 million for one sewage-treatment plant; nobody knows for sure what total metropolitan New York needs are. Also, many communities are at, or near, their legal or economic general debt limits, and thus find it difficult to borrow money. But legal debt limits are arbitrary, they can be changed; and economic limits are set by available revenues, and these can be increased.

Water and sewerage are services, and, as such, charges can be made for their use. The total income after operating expenses is highly predictable and can be used to pay off bonds. This is the way all private utilities operate. But public-water charges are, on the average, too low to provide the necessary revenue. Sometimes they do not even cover operating expenses, and even when they do, any surplus usually goes back into the city treasury to cover deficits from other services. One estimate is that if each person in the country would pay about 1½ cents more per day for water (an increase of about 50 percent over the mean U.S. per capita water rate), the accumulated deficiencies in water facilities could be wiped out by 1970 and that from then on new waterworks could be financed out of earnings. As for sewerage, few communities make any identifiable charge at all; operating costs are paid out of general taxes. Thus, even for the smallest capital expenditure, it becomes necessary to float a general bond issue.

NO PRESSURE ON CONGRESS

Rather than make the politically unpopular move of raising service charges, many communities talk wishfully about increased state or federal aid. They are not likely to get it. There are no figures available on the total amount of state aid for local water and sewer projects. But the states' general indifference to these local needs is indicated by the fact that currently only four states

(Maine, Maryland, New Mexico, and Vermont) are willing to give any grants at all toward the construction of sewage-treatment plants; the total amount of state funds appropriated in the U.S. is less than $7 million. In California, which estimates that $600 million should be spent on sewerage works through 1960, the only state aid to municipalities is a $1-million revolving loan fund. Some experts argue that the states should be doing far more than they are; they say the states should emulate Texas, which last year created a state water-development board that can issue up to $200 million in state general-obligation bonds for local water projects. Texas municipalities will save a considerable amount in interest charges because of the state's generally superior credit rating.

The federal government has spent practically nothing on municipal waterworks and sewerage systems since the massive WPA and PWA programs of the Thirties; since 1956 it has appropriated a trifling $50 million a year[1] for construction of sewage-treatment facilities. Last spring a bill to double the amount of sewage-treatment grants died in the House Rules Committee. And now there are indications that the whole program may be replaced by one that would relinquish some $145 million a year of federal telephone-tax money to the states. The states would not have to use this money for public works, and, judging by current state public-works policies, it seems unlikely that much of it would be used to build sewage-treatment works.

In view of the enormous pork-barreling potentials inherent in water and sewerage deficiencies—far greater, for example, than in river and harbor maintenance—Congress's lack of interest in the problem is surprising. But it also indicates the public's indifference to the problem: people don't even bring pressure on their Congressmen to get them federal help.

A QUARTER SAID NO

Water and sewer facilities will be a lot more costly in the future than they are now. The cheapest water sources are already

---

[1] There is also a federal loan program for public works, administered by the Community Facilities Administration, to help small communities that are unable to finance projects through normal channels.

being exploited. Increased demands in many areas will have to be met by transporting water much greater distances. Southern California, an extreme case, is now trying to put through a program that would involve building 400-mile-long aqueducts to bring water from the northern end of the state. More and more sewage treatment will be needed, and it seems almost certain that new and probably more costly processes will have to be used to remove inorganic matter that gets through today's plants; a little further in the future, but definitely in sight, is the need to deal with the wastes from nuclear-power generation, a fantastically expensive proposition.

But the basic problem in water and sewers is not money. Nor, for the time being at any rate, is it technology. The big problem is people. Last year, of the thousands of communities with inadequate water and sewerage facilities, only about 600 were stirred up enough to put bond issues up before the voters. In many instances the towns were under considerable state or federal pressure to clean up pollution. Yet the citizens of nearly one-quarter of these 600 municipalities—Costa Mesa, California, Warwick, New York, and La Grange, Ohio, to name a few—turned down the bond issues at the polls. "Some people won't do anything," says one disillusioned city official, "until we have another plague."

The Taxes Closest to Home*   _____

ROBERT LUBAR AND CHARLES E. SILBERMAN

Most of America's state and local governments look to be in a financial mess. It's a lucky governor or mayor who isn't facing a budgetary crisis, who hasn't found himself obliged to reach in every direction for new sources of revenue. New York City is considering a 10-cent tax on taxicab rides; Texas is thinking about seizing unclaimed bank accounts; South Carolina is eying pinball

_____

* June 1959

machines. Meanwhile the taxpayers, who are supplying some $46 billion to state and local governments, on top of $78 billion in personal, corporate, excise, and other taxes they have to pay to Washington, more often than not feel themselves very poorly served in return. The deficiencies in local administration are apparent on every hand: inadequate sewerage systems, streets poorly maintained, inefficient police forces, schools that are better than they used to be, no doubt, but that could be a great deal better—all the services, in fact, that affect the citizen most immediately and upset him the most when they deteriorate.

In the light of all this, it might surprise a good many citizens to hear that the state and local taxing apparatus of the U.S. has at least one characteristic greatly admired by tax experts. Though the system is full of patchwork and improvisations (like the federal tax system), it has shown a remarkable capacity for siphoning off its "share" of the growth of the U.S. economy. Today, in fact, it is generating three times as much revenue as it did ten years ago.

It is this ability of the state and local tax systems to grow with the economy that promises some relief to the harassed state legislatures and city councils. They may well be extricated from their holes by the sheer pull of economic forces. This article will presently attempt to show how this may come about. But to take the fullest advantage of the forces now at work, the apparatus does need overhauling and some enlargement. In proposing reforms of state and local tax systems, *Fortune* is attempting to appraise taxation in America against certain broad standards of equity and economic soundness. These articles have not undertaken to explore what is or isn't "politically feasible" this year or next, least of all in state and local taxation, where thousands of separate sovereignties are involved. The following recommendations are intended as a contribution to the continuing debate on tax policy that is taking place in most states and localities:

• In order to assure themselves an increasing flow of revenue without constantly having to juggle tax rates and search for new sources, the states should rely more extensively on broad-based taxes on personal income, corporation profits, and retail sales.

• Administration of property taxes must be improved so that assessments on property can be kept more nearly in line with market values.

• The states should work together to achieve some uniformity in the way they tax business; uniformity is important not only for equity's sake but to encourage the very economic growth that sustains the tax base.

THE TURNING POINT

The present financial troubles of the states and localities have been building up through thirty years of unusual stresses and strains. To begin with, the depression wiped out a good deal of the base of the property tax, which had been practically the sole mainstay of state and local revenues. The states, burdened with new relief and welfare expenditures, had to cast around for new revenue sources. During the war, though revenue was plentiful, they had to defer needed expenditures because of the shortage of materials and manpower. The states were still in the process of reconstructing their tax structures when they were hit by great new postwar revenue requirements. Not only did the population surge create new demands for public services, but there was a huge backlog of construction (particularly schools and highways) and a considerable lag in salaries (notably of teachers) to make up. States and localities found themselves particularly hard hit by inflation. Prices of the goods and services they have to buy (e.g., school buildings, hospitals, schoolteachers, and policemen) have gone up 83 percent since 1946 as compared with a rise of 48 percent in the general price level.

But now the situation may be at a turning point. To justify this conclusion, it is necessary to project the whole state and local financial situation into the next ten years. A look into the future is pertinent to this discussion because, although some of the reforms we have recommended above have a somewhat drastic sound to them, they are not nearly so drastic as reforms would have to be if the whole situation didn't have a fairly encouraging aspect. The fact is, during the next ten years, states and localities may well finance their services with less difficulty than in the past ten, and at the same time considerably improve them.

The extent of the "need" for more and better services is, of course, debatable. The U.S. has already reduced its famous "schoolroom shortage" more than many people realize; in water and sewerage systems, on the other hand, the deficiencies are greater than is generally known. The country is committed to a tremendous highway program; pressing claims can be made for hospitals and parks. Not only population growth but the extraordinary mobility of the U.S. population will be laying new burdens on state and local services throughout the 1960's. *Fortune* has predicted a $750-billion economy by 1970, and this in itself will require greatly increased expenditures for public services, which will be offset only slightly by declines in welfare and relief expenditures. *Fortune's* projection of such requirements indicates that state and local expenditures could rise to $85 billion by 1970, or double what they were in fiscal 1957.

A detailed projection, which confirms *Fortune's* over-all figures, was prepared [in 1959] by Dick Netzer of the Federal Reserve Bank of Chicago for a conference on public finance sponsored by the National Bureau of Economic Research. His basic assumption was that the population would increase 25 percent in the next decade. He makes three different forecasts of what state and local expenditures might come to in 1970, based on three different standards of public services. Just to maintain "constant" standards (i.e., about where they are now) for a rising population, states and localities might have to lay out $60 billion annually by the end of the next decade. What Netzer calls "moderate" improvement in services could cost another $10 billion. To bring about "substantial" improvement (i.e., up to the very top standards of today) Netzer projects a figure of about $85 billion. Top standards are, for example, those now set by the Chicago suburb of Glencoe, which spends two-thirds more on each school child than the national average. Some communities in 1970 may be satisfied with a good deal less than today's top standard. The trend, however, is toward substantial improvement, and $85 billion, by no means the highest figure that has been projected, is *Fortune's* best estimate of what the figure is likely to be. Such an expenditure would be 11.3 percent of a $750-billion GNP. State and local spending this year is running about 11 percent of GNP. In other words, a very high standard of public services can be achieved with no increase in the share of national output.

But specifically how will the states and localities raise the money? Netzer's conclusion is that the present state and local tax systems could provide most of it without any changes whatsoever. The state and local tax base will expand as the economy grows, and with a $750-billion GNP it will throw off about $67 billion of revenue, roughly $20 billion more than it does today. Part of the $18-billion gap between spending and income will be filled by some $11 billion in federal aid (a projection of current trends and of the aid levels assumed in present highway and other programs). This would leave a net gap of about $7 billion.

Part of the gap could be filled through additional borrowing. A high level of borrowing may be justified since about 30 percent of the spending will be for such long-lived projects as schools, roads, and hospitals. But the gap could also be closed by additional revenue from either an increase in rates or a widening of the tax base. A 10 percent over-all increase in rates of taxes now in force, for example, would yield an additional $4 billion. Or, if all states not now levying an income tax (seventeen of them) and a general sales tax (seventeen) were to impose these taxes and set rates at about the average prevailing in states that now have these taxes, an additional $8 billion of revenue would be raised.

THE "BIAS AGAINST ADEQUATE TAXATION"

Meanwhile the immediate financial problem is acute in many states and localities, and it may well grow worse in the next few years. While expenditures are likely to increase most rapidly in the early 1960's, revenues will be getting their big lift from the economy toward the end of the decade. Moreover, these projections are aggregate estimates, based on a nationwide average of expenditures and revenues. They suggest that the over-all problem is by no means hopeless, but they leave individual states and localities with many difficulties to overcome. All of the states and more than 100,000 cities, counties, towns, school boards, and special districts will not increase their spending at the same rate. Some have a great deal of catching up to do. Some states in the Southwest and Far West, for example, will be forced by an influx of population to spend faster than the national average. Other states do not now have a tax base broad enough to take advantage of economic growth. And some local governments need to overhaul their property-tax assessment so that the base of this tax will grow as property values increase.

Reforms of the type already suggested, however necessary, are not easy to bring off in state legislatures, which are notoriously shortsighted and susceptible to pressures. Moreover, most state legislatures are weighted on the side of rural constituencies and are not apt to look with sympathy on the problems of the cities, where populations are densest and needs are greatest. In any case, the tendency of politicians is to avoid doing anything decisive about taxes. "Politics," as a report on state constitutions pointed out, "tends to have a bias against 'adequate' taxation."

A contrast in two approaches to the state tax problem has been provided in 1959 by two neighboring and basically similar states, New York and New Jersey. Both have popular governors, elected by large majorities. In New York, Nelson Rockefeller's Republican party controls the legislature, while New Jersey's Democratic governor, Robert Meyner, has had to face a hostile majority. Both legislatures have been disinclined to take decisive action about taxes, and the interesting comparison is between the ways the two governors chose to cope with legislative stubbornness.

Rockefeller found, when he took office, that state revenues were falling further and further behind spending, which was rising at an annual $200-million rate. Rockefeller's response was a "pay as you go" policy and a stiff tax increase to back it up. It is arguable, of course, whether states can or should be placed on a truly pay-as-you-go basis, which means paying for all capital investments out of current revenue. The significance of Rockefeller's program, however, was not that he raised taxes as much as he did, but that he raised them in a way that offered the best assurance of an adequate flow of revenue in the future. He went straight to the most productive—and sensitive—part of the tax structure. He raised the top-bracket income-tax rate from 7 to 10 percent, and at the same time risked his political neck by lowering exemptions to create 400,000 new taxpapers and get more money from all.

Meanwhile, New Jersey's Meyner was accepting credit for having once again kept the long-standing bipartisan pledge of "no new taxes." New Jersey budgets have also been breaking records year after year, but Meyner has introduced only one new tax during his administration, a 1.75 percent corporation income tax enacted in 1958. Aside from this, the state tax system consists of a clutter of selective taxes; as the well-worn Jersey wisecrack goes, "You have no state taxes in New Jersey unless you drive an automobile, smoke, bet on the horses, drink, or die."

When its tax bite is measured in relation to per capita *income,* New Jersey ranks forty-fifth among the states. New Jersey keeps state aid to a minimum, leaving counties, cities, and towns to support their schools, their roads, and their hospitals on what they can raise from the property tax, which is haphazardly assessed and so inadequate that some counties can afford no more than $200 per pupil for their schools (vs. New York State's basic minimum of $330).

Sooner or later, most experts familiar with the state's finances agree, New Jersey will have to capitulate to a broad-based sales or income tax, or both. By the time some brave Jersey politician gets around to breaking the "no new taxes" pledge, Nelson Rockefeller's 1959 program may well be paying off in a soundly based "no new taxes" policy for New York.

THE FIRST AND LAST DOLLAR

Fortune's first recommendation in a program for reforming state and local taxes is *the adoption by all states of sales and personal income taxes.* Thirty-two states now levy each of these taxes, but only nineteen use both of them.

The general retail-sales tax is the largest single source of state revenue. But in 1957 it brought in only $3.4 billion, or 23.5 percent of the total tax yield in all the states. In the seventeen states that do not tax sales, opposition to the levy seems as firm as ever. The governor who advocates it always runs the risk of political extinction. Legislators find it more prudent, when revenue needs are pressing, to be "selective"—i.e., raise taxes on cigarettes, liquor, coin-operated machines, etc.

Opponents of the sales tax contend that it is bad social policy because it is regressive. The man on low wages, who has to spend a bigger share of his earnings on retail purchases than the rich man, pays a higher tax proportionately. If the sales tax were the only tax, it would indeed put a grossly unjust burden on lower incomes. But its regressiveness is less significant when it is considered in the context of the whole U.S. tax system, which is dominated by the steeply progressive federal income tax. And in any event, the tremendous rise in the per capita cost of government makes it inevitable that taxation becomes somewhat more regressive. Vast expenditures cannot be financed by "soaking the rich"; there simply isn't enough money at the upper income levels.

Most of the revenue must come from the income groups that in the aggregate receive most of the national income, and one reasonable way to get the revenue is by taxing people in proportion to what they spend. Moreover, the sales tax admirably reflects the state of economic activity, thereby enabling a state to reap growing revenues out of growing national output.

The rate at which the sales tax should be imposed is a matter for individual states to decide. It would depend on their revenue needs and economic conditions. In the thirty-two sales-tax states, rates now range from 2 to $3\frac{1}{3}$ percent. The top rate, levied in the state of Washington, has had no adverse economic effects there, and Washington is thinking of going to 4 percent.

"OUR MOST SALABLE ASSET"

The sales tax should be supplemented by the state income tax (1) because sales cannot bear the whole burden; and (2) because the great elasticity of the income tax gives it a unique advantage as a revenue raiser. As total personal incomes rise, the tax take rises even faster. (More taxpayers climb into brackets where they pay a higher rate.) Again it should be left to each state to determine how much progression it wants. A reasonable level is a rate scale rising to a 10 percent maximum, such as New York, Minnesota, and Colorado now have.

The income tax is the most useful generator of revenue in the thickly populated industrial states, where incomes are above average and where, in turn, government services are the most expensive. (Yet six populous states—Illinois, Pennsylvania, Michigan, Ohio, Texas, and New Jersey—which contribute among them almost a third of the entire federal income-tax yield, do not levy an income tax.)

Not a single state has adopted the income tax since 1937. Resistance to it has been particularly rigid since the 1940's when federal rates shot up so sharply. States eager to attract new industry feared that corporations would shun them if executive incomes were subjected to tax. The fact that Connecticut has no income tax, says a state official, "is our most salable asset."

This argument overlooks one important consideration. The privilege given the taxpayer of deducting his state income-tax payment from the income subject to federal income tax reduces his effective state tax to a much smaller figure than the rate schedule indicates. For a taxpayer in the federal 60 percent bracket, for instance, the effective rate of a state income tax is only 40 percent of the apparent rate. In New York the top tax rate is now 10 percent, beginning with incomes over $15,000. But after deducting his state tax from his federal return, a New Yorker with $16,000 taxable income pays only 2.5 percent more in total taxes than he would if there were no state tax. The percentage becomes even lower the higher the income.

Because the deduction privilege thus provides the state with some revenue at federal expense, it is an indirect form of federal aid. But this is a kind of federal aid that has much to commend it, because it leaves the decision making entirely to the states; they can raise money according to their needs and spend it as they see fit. As the first article in this series suggested, this is a good reason why a reformed federal income tax should retain the deduction for state income taxes.[1]

"OUR BIGGEST TAX HEADACHE"

The second of *Fortune's* specific recommendations is that *the states should make an effort to achieve greater uniformity in business taxation.*

In casting about for new revenue sources since the depression, the states have developed a welter of levies on business activity. They include flat license fees, taxes on capital stock, and gross-receipts taxes with arbitrarily fixed rates that differ from industry to industry. The inconsistency with which the states tax business is, of course, part of the price of states' rights: the states should be allowed to raise money the way they wish. But more uniformity in business taxes would be to the advantage of the states themselves: it would give the economy as a whole more freedom to grow.

In its markets and to a certain extent in its production, modern corporate enterprise has long since overflowed state lines. There

---

[1] Twenty of the thirty-two income-tax states allow the taxpayer to deduct his *federal* tax on his state return. This is a costly concession for the states to make. A Minnesota tax study estimates that federal deductibility costs that state one-third of the revenue it might otherwise collect from the income tax.

is hardly a big U.S. firm that isn't liable to taxation in several states. Varying tax conditions create unfair advantages and disadvantages, and thus distort competitive conditions.

Furthermore, the lack of uniformity sometimes makes the mechanical operation of paying taxes more costly than the taxes themselves. It may mean operating several different accounting procedures to satisfy different definitions of what is taxable, hiring extra lawyers to argue the fine points with various state and local authorities, and filing literally hundreds of tax returns every year. Union Carbide, for instance, submits 3,600 separate returns all together to states and localities, and according to Paul Smith, in charge of the company's tax problems, these complications and frustrations make for "our biggest tax headache."

A "FAVORABLE TAX CLIMATE"

One solution would be for the states gradually to replace the business taxes with one tax on corporation profits. Liability under this tax is fixed by a single common standard, net earnings. As the second article in this series argued, the corporation income tax has not hampered business expansion.

Thirty-five states already have some kind of corporation profits tax, and in 1957 they raised about $1 billion from it, with rates ranging from 1 to 8.8 percent. (Actually, the bite is only half that much, for the corporation deducts its state tax payment against its 52 percent federal tax.) But the states that do not levy it include some of the leading industrial centers, such as Illinois, Ohio, and Michigan, big states that conspicuously refrain from taxing personal income.

Opposition to the corporation tax springs from the same fear that it will frighten away industry. But corporate ideas about what makes a "favorable tax climate" are undergoing a revaluation. Taxes play a part in industry's choice of location, along with such considerations as nearness of raw materials, availability of labor, and access to markets. Some companies, however, are interested less in how much they have to pay in taxes and more in what they get for their money. Sophisticated corporations are aware that unusually low taxes usually spell a deficiency of public services. Scouts for new sites look for adequate highways for transporting goods and adequate schools for employees' children.

West Virginia is one state that has learned from painful experience that poor roads do more to scare industry away than high taxes.

There is increasing recognition of the fact that the corporation profits tax is the most equitable way in which industry can help finance the public services it requires. As a result, the tax has won converts in the corporations themselves and in the legislatures. As already noted, its adoption marked the only break in New Jersey's bipartisan "no new taxes" policy.

THE COURT'S SURPRISE

The corporation income tax, however, also raises some interstate problems. If a corporation manufactures and distributes in several states, who taxes what part of its net income? A series of Supreme Court decisions in the winter of 1958–59 answered this question in a way that surprised many tax lawyers. The Court ruled that a state could tax the income of an out-of-state corporation that merely sells within its borders. The decisions opened new doors for state revenue seekers (or at least kept old doors open, for twenty-five states had been taxing the income of "foreign" corporations before the test cases came up). Now those states that have been hesitant about stepping into the questionable territory of interstate commerce have a clear invitation to do so. Unless the states exercise restraint, some interstate firms could theoretically be taxed on more than 100 percent of their income. At present, tax liability is usually fixed according to elaborate formulas, which take into account the proportion of the corporation's property, payroll, warehouse facilities, and sales that fall within the taxing state. But there is a notable lack of standardization among these formulas, and no corporation is guaranteed against a ganging up on its income.

The Court rulings have pointed up the need for a common interstate formula. Differences could be composed by an agreement among the states, in which case, according to the Constitution, Congress would have to give its approval. The Senate has been holding hearings on a bill that would accomplish the same end more directly—and more efficiently—by authorizing the federal government to lay down rules for all states to follow in taxing interstate corporations.

THE HUMAN FACTOR

Fortune's third recommendation is *the improvement of local property-tax administration to keep assessments in step with market values.*

Before the depression, the property tax was the biggest source of revenue for both states and localities. It is now only a minor source of state revenue, but it continues to be the almost exclusive local tax, except in a few large cities. Thus in the aggregate revenues of all state and local tax systems, the property tax has declined from 62 percent in 1927 to 31 percent today. As a revenue source, it almost completely dried up during the depression of the 1930's; since the war it has made quite a comeback. Its 1957 yield, $13 billion, was triple that of 1945. Most of this gain resulted from the expansion of its base as property values rose.

This proved that the property tax, like income and sales taxes, is a good reflector of economic growth. But whereas rising income and consumption automatically throw off increased revenue, the degree in which advancing property values will produce a greater yield depends on a human factor—the efficiency with which thousands of individual assessors adjust tax liability to rising market price. A great deal has been done to improve assessment methods, but in many localities assessment is still left to untrained, poorly paid, occasionally venal, part-time petty officials.

Not only are these localities deprived of the revenues they would get if assessments were kept up to date, but individual taxpayers are often the victims of gross inequity. Time and again tax studies have cited vast discrepancies among assessments in the same county and among the counties in a single state. The studies have also shown that some pieces of property get by year after year completely untaxed. Another shortcoming is that lower-priced houses, whose value is more easily checked because they change hands more often, are taxed more realistically and therefore more heavily, proportionately, than high-priced property. A survey of Bethlehem, Pennsylvania, found that the average town assessment was 28.5 percent of real market value, but houses in the $50,000 class were assessed at only about 12 percent.

COMPUTERS AND AERIAL PHOTOS

The efficiency and equity of assessment can be improved, as has been shown in some areas, by giving the job to trained, full-time civil servants, whose technical background enables them to measure property values accurately. Some states are sending local assessors to school or making technical assistance available through equalization boards expressly set up to eliminate assessment anomalies. New York State is using electronic computers to keep its tax rolls up to date.

West Virginia has begun an ambitious operation that could prove a model for all other states where the property tax has been neglected. One of the first to relax the tax during the depression, West Virginia found that local assessment had deteriorated to the point where towns and counties could not function without great amounts of state aid, which the state treasury could ill afford. To bring assessments up to date, the state has arranged for the examination and microfilming of all property records, has hired professional appraisal firms to check values, and is sending out aerial-photography teams, using the latest photogrammetry techniques, to map the entire state for tax purposes. In one county this survey has already turned up no less than 700 parcels that had never been entered on the tax books. The ultimate goal is a uniform assessment of all West Virginia property at a minimum of 50 percent of true value.

A TAX ON HONESTY

Even if assessment procedure is revamped, however, property taxes are likely to play a declining role in state and local taxation. One reason is the increasing distaste aroused by one form of such taxation—the levy on personal (as opposed to real) property. This levy—when taken seriously—means an examination of bank accounts, securities, and even household goods including furniture, TV sets, automobiles, and clothing. Before the Civil War, when the levy was paid on slaves, it provided half the nation's revenue. Today it brings in 17 percent of the total property-tax yield. Local governments in all but three states retain the personal-property tax in their revenue system, although some make little effort to collect it, and others levy it by merely adding a nominal percentage to real-property assessments.

Personal property is almost impossible to assess accurately. Since the kind of snooping necessary for accurate assessment would never be tolerated, every taxpayer becomes in fact his own assessor, and the tax becomes a tax on honesty.

A SLUM MAKER

It may be necessary to lighten the burden of real-property taxation in certain circumstances where it has had bad economic and social consequences. The railroads, for instance, have a good case for relief from the tax. Real property—track mileage and terminals on choice urban land—is an inordinately large element in their assets, and the tax on it is a big cost item that remains fixed despite declining activity and falling earnings. The New York Public Service Commission has reported that while net earnings of railroads in New York State dropped 53.9 percent between 1955 and 1957, their real-property tax bill rose 9.3 percent. It appears likely that property-tax relief will commend itself to many communities as a way of giving first aid to the railroads in their steadily worsening situation. But this will have a profound effect on the tax base of many a town where the railroad is the biggest single taxpayer.

Then there are whole cities, particularly in the Northeast, where all forms of real property are bearing too much of a burden. Boston, which has the highest effective tax in the U.S.—$7.44 on every $100 of market value—has paid the price in urban decay; no one can afford to build in the heart of the city. Most big cities have found, in fact, that a high property tax hastens the development of slums by encouraging landlords to overcrowd and neglect their deteriorating (but still heavily taxed) properties.

The cities are finding, in fact, that programs for urban renewal cut deeply into the property-tax base. Housing developers demand, and get, substantial tax concessions. And the tax roll is constantly losing property that is set aside for parks, highway rights-of-way, and schools.

The burden on homeowners may also be growing too heavy. The property tax is the only tax now levied on what people own,

as contrasted with what they earn or what they spend. Furthermore, it is a tax on unrealized wealth; with diligent assessment,
tax liability will rise with the value of the property, but not
necessarily with the taxpayer's capacity to pay. The tax therefore
is no longer the measure of true affluence that it once was, and it
may wreak hardship on lower-income homeowners.

THE UNDERPRIVILEGED CITIES

Thus, while a great deal can and should be done to improve
methods of assessing property, more of local expenditures, in the
years to come, must be financed out of non-property revenue
sources. Most communities will continue to let the state do this
kind of taxing for them, counting on their passing on the proceeds
in the form of state aid. About 30 percent of what localities spend
is covered by state aid, and the proportion is likely to keep
growing.

The financial soundness of local governments will thus depend
increasingly on whether state aid is apportioned in accordance
with true need. The way aid is now passed out, particularly to
the big cities, leaves something to be desired. New York City's
dissatisfaction with state treatment is not unique. The grievance
of the cities does not stem from the fact that some of the taxes
collected from their citizens go to benefit rural communities;
such redistribution is the very purpose of state aid. But aid
formulas generally treat urban and rural localities as if their per
capita needs were equal and take no account of the steeper costs
the cities have to pay for their services. For instance, teachers'
salaries are higher, land is more expensive, and welfare outlays
are larger. A better allocation of state aid, however, will probably have to wait on a reapportionment of legislative constituencies to give cities the representation their population rates.

Meanwhile, the cities can bolster their revenues by levying
taxes on consumption. Retail sales are now taxed in 1,300 counties
and municipalities (including New York, Los Angeles, and
Chicago). Twenty-seven cities (among them Philadelphia, St.
Louis, and Louisville) even levy income taxes, most of them at
rates of less than 1 percent. Taxpayers in St. Louis and Louisville
pay three income taxes, since Missouri and Kentucky are income-
tax states. But the municipal income tax is not generally recom-

mended. It would be likely to hurt the city's economy and bring about an undesirable dispersal of industry. The taxing of incomes should be left to the state, but legislatures, both in making tax policy and in distributing the revenues, should give much more consideration than they now do to the financial needs of the metropolitan areas.

The cities could also obtain substantially more revenue from user charges and fees. These are intended to make consumers pay the full cost of certain services (for example, water, utilities, and special inspection required by commercial premises with safety, fire, or health hazards). But often the city government does not set its prices on a commercial basis, and the service is furnished at a loss. The beneficiary is thus subsidized out of the general tax fund. And some cities fail to exploit special opportunities for revenue of this kind. A city as motorized as Los Angeles could get a lot more out of parking meters than the $350,000 a year it collects now.

THE MICHIGAN MESSAGE

The emphasis of this article has been on raising enough revenue to meet inevitable increases in state and local expenditures. There is no doubt that a part of the necessary increases could be offset, if citizens and their governments were determined it should be done, by a better quality of administration. Reports of the "little Hoover commissions" in various states and cities suggest that the savings, on a national scale, would well finance a part of the additional services that will be necessary in the 1960's.

But meanwhile inadequate and inefficient tax systems are no real force for economy in government operation. Expenditures are rarely trimmed to meet revenue income. The spending decisions come first, and the taxes follow. At worst, when revenue turns out to be insufficient, the result is a crisis such as Michigan went through in the late 1950's, when it was strapped for cash to meet its payrolls. And chronic state and local financial crises lend plausibility to those who argue that the federal government should take on greatly increased responsibility for things like education, housing, and health, because the states cannot afford to keep them up to required standards.

An assured flow of revenue, drawn out of growing national income by broad-based taxes, will, on the other hand, strengthen state and local self-sufficiency. It will also eliminate the need for those hasty and often inequitable improvisations in the tax system that make both politicians and taxpayers unhappy.

What Can't Be Conserved* _____

EDITORIAL

The Supreme Court's decision in the Tennessee legislative apportionment case has been interpreted as a blow to conservatism. Senator Russell of Georgia even calls it "another major assault on our constitutional system." The Chicago *Tribune*, with characteristic plain speaking, says that the decision will hurt the Republican party by increasing the power of the Democratic urban machines, "which are nearly always on the side of unlimited spending, ever enlarging handouts, and all sorts of 'welfare' legislation." This hits a nail on the head but, as often happens with the *Tribune*, it's the wrong nail.

Those who defend the existing apportionments of many state legislatures support inertia, not conservatism. Indeed, it can be argued that the distortion of the legislative balance in favor of the rural areas has had a lot to do with the overconcentration of power in Washington and with the long-range decline of the Republican party. The business community, in particular, ought to be grateful for the Supreme Court's decision because business is often a victim of the lag between political ideas and the realities of a fast changing society. No doubt some lag is inevitable, but legislatures weighted with undue representation from rural areas put a heavy strain on the relation between business and politics. The Supreme Court's decision may, in the end, reduce the lag.

The Court held that the Fourteenth Amendment's promise of

_____
* *May 1962*

"the equal protection of the laws" to all citizens might be used as a basis for challenging the apportionment of seats in state legislatures. Not only in Tennessee but in at least forty other states there are serious discrepancies between population patterns and the distribution of legislative seats. Across the country these discrepancies are said to average out at a two-to-one advantage for the rural and small town voter as against voters in metropolitan areas.

The Court's decision, which impresses Senator Russell and many others as a wild innovation, can be seen from a different viewpoint as an effort to restore a principle that had broken down. In a representative democracy, the geographical distribution of representatives is supposed to follow, at least roughly, the geographic distribution of people. The central issue in the Tennessee case was whether the fairness of a legislative apportionment is always a "political question" or whether in some instances it can become a matter for the courts, including the federal courts. Two generations ago, certainly, ninety-nine lawyers out of a hundred would have agreed that the apportionment of a state legislature was no business of a federal court. During the nineteenth century there was many a horrid gerrymander of state voting districts with which the federal courts did not interfere. The theory was that if certain groups of voters were treated inequitably they could appeal to the sense of fair play in the general voting public, which might punish the party or group responsible for the gerrymander. This assumption did not always prove justified; sometimes the public apathetically accepted outrageous voting maps. But at least the positive act of redistricting gave public attention a chance to focus. In these circumstances, reliance on a "political remedy" was better than drawing voting maps in the courts.

The twentieth-century problem is different. The voting maps of most states have not been deliberately and outrageously gerrymandered. They were fair enough when they were drawn. But the people have gradually gerrymandered themselves by moving into metropolitan areas. Meanwhile legislators, elected on the basis of the old population maps, have quietly postponed reapportionment, which might cost them their seats. The "political remedy" is hard to apply to this kind of "negative gerrymander" because the public is not faced with a positive action it can reject. The fact is that year after year in Tennessee and other states the political remedy was not forthcoming.

The practical consequence has been for the disfranchised city voters and their mayors to turn increasingly to the federal government for the solution of problems for which the rural-dominated state legislatures are not willing to take responsibility. Many years ago Elihu Root, addressing himself to the danger of expanding federal power, said: "If the powers of the States are to be preserved and their authority is to continue, the States must exercise their powers. The only way to maintain the powers of Government is to govern." If the make-up of legislatures had followed the population shift, there would have been less unwholesome spread of the federal government's scope.

There are subtler and perhaps even more important political points involved. State legislatures are a kind of nursery of political leadership—and some twigs have been oddly bent. The Republican party, for instance, has declined in popularity partly because it impresses many voters as out of date. The quality of Republican leadership—including congressional leadership—has been influenced by the fact that rural Republicans have enjoyed an unfair advantage in state legislatures. Similarly, the actual South is not so detached from the realities of 1962 as the speeches of many of the South's political leaders would indicate. The stranglehold of the rural South on such progressive cities as Atlanta is reinforced by archaic legislative apportionment. Nor have many commentators noticed how the suburbs may be affected by the Supreme Court's decision. They, not the cities, are now the fastest-growing areas. The influence of the Court's decision will be felt over the next twenty years and may result in replacing some rural Republicans in state legislatures with suburban Republicans and some city Democrats with suburban Democrats. Will that be bad?

The Court has pointed a way out of a scandal that has gone on for decades. If the federal courts had refused to take jurisdiction, population shifts in the next twenty years would probably have brought worse distortion. Even under the new Supreme Court decision, no quick relief is assured. If legislatures decide to be stubborn, they can create exceedingly messy situations where state statutes may be held unconstitutional on the ground that they were passed by grossly unrepresentative legislatures. The hope is that legislatures will now move toward fairer apportionment rather than risk direct interventions by the federal courts. Minnesota, prodded by a 1958 federal district court decision, this year will permit the election of twelve additional legislators from Minneapolis. Other states, it is hoped, will react the same way—unless "conservatives" forget that in this fluid society nothing political can be conserved—nothing is worth conserving—except principle and the fundamental framework of decision. A rural dominance that has departed in fact cannot be frozen into political power without setting up other distortions that endanger the whole federal balance. The Supreme Court has not usurped any power; it has merely decided that state legislatures may be required to recognize the twentieth century.